PREFACE

Population Studies No. 41, *World Population Prospects as Assessed in 1963*, New York 1966.

All these published books have provided essential material for the present work. The reader will notice that they exclude extensive reference to interrelations between demographic factors and such matters as economic development, food supply and the use of resources. This restriction is deliberate for such is not the aim of this book. It aims, more modestly, to reveal the uniqueness of modern man as a procreative being and to indicate the revolutionary sociological and institutional implications of the actual or imminent achievement of what I term 'demographic immortality', or the expectation that he can achieve and hold a life span of three score and ten years.

Finally, I wish to thank two essential helpers in the production of this book: Mrs Helen Brown who typed the manuscript and Mrs Morag Cameron who prepared the diagrams and assisted with proof reading, bibliography and indexing.

Canberra, W. D. BORRIE
December 1969

emigration, gives the approximate answer. But what can be done where the records are deficient? This is where demography must be both a science and an art. One set of data has to be measured against another to see which may be accurate and which in error. For example, does a census population aged 0–9 correspond to the population recorded in birth statistics over the previous ten years and expected to remain alive until the census date? Or again, does the population enumerated at age 10–19 in a census bear the expected relationship to the population enumerated at ages 0–9 ten years earlier?[3]

Or yet again, if the level of literacy is low, or if marriage is known to occur at an early age and to be almost universal, or if the economy is 'underdeveloped' with the mass of the population living near Malthusian levels of subsistence, a trained demographer will regard birth rates below say 30 per 1,000 of population with considerable doubt: he will immediately suspect deficient birth registration. He must of course be careful, for human fertility patterns do not fit neatly into a few stereotypes *wholly* controlled by economic, educational or other clearly defined and measurable social and cultural variables. Yet the extensive (though as yet inadequate) knowledge which now exists of the interrelations of demographic, economic and social factors is sufficient to establish *some* regularities, the absence of which suggests both the sources of possible errors in the data and the methods that can be applied to eliminate them.

Now while these regularities may reasonably be expected to apply over very broad areas, they do not mean that there may not be a great variety of differentials in terms of birth, death and growth rates within each of those areas. The established fact that the birth rate of the North American continent as a whole averages 25 per 1,000 of population does not mean that there are not small sectors of population within that continent with totally different fertility patterns, and of course the Hutterites are known to be such a minority. Conversely, the established fact of a birth rate of over 40 per 1,000 in India, a country with over 500 million people, does not mean that no Indians have small families. Yet these exceptions do not invalidate a number of generalizations which are now held to describe the *average* patterns of broad population types.

It may now be asserted with some confidence that if a large area lacks the scientific and technical skills or the medical knowledge of

3

European man today, or if it has a low level of literacy, the chances of that area *as a whole* having a low birth rate or a low death rate are quite small. There appear to have been times when peoples who have not enjoyed the command over resources and the scientific, technical and medical knowledge which we associate with western Europe or North America today, have displayed a low fertility which has led to population decline; but when these cases are examined carefully they are generally found to be associated with other factors than, for example, a weakening of 'the will to live', or association with a 'higher' civilization. Thus the popular nineteenth-century view that many of the Pacific Islands' peoples were declining because of lowered fecundity, or physiological capacity to reproduce, following their contact with Western civilization, now receives little credence: the major checks to their population growth came from the ravages of new diseases introduced by their first contact with Europeans, not by any decline of 'the spirit' or of 'a will to live'.

In other words, in broad areas which may be defined as 'underdeveloped' in terms of such factors as modern technology, medical skills, degree of urbanization, industrialization, or literacy, we do not expect to find demographic patterns dissimilar from those considered to have applied in past centuries, that is with high fertility giving a *potentially* rapid rate of growth, but with this potential substantially if not wholly offset by a high level of mortality. Where these factors of technology, advanced medical skills, or a high degree of literacy have reached a 'developed' form, the population dynamics are likely to change markedly, and from the studies of contemporary populations undergoing these processes of change a body of theory is being built up which not only applies to the demographic situation today but which also helps to provide reasonable explanations about the quite distant past.

The rapid elimination of colonialism, particularly since the Second World War, has been associated with major changes in the social and technological structures of populations of many 'underdeveloped' countries, and indeed colonial control itself frequently introduced medical science and public health measures which drastically altered traditional demographic patterns by their control over disease. The nature of these changes has drawn attention to their uniqueness. For example, the methods used to eliminate malaria in recent years have had no precedent in human history. Nor is there any evidence to suggest that the level of infant mortality had ever before come anywhere near the situation where over 90 per cent of the babies born live beyond the age of 40 – which is now accepted as normal today among most nations of European stock, and which is a goal which may soon be reached in many of the non-European countries now in the process of industrialization.

Just as the study of demographic change in the contemporary world throws light upon the uniqueness of many of the vital indices of today, so the study of populations in areas where change has not yet occurred suggests patterns which have probably existed for aeons past. And inadequate as our knowledge yet is about many of the populations conforming to this latter type, more is known about them than ever before.

Thus, the study of the present is throwing light upon the past, partly by showing that many aspects of both the 'developed' and 'developing' countries today have systems of demographic controls that could never have existed in the past. Countries with controlled fertility and very low mortality, which may be more generally described as those with expectations of life around 70 years, fall into this category. Other countries have come under the influence of only one controlling factor, mortality, with the result that growth rates have soared upwards to levels that could not have held over extended periods of the past (or else numbers would long since have outstripped the means of subsistence) and which clearly cannot hold for long in the future (or else numbers will soon outstrip the means of subsistence). Finally there are the countries which appear to be a decreasing minority in number but which still contain a substantial part of the world's people, in which neither fertility nor mortality has been substantially affected by modern medical science, and in which demographic controls probably still conform basically to age-old patterns. These patterns can be broadly described as those in which high levels of fertility combined with high levels of mortality result in a relatively low growth rate. Again, it is obvious that over long periods of time in the past the average growth rate of the human species must have been at least as low as, and for much of human history much lower than, the patterns of these high-fertility–high-mortality countries in the world of today, or else the point of standing room only would not be a prospect of the future but would have been reached many centuries ago.

5

Thus estimating the world's population at any given point of time is a complicated exercise. For those parts of the world in which people enjoy high living standards, universal literacy, and with these, generally fairly accurate censuses and vital registration, the facts are reasonably firm; but for much of the rest of the world, where illiteracy is high and where census and vital records are often poor, the picture must be assessed on the basis of the data available. Here the records have to be reconstructed on the basis of analogy and of the increasing knowledge of patterns of human fertility and mortality in given socio-economic environments. Demographers have been very cautious in their use of these indirect measures, and this and the fact that censuses generally undercount rather than overcount people, almost certainly mean that global population estimates will tend to be too low. Thus the figure of 3,500 million people in the world in 1968 may well be an underestimate.

We will now consider the generally accepted estimates of the population of major land areas of the world and the expectations for the immediate future. Here 1960, with an estimated world population then of 2,990 million, will be taken as the pivotal point between past and future. Even the most cursory glance at Table 1·1

Table 1. 1 : Estimates of World Population (in millions)[4]

Year	World Total	Africa	Northern America	Central & South America	Asia excluding Asiatic USSR	Europe & Asiatic USSR	Oceania
1650	545	100	1	12	327	103	2
1750	728	95	1	11	475	144	2
1850	1,171	95	26	33	741	274	2
1900	1,608	120	81	63	915	423	6
1920	1,860	143	116	89	1,023	480	9
1930	2,068	164	134	107	1,120	533	10
1940	2,294	191	144	130	1,244	574	11
1950	2,515	221	166	162	1,381	572	13
1960	2,998	273	199	212	1,659	639	16

suggests some remarkable features. In the first place, according to these figures, *growth* has been a continuous process since 1650 and further evidence will be adduced in support of this view. (See especially Chapter 3.) Secondly, the *rate* of growth has also been accelerating continuously.

6

Considering the time-scale involved, the growth of human population to an estimated total of 545 millions in 1650 was a very slow affair. An average annual rate of about 0·005 per cent would have produced the population of 300 millions which is now generally accepted as approximately the upper limit of population at AD 0. Thereafter the pace seems to have quickened, and the population probably doubled over the next sixteen or seventeen centuries. But compared with this, the rates implied after 1650 in Table 1. 1 seem quite fantastic.

1 The increase to 728 millions in 1750 implied an annual average increase of 0·3 per cent for the previous century.

2 Over the next century the average growth rate rose to about 0·6 per cent a year.

3 From 1850 to 1950 the world's population more than doubled, growing from 1,171 millions to 2,515 millions, with an average annual increase of about 1 per cent.

4 By 1961 the world's population was estimated to be increasing at 1·7 per cent, and a continuation of this rate will mean that more people will be added to the world in the next half century than were added in the whole of human history up to 1961. The increase to be expected over the rest of this century alone, if current growth rates are sustained, will be more than the whole world's population in 1960.

Where has this increase come from? The pattern is summarized in the sectional columns of Table 1. 1. Clearly not all the increase has been among the areas which have reached relative affluence, that is Europe and North America. The discrepancy in growth rates appears greatest up to 1920. From 1650 to 1920 Europe and North America (which absorbed the greater part of Europe's 50 million emigrants) grew more than fivefold, compared with a threefold increase in Asia. By the end of the nineteenth century, western man was passing what was almost certainly the peak of his growth rate, a peak brought about less by an increase in his fertility than by his increasing mastery over agricultural and industrial resources, and by improvements in public health and, in the twentieth century, in medical care. His fertility had never been excessive; indeed, on the contrary, European man from at least the eighteenth century onwards was a most circumspect person who married relatively late in life and who had a modest birth rate which seldom seems to have exceeded 35 per 1,000 of population.

7

Nevertheless falling mortality kept pushing up growth rates, occasionally to 1·5 per cent a year, but more often to about 1·0 per cent; which may seem modest in today's world but which could not have existed for any extensive area and over long periods before the twentieth century.

From about 1900, however, a marked change began to appear in the patterns of world population growth. In the European world, and particularly in western Europe and overseas countries peopled by Europeans, birth rates began to decline more rapidly than death rates, thus slowing growth rates. The movement was accelerated during the great depression of the thirties, when birth rates fell so low in country after country that there was widespread fear of population decline. The years after 1945 brought some revival of birth rates, particularly in New World countries of European origin, such as the United States of America, New Zealand and Australia. The factors behind this apparent increase in fertility (which will be discussed in some detail in later chapters) were complex, but they brought no weakening of the forces of family planning and birth control which lay behind the decline of the birth rate since the late nineteenth century.

More striking than the revival of the birth rate in recent years in some western European countries, and in some oversea countries peopled by Europeans (USA, Australia and New Zealand), has been the sharp decline of fertility in eastern and southern Europe, in which birth rates had remained relatively high right up to the Second World War. Now they have come tumbling down to levels as low as anywhere in the world – for example Austria, Czechoslovakia, Hungary, Greece and Italy all have birth rates which now range between about 17 and 19 per 1,000 of population.

Yet quite substantial growth rates are still being sustained in many of these countries simply because of the extraordinary efficiency of modern controls over the factor of mortality. An infant mortality rate (i.e. deaths of children under 1 year of age per 1,000 live births) of 25 or even of 50, or an expectation of life at birth of over 60, and even up to 70 years, which is now simply taken for granted among Europeans, never existed until this century, and still only exists among the world's relatively affluent nations.

These new demographic controls of restricted fertility and low mortality have not brought about population decline. Low and stable birth rates and an expectation of life of 70 years can still produce a growth rate exceeding 1 per cent a year, or sufficient to double a population in 69 years – but they have kept the growth rates of many European and New World countries well below rates in the world's economically 'underdeveloped' areas, which cover most of Latin America, Africa and most of the half of the world's people who live in Asia. In the world's 'underdeveloped' areas the factor of mortality control has been increasingly effective, whereas the factor of fertility control has not been generally apparent. This sounds like the situation which prevailed in much of Europe in the latter part of the nineteenth and into the twentieth centuries. There is, however, a very important difference. Thanks to the advances in the medical and biological sciences, as well as in agricultural science, mortality rates have come tumbling down in many 'underdeveloped' areas with incredible speed compared with European experience. Asian, African and South American man has not had to learn the hard way how to eradicate the worst killing diseases. Western science has done this for him and he has been able to borrow the techniques, or to have them applied for him, and frequently to learn about them while he was either under colonial domination or at least within the sphere of influence of the Western nations.

So, as the rates of growth of the affluent sectors of the world have been slowing down and stabilizing, the rates of the low-income areas have been expanding quickly as the result of rapidly falling death rates, until now many of these areas have growth rates well above 2 per cent a year, with some over 3 per cent a year – rates which will double populations in about 34 and 23 years respectively.

While these very high rates can be explained primarily in terms of falling death rates, they are also the product of levels of fertility which are in many cases very much higher than rates which ever prevailed among European countries. As already emphasized, marriage age in these countries tended to remain relatively high, and at times quite high proportions of the adult populations did not marry at all. By contrast, marriage among many Asian peoples tends to occur at very young ages and to be universal. This is particularly true of India where the average age of marriage is about 16 years.

The effect of these variations in trends is apparent in Table 1. 1. As the growth rates of the European world have tended to stabilize, those of the Latin American, African and Asian worlds have been

9

leaping ahead. From 1900 to 1960 Europe, including Asiatic USSR, increased by one-half, compared with 81 per cent increase in Asia, a 128 per cent increase in Africa and a 237 per cent increase in Central and South America. This last case (and also North America, with an increase of 146 per cent) shows the influence of large-scale immigration over this sixty-year period.

There are of course considerable variations of fertility and mortality within these broad regions. The presentation of almost 56 per cent of the world under the one heading of 'Asia' is perhaps stretching the theory of typology to the limit; but it nevertheless remains true that very few of the countries within this category of 'Asia', or for that matter in the broad areas covered by 'Africa' or 'Central and South America' have demographic patterns or population structures in any way similar to those which are now dominant in 'Europe' or 'North America'. Just how similar the patterns of individual countries had become by 1960 within many of these broad areas, and how far they differed as between the 'developed' and 'underdeveloped' areas, is illustrated in Table 1. 2.

One important aspect of Table 1. 2 is the fact that no country was showing a decrease in population, and that very few countries – and all of them in Europe – were increasing at a rate slow enough to prevent a doubling of population in considerably less than a century. Some countries – for example Ghana, Tunisia, Taiwan and Malaya – had rates of increase exceeding 3 per cent a year, which is sufficient to double a population every twenty-three years.

The growth of populations is a function of the relationship existing between births and deaths rather than of the absolute level of either factor. Western people generally have in mind countries with high birth rates when they are thinking of 'the population problem' or 'overpopulation'. Yet high *birth* rates have not always been associated with high *growth* rates. Indeed throughout the greater part of human history the controlling factor in population growth has not been the level of the birth rate, but the level of the death rate. This perspective comes to the heart of the Malthusian theory that population growth tends to outstrip the means of sustaining life. If by 'sustaining life' is meant not merely subsistence, but the ravages of disease, wars, pestilence and all the other catastrophes afflicting mankind, the Malthusian proposition has held substantially true over a great part of human existence. For most of that history reproduction has been an appallingly

Table 1. 2 : Illustrative Growth Rates (Rates per 1000 of population)[5]

Area		Year of Estimate	Birth Rates	Death Rates	Natural Increase
Africa	Ghana	1958	52·4	20·9	31·5
	Tunisia	1958	47·0	9·6	37·4
	Mauritius	1958	38·5	10·9	27·6
Asia	Taiwan	1958	41·7	7·6	34·1
	Fed. of Malaya	1958	43·2	11·0	32·2
	India	1958	39·1	19·4	19·7
	China (Mainland)	1957	34·0	11·0	23·0
	Thailand	1956	42·0	20·0	22·0
	Japan	1959	17·5	7·4	10·1
South America	Argentine	1959	22·6	8·1	14·5
	Chile	1958	35·5	12·1	23·4
	Ecuador	1958	45·9	15·2	30·7
	Venezuela	1958	44·7	9·4	35·3
North America	USA	1960	23·6	9·5	14·1
	Canada	1959	27·9	8·1	19·8
Europe	Austria	1958	17·1	12·2	4·9
	Czechoslovakia	1959	16·0	9·7	6·3
	France	1959	18·3	11·2	7·1
	West Germany	1959	17·6	10·8	6·8
	Greece	1958	19·0	7·1	11·9
	Italy	1959	18·4	9·3	9·1
	Spain	1960	21·9	8·9	13·0
	Sweden	1960	13·6	10·0	3·6
	United Kingdom	1959	16·9	11·6	5·3
	USSR	1959	25·0	7·6	17·4
Oceania	Australia	1959	22·6	8·9	13·7
	New Zealand	1959	26·5	9·1	17·4

inefficient business, requiring a high rate of conception on the part of the human female for the *replacement* of each generation, let alone its *increase*. The rate of increase of 1·7 per cent or more a year which is estimated to prevail in the world around 1960 and which, if sustained, will double the world's population again in a mere forty years, clearly could not have prevailed over long periods of the past; otherwise, as already emphasized, the point of 'standing room only' would not be a prospect but would have been attained aeons ago.

Arithmetical calculations to prove this point have often been amusingly made. The simplest one points out that with a constant annual rate of increase of 1·2 per cent a year (compared with a world figure in 1960 of say 1·7 per cent), the world's present population could have been derived from a single couple living in the year AD 0. More fanciful is the calculation which estimated that a single couple living 6,000 years ago and increasing at the rate of 1 per cent a year would have produced a population so vast today that there would now be standing room, not just upon the entire surface of the earth, but on the surface of a sphere with a radius fourteen times the orbit of the planet Neptune. Clearly, therefore, estimated current rates of growth of the world's population must have existed for only a very brief part of human history.

Considered in relation to the life-span of a single human being, the elapse of time since 1650 (that is approximately the point at which the world's populations considered as a whole began to grow at unprecedented rates) is too great to justify the use of the term 'explosion' to describe demographic events since then. Yet the fact remains that over the past two or three centuries systems of demographic controls have been established, over increasingly large sectors of the world, which are unique in human history. These controls, which may be briefly described as an unparalleled low level of mortality and extensive control over fertility, have for the first time brought about a reasonably efficient system of reproduction in most of the richer and more literate sectors of the world. The two factors of fertility control and mortality control have had to go together, otherwise death control, which slowly increased its efficiency with improving living standards and with the pioneer developments in medical science and public health of the nineteenth century, would have brought about continually increasing growth rates. In fact, however, there is no example of *nations* of people behaving in this way. Some small minority groups, such as the Hutterites, have failed to establish effective fertility control in situations of extremely efficient death control; but there is no example of a European nation in which fertility has not been greatly reduced in response to efficient death control, although there are cases where birth control has preceded really effective death control.

By efficient death control is here meant levels of death rates which prevailed around 1960 throughout virtually all European countries (including European USSR) and many countries peopled by Europeans, that is with infant death rates per 1,000 live births between about 20 and 50, with some 90 per cent of females born living to the end of the child-bearing period, and with expectations of life at birth between about 65 and 70 years. Such conditions were unknown to mankind until the twentieth century; but whereas they were so laboriously attained by the pioneering efforts of Western peoples, now the death control aspect is rapidly achieving remarkable success by applied *Western* science in much of the world's low income, illiterate and semi-literate areas. The result, in the form of unprecedented levels of growth rates, is seen in Table 1. 2, for in very few of these areas has the birth rate yet come under control.

Will fertility control follow, as it did in the European world, to bring about a new and efficient demographic balance in the Asian, African and Latin American sectors of the world, where birth rates remain at 40 or more per 1,000 of population?

Western demographers and economists, after examining the cycle of movements of death, birth and growth rates among the Western nations have been struck by other associated features. As death rates declined urbanization and industrialization increased; these phenomena were also associated with the growth of universal literacy, increasing social and occupational mobility, rising material living standards; and as death rates fell in the face of these great advances in the social, technical and scientific fields, so increasing control was exercised over fertility. By the twentieth century the situation had been reached where three pregnancies in a woman's life could produce the same level of population growth as six or more pregnancies in the pre-industrial days.

These observations form the basis of the demographic 'transition theory' which was so widely used to explain the trends in vital rates from about the end of the eighteenth century through to the present day. A few exceptions were admitted, such as France and Ireland where the decline in fertility had little positive association with either changes in mortality or industrialization; but there were many more countries for which the transition theory offered a very reasonable explanation. Furthermore, events over the past twenty years in eastern and southern Europe give much support for the theory, because levels of education have been raised, the pace of industrialization and urbanization has quickened, *per capita* incomes have risen, and death rates have fallen rapidly; and everywhere these phenomena have been followed or accompanied by birth rates which have declined from levels of thirty and more to twenty and lower, as illustrated in Table 1. 2. Recent attacks upon

13

the original theories of the 'transitionists' have not weakened their basic validity for much that has already happened and have tended to endow the originators of the theory with a prescience which they never claimed.

Transition theory did draw attention to the basic social, economic and cultural changes that had usually accompanied the growth of relatively efficient reproductive systems, and thereby suggested that *future* declines in fertility would probably be expedited if these preconditions could be established – industrialization, increasing urbanization, literacy, and death control. The establishment of the first two of these trends at least presumes an economic breakthrough to the point where capital investment succeeds in raising *per capita* incomes above bare subsistence levels; but this is just where the problem of so many Asian and Latin American countries is so difficult, and so very different from the situation with which Europeans were faced when they began their economic advance. The populations of these European countries were usually small and their natural resources great, and they discovered and colonized vast new continents in America, Africa and Oceania. By contrast most of the areas which suffer today from high birth rates, declining death rates and expanding *demographic* growth rates, are already relatively densely populated, cannot enter into extensive world trade because their very poverty presents an almost insuperable balance of payment prospect, and can hardly keep production up to, let alone ahead of, population growth. If they can manage to keep food production up with population growth, applied science can rapidly push death rates down. Even today there are relatively few Asian countries with expectations of life at birth below 45 years, whereas a century ago there were few anywhere near that level.

Success in reducing death rates through the eradication or control of killing and infectious diseases has been more successful than economic growth. Eventually the latter must follow the former if the disaster of overpopulation is to be avoided, or unless the traditional cycle of the demographic transition experienced in much of the western world can be short-circuited; that is if effective fertility control can precede industrialization thereby assisting the process of economic growth. This is just what a number of the leaders of today's 'underdeveloped' areas, especially in Asia, are working for. Despite their frank and rational attitude to the whole question of birth control, success is so far not very apparent, with the one very clear and significant exception of Japan, and with some signs of declining fertility in some smaller Asian countries (Korea, Taiwan, Singapore); but it should be remembered that the attempts to bring about birth control first, or at least in association with the early processes of economic development, have only been strongly in evidence since the Second World War, and success can hardly be expected within less than a generation of thirty years or so. The degree of success may in the end turn less upon industrialization than upon the eradication of illiteracy.

Detailed discussion of the nature of the demographic transition of western powers and of the high growth rates of today's under-developed countries will follow in subsequent chapters; but in concluding this introductory survey attention should be drawn to two further elements which will be important in these later discussions, namely density and structure.

Population density alone has little significance; it is related to other factors such as rainfall, fertility of the soil, and access to external resources through international trade. Parts of the world are uninhabited because they are uninhabitable, mountainous, snowbound or desert. Some of the most densely populated areas are at the same time also amongst the world's most prosperous areas. Central Europe, with 130 persons per square kilometre in 1950, and Japan and the Ryukyu Islands with 225 persons, are the world's most densely settled, but by no means poorest regions. Temperate South America, with only 6·5 persons per square kilometre in 1950, is a sparsely settled region but also a region with low *per capita* income. Southern and Eastern Asia, with relatively high densities of about 40 and 55 persons per square kilometre, are also amongst the world's relatively low-income regions.

Obviously, there is a variety of situations, with little positive correlation between density and economic standards. Adequate capital for investment, the skills to develop and use resources and trade are the basic factors which determine population carrying capacity over major regions. Of course there are areas, such as the valleys of the Ganges in India or the Yellow River in China where the man–land ratio cannot be increased; and as the world's population rushes forward towards the 6,000 millions mark, as suggested in Table 1. 1, there will be many other areas in which this man–land ratio will approach the maximum limit.

These increasing densities will mean increasing poverty if man–land ratios are increased. They can, however, mean improved economic welfare if they are associated with major transfers of future generations from the land to productive non-agricultural employment in urban areas. This point can best be illustrated by a brief glance at the differential structures of populations between high-income and low-income regions.

Table 1. 3 : The Composition of Populations of major Regions, 1960 (Percentage in each age group)[6]

Age	World	Africa	North America	Latin America	East Asia	South Asia	Europe	Oceania	USSR
0–14	36·4	43·1	31·3	41·7	36·1	41·0	25·7	31·7	30·8
15–64	58·7	54·2	59·7	55·0	59·7	55·9	64·5	60·5	63·0
65+	4·9	2·7	9·0	3·3	4·2	3·1	9·8	7·8	6·2

As already emphasized, countries of controlled fertility tend also to be countries of low mortality and of high expectations of life; relatively few infants who are alive die until middle life. Consequently the populations of these regions have much higher proportions of their numbers in the adult age groups than do areas of high fertility and relatively high mortality. In the latter type of population a high proportion will be children below working age. In Latin America, Africa and Asia about 40 per cent of the population is between the ages of 0 and 14 years, compared with only 28 per cent in North America, 26 per cent in Europe and 31 per cent in the USSR. The contrast between these population types is best illustrated by population pyramids, or profiles, which give a composite picture of the age and sex structure at a selected point of time. The countries selected for this purpose in Figure 1. 1 illustrate typical high, medium and low growth types.

It has already been made clear that this illustration of a basic typology does not mean that each major region, to which reference is usually made to illustrate areas of 'high', 'medium' or 'low' growth, is homogeneous. For one thing the regional boundaries used are generally those of a nation-state which happens to be the administrative unit for which aggregate statistics of births and deaths are available. But no nation-state consists of a homogeneous

Figure 1.1 : Population Pyramids illustrating Different Population Types

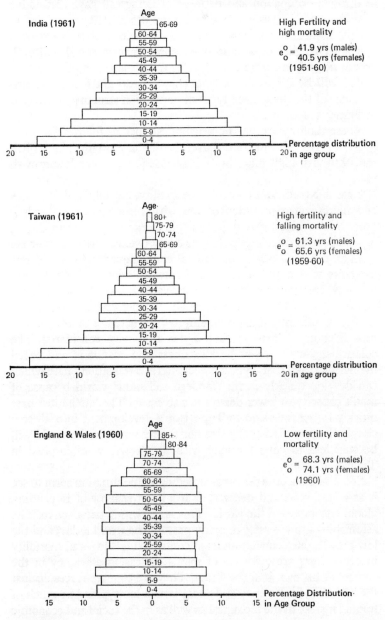

India (1961)

High Fertility and
high mortality

$e_0^o = $ 41.9 yrs (males)
       40.5 yrs (females)
(1951-60)

Percentage distribution
in age group

Taiwan (1961)

High fertility and
falling mortality

$e_0^o = $ 61.3 yrs (males)
       65.6 yrs (females)
(1959-60)

Percentage distribution
in age group

England & Wales (1960)

Low fertility and
mortality

$e_0^o = $ 68.3 yrs (males)
       74.1 yrs (females)
(1960)

Percentage Distribution
in Age Group

17

population: few are ethnically homogeneous; all have differentials of income, occupation and patterns of living; all have distinctive characteristics between urban and rural areas. Patterns of differentials of fertility and mortality run through all these sub-strata and are changing over time in response to new social, cultural, economic and scientific stimuli. Yet these more complex factors, which will be discussed in later chapters, do not lessen the importance of the three basic types of population structure illustrated in Figure 1. 1.

These three types may be briefly described as follows:

Type 1 No efficient control over fertility or mortality; high birth rates but also high mortality with consequently very low growth rates.

Type 2 No efficient control over fertility, but falling death rates and increasing expectation of life with consequently expanding growth rates which may quickly begin to exceed 3 per cent a year, or sufficient to double populations every twenty-three years or so.

Type 3 A high degree of rational control over fertility and low mortality with expectations of life between approximately 65 and 70 years, and with a return to a reasonable balance between births and deaths and with growth rates about 1 per cent or less.

The significant points to be emphasized here are that Type 3 is new in human history; that Type 1 is now considered, like colonialism, evidence of backwardness and economic and social inefficiency; and that Type 2 is accepted as a transition phase which can develop quickly in this modern 'scientific' world because of man's capacity to lower death rates so easily. The latter must pass quickly into a reversion to Type 1 or a development into Type 3 simply because neither the size nor the resources in the world will be sufficient to cope for long with the growth rates implied in Type 2.

Some who observe the present demographic situation seem to see it as a static one and decry it as if a great shadow of impending gloom encompassed the world. This is the wrong perspective. The astonishing growth rates in many parts of the world today, and the low growth rates emanating from controlled fertility and mortality in other parts are evidence of man's increasing efficiency in the control of his own biological fate. They are counter-forces against the appalling inefficiency and waste which has typified so much of human history in the biological as well as in the social and economic

Figure 1.2 : History of the World's Population Growth

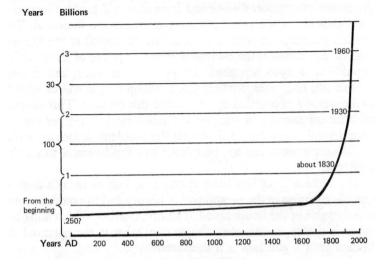

Figure 1.3 : Rates of Growth of World Population

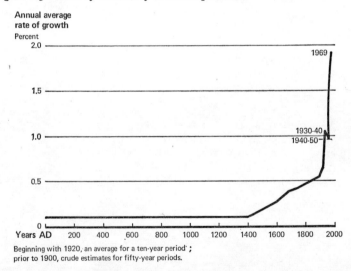

Beginning with 1920, an average for a ten-year period ;
prior to 1900, crude estimates for fifty-year periods.

spheres. The emphasis should not be that half of mankind is still illiterate and undernourished, but that half the world has escaped sufficiently from the waste and ignorance of the past to become literate and to be confidently expecting heritage of three-score-and-ten years. This is a tremendous achievement; but the completion of the victory for the other half of the world which is still bound by the chains of squalor, disease and ignorance will become increasingly difficult as the pressures upon resources are increased. To emphasize again the elementary statistics presented at the beginning of this chapter, the estimated annual increase of the world's population in 1960 was about 1·7 per cent or more; and if this growth rate continues, another 3,000 million people will be added to the world's population by the end of this century. This simple arithmetical exercise in compound interest rates of 1·7 per cent a year is surely sufficient to show that the problems associated with population growth are not peripheral but fundamental to man's existence.

The remainder of this book attempts to look at today's demographic situation in the perspective of history and to examine more closely some of the issues ahead. The first question which must be asked is the apparently very simple one: what is the potential of human growth and how is it measured?

Chapter 2

The Numbers Game: Counting Mankind and Measuring Growth

The first essential for the study of population movement is, of course, adequate data. Western peoples no longer seriously question the necessity of regular censuses and of the compulsory registration of births, marriages and deaths. Censuses are required for many reasons: they provide periodical stocktakings, not merely of population growth, but also of social capital and of the distribution of people and resources, and in this way they are important aids to the ordering of the economic and social affairs of nations. Birth, marriage and death records are also required for many social and legal purposes and are not merely data for the demographers. Nevertheless they remain the essential keys to the development of the science of demography, and until the habit of census-taking and vital registration becomes universal, many doubts will remain about the exact population of the world and of its exact rate of growth. Fortunately most of today's 'underdeveloped' nations are also realizing the importance of regular population counts as basic to effective social and economic planning, and although the results of such censuses are not always as exact or complete as either the government officials or research workers might wish, there remain relatively few countries in which governments do not aim to maintain a regular census and record vital data. The substantial advances which have been brought about since the Second World War in these matters owe a great deal to the work of the Statistical Division and the Department of Economic and Social Affairs of the United Nations.

Yet recognition of the importance of the census and vital registration came slowly and was associated essentially with the growth of the modern nation-state.[1] For many centuries after the fall of the Roman Empire there were no regular population counts throughout most of the European world. On the other hand, many enumerations were carried out in China from the Han dynasty up to modern times, although their accuracy is still controversial. One of the duties of the Roman Censors was to report upon the numbers of people, but no records remain of their labours. With the break-up of the Empire the habit of population counts ceased, and indeed was virtually impossible in the disintegration that followed. When reorganization came again some attempts were made to count hearths or dwelling units for the purpose of raising taxes. In 1328, for example, Phillip VI of Valois imposed a fiscal levy based upon a count of hearths to provide funds for an attack on Flanders. In 1085–6, William the Conqueror began collecting details in England of the type of cultivation, the numbers of inhabitants on the various estates and of their respective classes. An attempt was also made to classify the information collected in order to provide a description of the prevailing conditions.

Such population counts were rare and it was not until the seventeenth century that serious attempts were made among European peoples to maintain regular records and to analyse trends in population in terms of the factors determining growth or decline. For these purposes parish records of baptisms and burials provided the main source of data. In 1662 John Graunt published his *Natural and Political Observations made upon the Bills of Mortality*, a work based upon a study of the burials and christenings of a population of about half a million persons in the vicinity of London for which records had been maintained from 1592. Thirty years later Edmund Halley constructed a life table based upon births and deaths recorded in the church records of Breslau in Silesia.

These were the pioneer efforts in the field of demographic science, but adequate data were few and far between; censuses were unknown and anything approaching accurate vital records were restricted to a few areas. A step towards better data was taken by the proposal of the English parliament in 1694 to levy taxes on marriages, births and burials; a proposal which implied the exist-ence of accurate records. This scheme was not carried through, but by this time hearth tax records were being kept and it was from these that an estimate of houses, as required for administrative purposes, was provided in 1690. From these records Gregory King prepared his estimate of the population of England and Wales in 1695 by applying different ratios of persons per house in various areas. His estimate of 5·5 million persons in England and Wales in

1695 was the first serious attempt to count the population of the nation since the Domesday Survey.[2]

Similar developments had been occurring in France, where a population count during 1693 was intended to facilitate the distribution of food during a period of severe shortage. The most complete records in Europe before the nineteenth century were, however, to come from the Scandinavian countries. The proper recording of vital events became a matter of some importance during the Reformation. The Council of Trent (1545–63) also laid down rules about the proper recording of baptisms, marriages and burials in Catholic parishes. It was not, however, until 1748 when a Swedish law stipulated that records were to be completed each year by the pastor of each parish giving details of births, marriages and dissolutions of marriages, deaths by age, sex and cause, and numbers of persons in each household, that parish records provided the basis of a *national* register. This law began the longest series of demographic data of modern times.

About the same time special population counts, or censuses as we now know them, were beginning to occur. The hearth count in England and Wales in 1690 has already been mentioned. A population count was also made in French Canada in 1666. A census was taken in Ireland in 1703. In 1748 Frederick the Great of Prussia initiated a number of enumerations of the population. In the United States of America, the constitution stipulated that a count of the population should be made within three years of the first meeting of Congress and within every subsequent period of ten years and the first census was carried out in 1790. England and Wales commenced the first regular decennial census in 1801. In France quinquennial censuses also began in 1801. Many of the 'New World' countries to which Europeans emigrated carried out enumerations from their earliest settlements. In New South Wales, the first British settlement in Australia, a census was taken in 1828 when the population consisted of only about 30,000 persons. Thereafter counts were taken at fairly regular intervals of approximately ten years in all the Australian colonies. New Zealand took similar measures soon after British sovereignty was declared in 1840, with the initial census in 1856 and five-yearly censuses thereafter. In British India decennial censuses began in 1871.

The spread of the habit of regular population counts, which coincided with the rise of great nation-states in Europe and of new lands peopled by Europeans overseas, was accompanied by increasing attention to more adequate systems of vital registration.[3] The pioneer efforts of Sweden in this regard were followed by similar developments in Norway. A national system of civil registers was begun in England and Wales in 1837, although compulsory registration of vital events was not introduced until 1874. International conferences, which began in 1853 in Brussels, stimulated activity in the organization of official statistical services, and again those most enthusiastic in the cause were some of the newly settled countries outside Europe. By 1860, for example, all the Australian colonies and New Zealand had introduced compulsory registration of births, deaths and marriages.

The gradual improvement in the scope and quality of basic data was marked, not unnaturally, by a widening interest in the study of populations. The pioneer work of Graunt, Halley and King in England was matched by studies in other countries. Johann Sussmilch, for example, a Lutheran clergyman, set about examining the apparent regularities over time in marriage, births and deaths which had been observed by Graunt. His first work was published in 1741; the second edition of two volumes issued in 1761–2 ran to 1,200 pages with an appendix of 68 tables. He collected and analysed the vital statistics of over 1,000 parishes in Brandenberg, and took counts in cities and provinces in Prussia, comparing his findings with studies in England and elsewhere. He computed ratios of the relation of births, marriages and deaths to the population. He also constructed life tables for urban and rural areas of Germany. Unlike Graunt, who concluded from his London study that burials tended to exceed baptisms, Sussmilch found that births tended to exceed deaths, thus providing a steady increase in population. Sussmilch considered that governments should be concerned to sustain such growth and this view came to be widely accepted in western Europe in the eighteenth and nineteenth centuries.

These early statistical studies of the relation between births and deaths and of the social implications of these trends, which became known as 'political arithmetic', necessarily contained much speculation, because however good the vital records with which they were concerned, they usually lacked any accurate knowledge of the populations to which they referred: the census was a later development. Nevertheless some of the observations led to theoretical propositions which have stood the test of time remarkably well. Sussmilch's observation of a tendency of populations to increase was followed by propositions about the possible maximum rate of increase of human populations and of the relation between this and available resources. Here was the relation between 'political arithmetic' and 'political economy' which was to be elaborated by such writers as Benjamin Franklin in America, and particularly by Thomas Malthus in England. In 1755 Franklin had postulated the theory that Europe was carrying about as many people as food resources would allow and that population would therefore increase only slowly in the future because of this limit of subsistence. He also considered that in a young country like the United States where there was still no apparent limit to the available food supplies in relation to existing population, population could double in twenty-five years. About the same time a Scottish cleric, Robert Wallace, in his book *Various Prospects of Mankind, Nature, and Providence* (1761) also referred to the tendency of populations to outgrow food supplies. Even if a perfect society could be set up, he argued, it would soon be destroyed by excess numbers and soon war, 'unnatural customs', fraud and force would prevail to reduce mankind 'to the same calamitous condition as at present'.[4]

Here were the forerunners of the views that were to be developed by the Reverend Thomas Malthus, whose work *An Essay on the Principles of Population* was first published in 1798. This work was substantially revised and developed in the second edition of 1803,[5] and six editions were published in his lifetime. Whatever the flaws in Malthus's theories of the relation between population growth and resources, his work remains a substantial exercise in political arithmetic. His data from the early censuses of the United States and New Spain supported his thesis that population, if unchecked, could increase in a geometrical progression in a manner which would double it every twenty-five years. This implies an annual rate slightly below 3 per cent. This and even higher rates are found in quite a number of countries today. He was also aware of some technical problems concerning the measurement of fertility, such as the importance of relating births of a given year to the marriages from which they occurred and not merely to the population as a whole in that same year. These statistical exercises were used by Malthus merely as illustrations of his major law, namely, that population tended to outstrip resources unless held in check by moral restraint, or by an increased mortality arising from his 'positive' checks of 'misery' and 'vice', which covered a multitude of sins ranging from wars and infanticide to plague and famine.

The controversy which Malthus aroused concerned his broad theoretical concepts, rather than his empirical data. Indeed statistical analysis entered little into the battle. Until well into the nineteenth century the only substantial advance on Malthus in regard to the statistical measurement of fertility was Michael Sadler[6] who assembled considerable data from the census of the United States of America for 1820 and from that of Ireland for 1821 to support his theory that there was an inverse relation between population density and fertility, and that fertility tended to be checked by the growth of cities and by increasing wealth. He also seems to have been the first to use the ratio of children to women of child-bearing age as a measure of fertility.

Generally, however, fertility was not considered a 'problem', particularly as time and the agricultural and industrial revolutions seemed to be proving Malthus's major thesis quite wrong. The main social concern in many of the western European countries was rather with the level of mortality. The task of measuring the risk of death also became an important factor in the management and expansion of life insurance operators and with more frequent and more accurate censuses and vital data mortality rates specific for age and sex could be calculated. These were fundamental elements in the development of actuarial science and in the construction of life tables. Studies of the causes of death related to age were also aids to the measurement of the effectiveness of public health schemes and preventive medicine. It was not until the discovery that birth rates were declining towards the end of the century that renewed attention was given to the matter of fertility. Throughout most of the European world population growth had come to be accepted as a sign of national vigour and integrity, and a decline in birth rates tended to be associated with national degeneracy, hedonism and selfishness, and to be considered contrary to the basic ethical principles of Christianity.

More will be said in Chapter 4 of the reaction of Western man to these trends: the reason for mentioning it here is merely to suggest that it probably helps to explain the increasing attention focused upon fertility studies towards the end of the century. These studies were assisted by the improvement in vital data as the compulsory registration of births and deaths became widespread practice, by the introduction of more demographic questions in census schedules, and by the trend towards the establishment of national, provincial and even municipal statistical offices. Sociologists, especially in France where the decline in the birth rate was apparent from the early years of the nineteenth century, were also becoming increasingly interested in studies relating to the family. Le Play,[7] for example, writing between 1855 and 1871, sought to explain the decrease in French fertility in terms of the changes in the rules of inheritance, and in 1890 Arsène Dumont[8] developed his famous theory of the decline in fertility in terms of greater social mobility or 'social capillarity'. Much of this theorizing was speculative and went far beyond what could be measured by available statistics. Many of the best statistical analyses of fertility trends come from official inquiries, two excellent examples of which are the 'Royal Commission upon the Decline of the Birth Rate and on the Mortality of Infants in New South Wales' (Australia) in 1904,[9] and the general inquiry by T. H. E. Stevenson,[10] the Registrar General, into the fertility of marriages in England and Wales based upon the data obtained in the census of 1911.

By the early years of this century the study of population movements and trends had been revived in many parts of the European world. This was stimulated by the knowledge, by now widely ascertainable from reliable systems of vital registration as well as from more accurate censuses, that the rate of population growth was slowing down as a result of a marked decline in birth rates. In some cases, such as the official inquiry referred to above in New South Wales in 1904, the haunting fear that nations must wither away because of declining fertility was already present. To some extent the awakening interest was scientific rather than political and was concerned to measure not merely national growth rates, but also differentials within a given society, such as by social and economic class, by urban and rural areas. Yet the motivation of many of these works was the threat to national prestige which was felt to be implied in the trends and differentials being analysed. This was the case with one of the pioneer studies in the field of differentials, *On the Relation of Fertility in Man to Social Status and on the Changes in this Relation that have taken Place during the Last Fifty Years* by David Heron, a study based upon London

27

and published by the Drapers' Company Research Memoirs as Vol. I of a series, *Studies in National Deterioration.*

The work of men like Dumont in France, Heron and Stevenson in England, and Coghlan in Australia, was matched by new studies of fertility and mortality in many other countries; Westergaard in Denmark, Willcox and Hill in the United States of America, and Beneduce and Gini in Italy. There was also a renewed interest in the great movement which had led to the peopling of the Americas and Oceania; ranging from Frederick Jackson Turner's imaginative concept of the *Significance of the Frontier in American History,* published in 1893, to the detailed statistical work in countries of origin by such scholars as Gustav Sundbörg of Sweden.[11]

The advancement of knowledge in all these fields depended upon better analytical tools and better data. But what kinds of data? The scientific interests in population which were now developing implied much more than the simple measurement of growth rates at any point of time, by the subtraction of deaths from births and the expression of the difference as a ratio of the total population. They implied rather analyses of the whole structure of populations, of the manner in which growth rates were affected by changes in age structure, marriage patterns, degree of urbanization, and social and occupational mobility. Nor was growth and quantity of population the only issue: increasing interest was being displayed in the qualitative aspects of population change by the eugenicists and, in the New World countries in particular, by the advocates of selective immigration policies.

Thus the definition of terms and new techniques of measurement became important. Simple *birth* and *death* rates per 1,000 of total population were not enough; births and deaths had to be measured against the segments of the population to which they applied, and to be specific for age and sex. Whereas mortality had been the factor which received most attention in the nineteenth century, increasing attention was now being given to the measurement of fertility. But how was fertility to be measured?

A distinction needs to be made here between *fertility* and *fecundity.* The latter may be defined as the maximum physiological capacity of the human female to conceive; but even today this cannot be precisely measured because there remain many unsolved questions relating to such matters as the onset of menarche and ovulation, the precise duration of the fertile period within each

28

menstrual cycle, the duration of anovulatory cycles after pregnancy, and the relation between age and fecundity. In any case, considered within the context of *society*, instead of as a purely physiological phenomenon, *fecundity* has little meaning, because social customs, religious practices, economic forces and many other factors impose limitations which always keep actual reproductive performance below physiological capacity.

Hence, socially, the only meaningful concept is that of fertility, or the *actual* reproductive performance of women or, for that matter, of men. The reason why human fertility is usually measured in terms of the female is obvious; the reproductive span of the female can be defined as covering the period between menarche and menopause, but there are no clearly definable limits in the case of males.

Assuming that a woman's fertile years lie between ages 15 and 49, that is a period of thirty-five years, and that she was married throughout the whole of this period, it might be quite possible for her to have up to twenty conceptions; but this is much above the *average* figure known to have existed in any community. In no society do all women marry at the onset of puberty, or stay married until menopause. Some do not marry at all; some marry and are widowed or die during their child-bearing years; some marry but are infertile because of their own or their husband's sterility. Moreover, not all conceptions result in live births. Many societies also have customs which forbid or restrict intercourse for long periods after the birth of a child. Thus there are many biological, social and environmental factors which reduce average fertility well below the theoretical maximum, and the highest known *average* number of births to women by the end of their child-bearing years is about ten. This seems to have been the level attained by the early settlers in French Canada in the seventeenth century. The nearest modern approach to this is found in the Cocos Islands with a total of about 8·8 children, or the anabaptist Hutterites of North America whose fertility in 1946–50 also implied an average of about eight children by the end of the child-bearing period.

These concepts of *age-specific fertility* and of *total fertility* enable comparisons to be made between populations which may vary greatly in age composition and provide a summary picture of the number of births to be expected from a woman living through the whole child-bearing period. This idea of standardizing to a common base is essential to many aspects of comparative demographic analyses. For example, the very great difference between the total fertility of Australia (3·29 in 1957–9) and of the Cocos Islands as given in Table 2.1 is due to two factors: Australian women cease having children at an earlier age and have lower age-specific fertilities at each age, compared with the Cocos women. But there remain a number of variables which are important to an understanding of the growth of human populations and which are not revealed in Table 2.1. Differentials in the frequency of marriage

Table 2.1: Examples of High Fertility: Age Specific Fertility Rates per Woman, together with Total Fertility[12]

| Population | Age Group | | | | | | | Sum of Specific Rates, × 5 (i.e. Total Fertility) |
	15–19	20–24	25–29	30–34	35–39	40–44	45–49	
Cocos Islands 1932–7	0·130	0·378	0·442	0·294	0·280	0·216	0·024	8·820
Hutterites 1946–50	0·120	0·231	0·383	0·391	0·345	0·208	0·042	8·600
Brazil 1940	0·082	0·256	0·308	0·271	0·207	0·127	0·041	6·450
China Yangtze Area 1931–5	0·078	0·325	0·322	0·260	0·207	0·083	0·005	6·400
Mauritius 1958	0·144	0·306	0·263	0·229	0·155	0·054	(0·020)*	5·855

*Estimated

are not included, and the differences between the Cocos Islands and Australia could conceivably be accounted for by different proportions of people married by each age. Nor does the Table indicate the proportion of women who marry who will live to the end of the reproductive period; the high-fertility rates of women in the later years of their child-bearing lives may be counterbalanced by the fact that they may be very few in number. Australia, for example, is a country of very low death rates, with a very high proportion of those who marry living to the end of the child-bearing years, so that relatively low age-specific female fertility rates are compensated for to some extent by the relatively large

30

number of women surviving. Conversely, the Yangtze area in 1931–5, in Table 2. 1, probably suffered high mortality which would thus tend to offset the effect of high specific fertilities of higher ages upon growth rates. In short, in conditions of low mortality a total fertility of 3·29 in Australia might achieve a growth rate as high or higher than total fertilities of 6 in areas of high mortality.

The relation between mortality rates and growth rates has, however, more to do with the levels of deaths in the early years of life than with the proportions entering the child-bearing cycle who live through to menopause. In countries like the United States of America, England and Wales, Sweden, New Zealand or Australia, only about 2 per cent of babies die in their first year of life; but in other countries where nutritional standards are low and where modern medical science is unknown, more than 20 per cent of babies might die in infancy. This was probably the case in many parts of India, Africa and Latin America until quite recently; and as the factors which cause high mortality in infancy generally tend to sustain relatively high death rates in later years as well, the differential between the low mortality and high mortality countries goes on increasing. Thus in high mortality conditions, the survivors of 1,000 births may only be 750 at age 1 and 450 at age 45; whereas in low mortality conditions 980 might survive to age 1 and over 900 to age 45. When mortality is improving, with consequently higher proportions of people living through the child-bearing years, declining age-specific fertility rates or decreasing proportions of women married are not necessarily accompanied by lower population growth rates.

These few illustrations are given to indicate both the quite complicated web of variables which may operate to affect population growth and structure and the refinements which must be achieved in the basic statistics before these variables can be taken into account in indexes of measurement. The first essentials in demographic measurement are accurate records of births and deaths; but in order to understand the implications of 'crude' measurements derived from these, such as birth and death rates per 1,000 of total population, the basic data need to be 'refined' – births need to be related to mothers by age and deaths to age and sex. To get further towards ideal refinements it becomes necessary to record the proportion of the males and females in a population who are married and to relate births not merely to mothers' ages, but also to such factors as parity of births, age of mother at marriage and duration of marriage.

No country has attained the ideal situation with regard to the measurement of fertility, or mortality. The requirements of the statistician or demographer have not been covered by what governments have been prepared to demand from people in a census. Nevertheless, great improvements had occurred by the early twentieth century in the collection of vital data and in the demographic material of censuses in many European and overseas countries. The studies of fertility in the censuses of British countries in 1911 bear witness of this; and the quality of the demographic data in the censuses of the United States was some compensation for the absence of a national coverage of birth registration until 1933. Some of the most striking advances in census and vital data were again to come from newly settled countries far from Europe or America. In Australia, for example, the censuses of 1911 and 1921 presented quite comprehensive analyses of family size by such factors as age, duration of marriage, geographical area and occupation. The year 1908 saw the beginning of the collection of Australian birth statistics by age and duration of marriage of mothers. From the demographer's point of view one of the benefits bestowed by colonial control in some Asian countries was the development of regular (and often reasonably accurate) censuses. India, with a continuous series of decennial censuses from 1871, is a good illustration of this point.

In the western European world the improvement in the quality of the census and vital statistics was accompanied by increasing attention to the analysis of fertility and growth trends. The realization that simple birth and death rates measured against the total population would vary according to age and sex composition, as well as to the proportions of the populations marrying and the age at marriage, encouraged attempts to control these variables through standardization and to find a synthetic index which would determine the 'true' or 'intrinsic' rates of increase and which would indicate the extent to which a population was above or below replacement level. The fact that births exceeded deaths at a given moment did not necessarily mean that a population's fertility was above replacement level in the long run, but might arise wholly from the fact that the age composition was temporarily biased in ways which would both accentuate the birth rate (that is with a high proportion of women in the child-bearing age groups) and deflate the death rate (for example, with relatively few people in the older age groups, or 'exposed to the risk' of dying).

The idea of a reproduction rate was related to the concepts of *age-specific fertility rates* and the *total fertility rate*. The latter, which is the sum of the age-specific fertility rates divided by the total number of women of child-bearing age, provides a synthetic index of the number of babies who would be born to women during their child-bearing years according to the fertility experience of a given year. If we multiply the age-specific birth rates by the ratio of female to total births, and allow for the number of these female births expected to die before they grow up to replace their mothers, then we have a concept of a net *replacement* or *reproduction* rate.

The first net reproduction ratio was computed in 1884 by Richard Bockh, Director of the Berlin Statistical Office. In the 1920s and 1930s the *gross* and *net reproduction rates* were widely used, the former as a measure of fertility and differing from the 'total fertility rate' only in so far as it used only *female* instead of *all* births; and the latter as a measure of the rate of growth or decline that would occur if the rates of fertility and mortality at the time of measurement remained constant over time. The classic work in this field was R. R. Kuczynski's *The Measurement of Population Growth : Measurement and Results*, which was published in London in 1936 and which included reproduction rates for almost every country for which the necessary basic data were available.

A few years before Kuczynski's book was published important studies in the United States of America were aiming to solve the riddle of the 'true' or 'intrinsic' rates of growth of populations by allowing for the variations in birth and death rates brought about by changing age composition. In 1925 Louis I. Dublin and Alfred J. Lotka published an article 'On the True Rate of Increase, as Exemplified by the Population of the United States, 1920'.[13] They showed that if fertility and mortality remained constant, age and sex composition would eventually become fixed or 'stable', thus giving a constant growth rate. Lotka then went on to develop a general theory of the interrelation of the processes of fertility, mortality and growth rates based upon this principle of the stable population. As one commentator has written, 'Lotka's contribution

33

to demography can be likened in some respects to that of Newton to physics. Both achieved a synthesis in analytical theory which had far-reaching significance, and both set a frame for new empirical investigations.'[14]

Stable population theory has been shown to be of limited value in the demographic situation which has developed in the European and Western World since Lotka was writing. The great fluctuations in fertility following the years of economic recession in the 1930s and the 'baby boom' and 'marriage boom' of the years following 1945, have introduced age structures far removed from the 'stable'. Kuczynski's reproduction rates have also tended to be discarded for similar reasons. Stable population theory has been important as an aid in assessing the growth rates of many of the world's high-fertility areas in which vital data have been deficient, for here age and sex structures have been much closer to the stable situation and where intercensal growth rates have been known, stable population theory has enabled the probable birth and death rates to be calculated.

While regular censuses are now established in the majority of countries, their accuracy is often in doubt, and in many of those areas in which growth rates are highest and the ratio of available resources to population lowest, annual vital data are still extremely deficient. Consequently the demographer still has to rely a great deal upon quite elementary measures or upon interpretative theory to assess trends in population growth.

The main emphasis in modern demography has been a tendency to turn away from mortality and to concentrate upon fertility and the study of factors that can reduce birth rates enough to close the expanding growth rates. Attention has turned from summary measures which synthesize the fertility of women living within the child-bearing years at a given point of time to the study of the fertility of 'cohorts' of women born at a given time or married at a given age, by tracing their fertility performance through their reproductive life-span. When do women marry? How soon do they start bearing children? What are the intervals between births? When do they cease having children? How many children do they have at given durations of marriage? What size of family do people want? What kinds of birth control do people practise, and why? These are some of the basic questions to which demographers are directing their attention today, and as few countries provide the necessary official data, much of the basic material has had to be collected by sample investigations in the field. Greater understanding of the marriage patterns and family building processes in areas of high fertility can elucidate the nature of the problems that must be solved before fertility can be reduced; and the study of low-fertility societies can suggest possible ways and means of achieving this. Quite apart from the relevance of these studies to the solution of 'problems' they also emphasize the unique factors in the demographic situation of the world today, and those factors exist in the extraordinarily high growth rates of the world's underdeveloped areas almost as much as they do in the efficient reproductive systems of the world's high-income developed countries with their controlled fertility and, historically speaking, extremely long expectations of life. For a proper understanding of the uniqueness of today's demographic situation it is necessary to go back in time to try and understand the essential features of the pre-industrial world, to study the factors that gave rise to a process which has culminated in a world growth rate of 1·7 per cent or more a year – a rate sufficient to double population in about forty years.

Figure 2.1 :
Countries taking a Census c. 1960 (shaded areas)

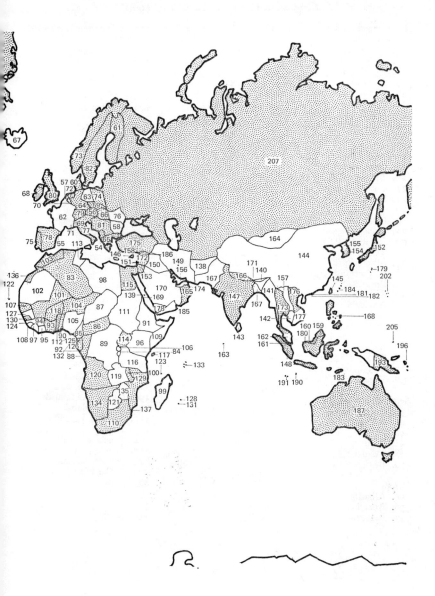

(See next page for key.)

Countries Taking a Census c. 1960

North America
1. Canada
4. Dominican Republic
5. El Salvador
8. Honduras
9. Jamaica
10. Mexico
12. Panama
13. Canal Zone (Panama)
14. Trinidad & Tobago
15. USA
16. Antigua
18. Barbados
19. Bermuda
20. British Honduras
21. Cayman Islands
22. Dominica (UK)
23. Greenland (Dan.)
24. Grenada
25. Guadeloupe
26. Leeward Islands (UK)
27. Martinique
28. Netherlands Antillies
29. Puerto Rico
30. St Kitts-Nevis & Anguilla
31. St Lucia
23. St Vincent
35. Turks and Caisos Islands
36. Virgin Islands (UK)
37. Virgin Islands (US)
38. Windward Islands

South America
39. Argentina
41. Brazil
42. Chile
46. Peru
48. Venezuela
50. British Guiana

Europe
54. Albania
56. Austria
57. Belgium
59. Czechoslovakia
60. Denmark
61. Finland
64. Germany (FR)
65. Greece
66. Hungary
68. Ireland
69. Italy
70. Luxembourg
71. Monaco
72. Netherlands
73. Norway
74. Poland
75. Portugal
78. Spain
79. Switzerland
80. UK
81. Yugoslavia
82. Sweden

Africa
83. Algeria
86. Central African Republic
88. Congo (Brazzaville)
90. Dahomey
92. Gabon
93. Ghana
100. Malawi
101. Mali
103. Morocco
104. Niger
107. Senegal
110. South Africa
112. Togo
114. Uganda
115. United Arab Republic
118. Upper Volta
120. Angola
122. Cape Verde Islands
124. Equatorial Guinea
125. Fernando Poo
126. Rio Muni
129. Mozambique
130. Portuguese Guinea
131. Reunion

132. St Thomas and Île du Prince
133. Seychelles
134. South West Africa
136. Spanish Sahara

Asia
146. Cyprus
147. India
148. Indonesia
151. Israel
152. Japan
153. Jordan
154. Republic of Korea
159. Malaysia (Sabah)
160. Sarawak
165. Muscat and Oman
166. Nepal
168. Philippines
171. Sikkim
172. Syria
173. Thailand
175. Turkey
176. North Vietnam
180. Brunei
181. Hong Kong
182. Macau
183. Portuguese Timor
184. Ryukyu Islands

Oceania
187. Australia
188. New Zealand
189. Western Samoa
190. Christmas Islands
191. Cocos Islands
192. Norfolk Islands
193. Papua
201. American Samoa
202. Guam
203. Johnston Islands
204. Wake Island
205. Nauru

USSR
207. USSR

Countries Not Taking Census c. 1960

North America		
2. Costa Rica	89. Congo (Leopoldville)	145. China (Taiwan)
3. Cuba	91. Ethiopia	149. Iran
6. Guatemala	94. Guinea	150. Iraq
7. Haiti	95. Ivory Coast	155. North Korea
11. Nicaragua	96. Kenya	156. Kuwait
17. Bahama Islands	97. Liberia	157. Laos
32. Monserrat	98. Libya	158. Lebanon
33. St Pierre & Miquelon	99. Madagascar	161. Singapore
	102. Mauritania	162. Malaya
	105. Nigeria	163. Maldive Islands
South America	106. Rwanda	164. Mongolia
40. Bolivia	108. Sierra Leone	167. Pakistan (East and
43. Columbia	109. Somalia	West)
44. Ecuador	111. Sudan	169. Qatar
45. Paraguay	113. Tunisia	170. Saudia Arabia
47. Uruguay	116. Tanzania	174. Trucial Oman
51. Falkland Islands	117. Zanzibar	177. Republic of Viet-
52. Surinam	119. Zambia	Nam
53. French Guiana	121. Bechuanaland	178. Yemen
	123. Comoro Islands	179. Bonin Islands
Europe	127. Gambia	185. Aden
55. Andorra	128. Mauritius	186. Palestine
58. Bulgaria	135. Southern Rhodesia	
62. France	137. Swaziland	Oceania
63. Germany (East)		194. French Polynesia
67. Iceland	Asia	195. New Caledonia
76. Romania	138. Afghanistan	196. British Solomons
77. San Marino	139. Bahrain	197. Fiji
	140. Bhutan	198. Gilbert & Ellis
Africa	141. Burma	Islands
84. Burundi	142. Cambodia	199. Pitcairn
85. Cameroon	143. Ceylon	200. Tonga
87. Chad	144. China (Mainland)	206. New Hebrides

39

Chapter 3

The Populations of the Ancient and Medieval World

J. C. Russell[1] introduces his study, *Late Ancient and Medieval Population* with a quotation from one medieval historian, Lot, about another, Pirenne. Lot is stated to have quoted Pirenne as writing that 'Demography is perhaps the most important of all social sciences'. Demographers can appreciate the tribute, but, as Russell also emphasizes, population history was long lost among the maze of political, economic and social histories. Modern research by historians and demographers is slowly adding to knowledge of population trends before the nineteenth century, but there is still much uncertainty, and many still take as their starting-point estimates from the middle of the seventeenth century. This emphasis upon the seventeenth century is not surprising, for it is approximately the dividing line between studies which must be highly speculative and those which, in some countries, could be based upon reasonably reliable data. As already emphasized in Chapter 1, the habit of collecting statistics of baptisms, burials and marriages and of enumerating national populations began to take hold in Europe from the seventeenth century, after periods for which only the scantiest data have been found.

The tribute of Pirenne to demography and the desire of demographers to prove his point provide perhaps one reason why they have remained reluctant to speculate about either the remote past or the distant future. Naturally they have preferred to stick to analyses based upon observable data. Yet there remain just enough fragments about earlier times to tempt the historian and demographer to reconstruct their population history. One notable and massive attempt to carry this reconstruction back to the beginning of the Christian era was made towards the end of the nineteenth century by the German scholar, J. Beloch, particularly in his *Die Bevölkerung der griechisch-romanischen Welt* (1886). Critical reassessments of Beloch's work and the more recent studies by such scholars as J. C. Russell, referred to above, and by Abbott Payson Usher of Harvard University, whose *History of Population and Settlement in Eurasia* was first published in 1930,[2] may not, as indeed they cannot, provide final answers to the riddles of the past, but they do show conclusively enough that earlier theories about 'the great populousness' of ancient times, which were common amongst writers in the late eighteenth and early nineteenth centuries, were certainly fallacious. For example, Robert Wallace, Moderator of the General Assembly of the Church of Scotland produced in 1753 *A Dissertation on the Numbers of Mankind in ancient and modern Times: in which the superior Populousness of Antiquity is Maintained.* He concluded that Europe had been more densely populated between the siege of Troy and the conquests of Alexander than it was in his own time. Similar views were even more extravagantly expressed by Montesquieu who maintained that, in general, the countries of Europe had larger populations in Charlemagne's day than in the mid-eighteenth century and that by the latter time population was scarcely a tenth of what it had been in ancient times. Wallace's opinions were challenged by David Hume, who, in the tenth book of his *Political Discourses* (1752), attacked Wallace's manuscript even before it was published. Hume argued that in conditions of slavery, wholesale murder and barbarism, together with unstable government and limited and fluctuating trading areas, population growth would not be encouraged. He doubted if antiquity had anything to compare, in the way of riches or numbers of people, with those provided in his own day within the area bounded by a circle of two hundred miles' radius taking Dover or Calais as the centre.

While the disintegration of the Roman Empire, with the resulting fragmentation of economic and political units within Europe, may have re-created conditions – the so-called 'Dark Ages' – which were inimical to rapid population growth, a study of the conditions and patterns of growth of *modern* populations at least tends to support Hume's general proposition rather than that of Montesquieu or Wallace concerning *ancient* populations. The position appears from all available evidence to have been the reverse of Montesquieu's argument, with the late eighteenth-century population, not ten times but perhaps at least three times that of the world at the time of Julius Caesar. The population of the Roman world was again almost certainly greater than that of the still more ancient world, although over time there were even then probably moderate upsurges of growth in response to migration to new lands or as the result of technical innovation, followed by periods of stability and even decline. But over the *long* term, the evidence is in favour of slow growth, not of secular decline.

Accounts of the prehistoric and early historic periods offer the following propositions about mankind's earlier growth.

1 During the palaeolithic age, beginning about 1,000,000 BC and terminating about 25,000 BC, the average increase per generation must have been very low, for otherwise the world would have been quite densely populated by the latter date. This view is supported by the fact that the present population of the world could have been produced from two dozen individuals living 100,000 years ago with an average annual natural increase of only 0·02 per cent.

2 With the retreat of the last great ice-cap beginning about 25,000 BC the areas of forest and grass lands extended, leading to the cultivation of plants and the domestication of animals from about 7000 BC. The growth of village farming followed in an expanding area from focal points in southern Asia (India) and south-west Asia and North Africa. A similar but somewhat later movement occurred in America.

3 A recent American writer, Edward S. Deevey, has estimated that population had grown from 86·5 million in 4000 BC to 133 million at the beginning of the Christian era, but this last figure is not supported from other sources, which put world population at AD 0 between 200 and 300 million.[3]

4 This great upsurge was the result of the regulation of water and soil resources through the building of dykes, irrigation and terracing, which, beginning in the Lower Nile region and in Mesopotamia in about 4000 BC, led to increased food supplies, urban communities and increasing efficiency in the use of resources and labour. Similar developments after 3000 BC in the Indus region of western India led to the growth of a great city-centred civilization there. This was followed by a similar trend in the great flood-plain of the Yellow River in China. Comparable developments occurred in the northern Andes and lower Mexico.

5 By AD 0 great trading civilizations, with established industries as well as agriculture, had been established; and while succeeding centuries continued to be beset with ravages of disease and plague, population growth continued, almost certainly at a much faster

rate than in ancient times, until by 1650 there were estimated to be between 465 and 545 million people in the world compared with only 200 or 300 million in AD 0.

What then was the nature of this growth in the various sectors of the world? J. Beloch's great work of 1886 still stands as the classical study of the Roman world at the beginning of the Christian era. His estimates of the population of the Roman Empire in AD 14, that is at the death of Augustus, are given in Table 3. 1. Subsequent

Table 3.1 : Population of the World about AD 14 according to J. Beloch

	Number in thousands	Density per sq. mile
Europe		
Italy	6,000	62·2
Sicily	600	59·5
Sardinia-Corsica	500	39
Iberia	6,000	26
Narbonensis	1,500	39
Gaul	3,400	16·3
Danube	2,000	12·2
Greece	3,000	28·6
Total	23,000	26
Asia		
Asia (Province)	6,000	114
Asia Minor	7,000	44
Syria	6,000	143
Cyprus	500	135
Total	19,500	77·5
Africa		
Egypt	5,000	465·0
Cyrenaica	500	85·5
Province of Africa	6,000	39·0
Total	11,500	67·5
Roman Empire	54,000	41·5

scholars have tended rather to raise Beloch's figures to higher levels than to challenge their basic validity.

On the other side of the world lay the great land mass of China, where two census reports of the Han dynasty gave totals of 59·5 million in AD 2 and 50 millions in AD 156. These estimates did not cover the entire area of China, and were revised upward by Usher[4] to include the whole of China according to its 1930 boundaries, with 71 million in AD 2 and 60 million in AD 156. The figure for AD 2 is the same as another estimate by J. D. Durand published in 1960.[5]

In India the position in pre-Christian and early Christian times remains even more uncertain than that for Europe or China. Professor Kingsley Davis,[6] after briefly reviewing early evidence, concludes:

. . . putting the evidence from archaeology, literature and history together, we reach the conclusion that before the Christian era, India had a substantial population, first because of its advanced technology, and second because of the fertile environment for the application of this technology. . . . This view is confirmed by Pran Nath, who after careful examination of the evidence believes that the population of ancient India, say around 300 BC, was between 100 and 140 million.

Some of that supporting evidence indicated that one small kingdom had thirty-seven towns of over 5,000 inhabitants, and that India's first real empire under the sway of Chandragupta (c. 321–297 BC) left records indicating a standing army of some 700,000 men, the maintenance of which would have required a very substantial population.

These estimates at about the beginning of the Christian era for the Roman Empire (54 m.), China (71 m.) and India (lower estimate of 100 m.) add up to 225 million. Allowing for populations of Africa south of the Sahara, south-eastern Asia, northern Europe and the Americas, a world total of some 300 million or higher would seem to be reasonable; and if so, and if the higher estimate of 545 million at 1650 is also accepted, the average rate of growth in between was, by today's standards, very low – little more than 0·1 per cent – but nevertheless this was also much above long-run trends in the pre-Christian world. Again, however, the fluctuations that must have occurred in the period AD 0–1650 within specific areas and within specified periods of time remain very difficult to determine, particularly until at least the fourteenth century.

Beloch concluded that the population of the Roman Empire increased through the first and all or part of the second century after Augustus, and perhaps then remained fairly constant until the end of the fourth century, with divergent trends in different parts of the Empire. In Egypt and Asia Minor, which were densely settled areas, the gap between resources and population was narrower than in many other areas, and the conclusion is that population growth was therefore probably slower than in many of the western provinces. From the evidence of the historian, Polybius, the citizen population of the Greek states appears to have decreased from the time of Pericles (490–429 BC) as a result of losses through wars, epidemics and emigration, followed by declining birth rates as the result of both the relatively low proportions marrying and the prevention of births after marriage. Similar demographic factors appear to have led to natural decrease in later Roman society from about the end of the second century AD.[7]

There is little direct evidence relating to the demographic trends which followed the disintegration of Roman authority. The agricultural and industrial arts and the improvements in overland communications which accompanied the spread of Roman authority would have created conditions which favoured population increase, but these were offset in some areas by the destruction caused by the barbarian invasions from the east. These invasions were particularly severe in the region of the lower Danube, but farther west, in Italy, southern France and Spain, the invaders tended to be absorbed into the existing population without serious disruption. Generally, so far as can be judged from historical evidence, the pattern from about the fourth to the fifteenth centuries seems to have been one of population decline in the east, including Mesopotamia, Persia, Turkestan and Egypt, but of slow increase towards the west, with the possible exception of Spain which suffered severe disruption as a result of invasions from both Europe and North Africa.[8]

In the case of Britain, population estimates relating to Roman times and based upon archaeological evidence, range between 0·5 and 1·5 million, with majority support for a figure around 1 million or higher. From then on the demographic picture remains very uncertain until the Domesday survey of 1086. Some estimates based upon this survey place the population of England at about 1·8 million to 2 million, which figures were derived by using a multiplier of six to convert households to people. J. C. Russell, in his study, *British Medieval Population*,[9] argues that, although evasions of the Domesday Survey were numerous, the multiplier of six to a household is too high and he reduces the figure to 1·1 million. Even if the upper figure is used, this implies a very slow rate of increase in England over the first ten centuries of the Christian era. If the lower figure is taken, this could imply virtually no increase when compared with the estimate for Roman Britain.

From this point, however, there was fairly clearly a considerable acceleration of growth in England until the middle of the fourteenth century, although monastic records suggest that the rate of increase had slowed down a century before the great catastrophe of the Black Death struck in 1348. The population was then estimated to be 3·7 million; Russell puts the population in 1377, thirty years after the onslaught of the Black Death, at only 2·5 million, and further concludes from detailed examination of the inquisitions post-mortem that 'the plague reduced the population probably about 50 per cent by 1400' – that is 50 per cent below what it would have been by 1400 had plague not occurred. The immediate destructive force of the Black Death is suggested in Russell's estimate that the population may have fallen by 20 per cent in three years, 1348–50. Just what age groups were most severely struck by the Black Death and later visitations of plague in the remainder of the fourteenth century are difficult to assess. Russell concluded that it killed off more men than women, and that in general the mortality was least severe among the very young and most severe amongst the old. If this was the pattern of mortality it would have tended to increase the birth rate as the young children least affected by plague grew to marriageable ages, even without any change in the fertility of marriage, and so a revival of natural increase could have been expected again by early in the fifteenth century. This in fact seems to have occurred.

An economic historian, Postan,[10] has argued from the assumption of a positive correlation between prices and population movements in medieval times that downward trends in prices implied that the population must have begun to fall in England about 1330, or almost twenty years before the Black Death. Whatever the cause of such a decline, there can, however, be little doubt that the Black Death and other visitations of plague were undoubtedly the main check on population growth between the eleventh and sixteenth centuries. Even so, recovery after the fourteenth century must have been considerable because there now seems good evidence that by the close of the seventeenth century the population of England and Wales was over 5 million. The best-known estimate is that of Gregory King which gave a figure of 5·5 million in 1695. Careful appraisal of King's data and methods has tended to support his conclusion, although Professor Glass has suggested that King's estimate might be reduced to 5·2 million.[11] However, the essential soundness of King's figure remains.

In northern Europe the pattern of growth appears to have been broadly similar. In the case of France, estimates suggest an increase from approximately 6 million in the early Christian era to 8·5 million under Charlemagne at the beginning of the ninth century. Thereafter, as in England, growth seems to have been more rapid. A survey of hearths made in France in 1328 was examined by E. Levasseur in his work, *La Population Française*, published in 1889. He applied a multiplier of 4 to convert 'hearths' to 'people' and in this way estimated a population of about 20 million. Another French scholar, A. Landry,[12] suggests a similar figure. The Black Death affected the French population much as it did that of England. Thereafter France suffered further checks which prevented the recovery that was apparent in England from the beginning of the fifteenth century. The Hundred Years War was followed in the later fifteenth century by the Wars of Religion, by which time numbers appear to have been reduced to some 16 million. The estimated 20 million of 1328 does not seem to have been attained again in France until the seventeenth century.

One estimate of the population of Europe in the seventeenth

Table 3.2 : Population of European area in the Seventeenth Century, according to Riccioli (in millions)

Italy (with Sicily and adjacent islands)	10–11
Spain (with Portugal and Sardinia)	10
France	19–20
Great Britain and Ireland	4
Lower Germany, Holland and Zeeland	4
Upper Germany	20
Illyria, Dalmatia, Greece and the Islands	10
Macedonia, Thrace, Moesia	6
Poland, Lithuania, Pomerania	6
Denmark, Gotland, Sweden, Norway, Livonia and other northern lands	8
Total	97–99

century which has often been quoted by later writers is that of Riccioli,[13] a learned Jesuit priest who was chosen by the Roman Catholic Church to defend its attitude towards the heretical doctrines of Copernicus and Galileo, and who later, according to W. F. Willcox,[14] compiled 'obvious conjectures and essays concerning the true volume of mankind'.

Some of Riccioli's guesses are probably on the low side (e.g. Great Britain and Ireland) but in many instances they bear a close resemblance to later figures prepared by Beloch in 1900, which are given in Table 3. 3, but which excluded the Greek and Macedonian regions.

Table 3.3: J. Beloch's population estimates for European countries in the Seventeenth Century

	Number in millions	Density per sq. miles
Italy	13	114
Spain and Portugal	10	44
France	16	88
England and Wales	4·5	78
Scotland and Ireland	2	32
Netherlands	3	104
Denmark	0·6	39
Sweden, Norway, Finland	1·4	2·5
Poland with Prussia	3	36·9
Germany	20	73
Total	73·5	50

Obvious features in these and Riccioli's figures compared with A D 0 are the much greater densities and the movement of the great centres of population to the north and west. By the seventeenth century, the European area and not the Mediterranean and Byzantine zones dominated the scene.

After reviewing the data on world population growth and distribution until the seventeenth century Usher[15] reached the following conclusion:

None of the centres of massive modern population was maturely settled at the beginning of the Christian era. North-western Europe may be classed as a frontier, India and China were in early phases of the intermediate stage of settlement. In the Near and Middle East settlement was mature, but the absolute mass of the population was not large, because the areas capable of significant settlement were small. . . . By the fourteenth century the progress of settlement in Europe was notable, and growth continued throughout the fifteenth and sixteenth centuries. At the close of the sixteenth century India was still incompletely settled, though portions of the Ganges Valley were beyond doubt maturely settled. China was only on the verge of the period of notable development that established the modern patterns in her density map. Thus we may say that the Mediterranean region achieved substantial maturity of settlement by the beginning of the Christian era. North-western Europe achieved maturity of settlement, with some areas excepted, by the close of the sixteenth century. India and China did not achieve full maturity of settlement until the early part of the nineteenth century.

The situation of India and China, and particularly the latter, throughout these centuries requires further consideration.

The precise trends in India during this period remain even more conjectural than elsewhere, but much of the splendour of pre-Christian times had gone and, according to figures quoted by Kingsley Davis,[16] the population may not have been any greater in 1650 than it was in AD 0. By contrast, Ceylon, through extensive development of irrigated agriculture reached a zenith in the twelfth century, and although some consider an estimate of 20 million excessive for this period, the population may nevertheless have been considerably greater than it is today.

Recorded statistics in China indicate little change in the population – and perhaps even some decline – between AD 2 and 156. Durand,[17] after multiplying the recorded number of households by a factor of 6, estimates 71 million Chinese in AD 2 and 62 million in AD 156. As with the fall of the Roman Empire in the West, the disintegration of the Han empire in China in the third century AD created conditions in which only fragmentary population records were made. The censuses again operated with reasonable efficiency in the eighth century under the T'ang dynasty, but if they were accurate, they reveal a decrease compared with the first century. Durand suggests that, compared with 71 million in AD 2, the population may have been as low as 37 million at the beginning of the eighth century and possibly did not rise above 52 million until over a century later. By contrast, Durand's interpretation of Sung Dynasty figures of the eleventh century, when China was again united after a long period of disintegration, suggests a steady upward trend from perhaps 60 million in 1014 to 123 million

49

in 1193. The actual census figures of persons and households recorded over this period implied average households varying from about 2 to 2·2 persons. Durand assumes both that these refer only to *males* and that there was serious undercounting. Consequently he applied a multiplier of 6 to recorded households to provide the revised estimates quoted above. If his estimate of 123 million in 1103 is correct – and the arguments he presents for using such a high multiplier are not entirely convincing – it suggests that China again suffered population decline after it fell to the Mongols in the early thirteenth century. A census in 1290, ten years after Kublai Khan became Emperor of all China, recorded 13,196,000 households and 58,835,000 persons, that is 4·5 persons per household. This total apparently did not include those of the old regime who had fled to the mountains and rebels in arms, but these alone could not account for the rapid decline in population implied in these figures, compared with 123 million at the beginning of the twelfth century. Durand concludes that the Mongol records were very incomplete on the grounds that many areas were not covered by the Mongol censuses, but the Mongol figures on the other hand do fit fairly well with a series of censuses under the Ming Dynasty beginning in 1381, which are summarized in an article published by O. B. van der Sprenkel in 1953.[18]

The Ming system of population records, running from 1381 to 1620, deserves comment, for they suggest an official concern about censuses not paralleled elsewhere until the middle of the eighteenth century.

The Ming records were based on a system of permanent registers. The primary units of the organization were the *chia*, composed in principle of eleven households; above these were the *li* comprising ten *chia* plus widows, orphans and others who were exempt from taxation and not assigned to any *chia*. Each year forms were printed from word blocks, and distributed to householders who were then required to complete them by entering details of numbers of persons, occupations and property. The forms were then collected by *chia* leaders and sent to *li* chiefs who passed them on to the *hsien* office where they were checked and counted and then compared with earlier records. Where no increase in population was shown the forms were returned to the local officers who had then to reinvestigate the matter.

Now the main purpose of the Ming system was fiscal, and people may have tended to evade enumeration, particularly those who could come under the protection of powerful rural interests or who could bribe the collectors. From such evidence Ping-ti Ho concludes in his *Studies on the Population of China*[19] that the Ming population counts became increasingly inefficient. As presented by O. B. van der Sprenkel, the Ming figures show the following populations:

	Persons	Households	Persons per household
1381	59,873,000	10,654,000	5·6
1431	50,656,000	9,705,000	5·2
1481	62,458,000	9,128,000	6·8
1532	61,713,000	9,443,000	6·5
1578	60,693,000	10,621,000	5·7
1620–6	51,655,000	9,835,000	5·3

Durand concludes that these Ming statistics became virtually useless in the fifteenth century as indicators of population trends. Ping-ti Ho is of much the same opinion and, on the basis of provincial records of northern and southern provinces, records of land use, crop production and trends in the price of rice; an analysis much like that of Postan's study of England in the fourteenth century; comes to the conclusion that population at the end of the Ming period was probably nearer 150 million than the recorded 52 million. This higher figure is the same as that derived by Carr Saunders[20] from working back from the more reliable records of the late eighteenth century. It should also be noticed that Willcox, who put China's population in 1659 at 70 million in his first estimates of 1931, subsequently revised these upwards to 113 millions in his 1940 estimates published in his *Studies in American Demography*.[21] Wherever the exact figure lay (and the many conjectures show how little trust can be placed in the *chia-li* system, which on the face of things seemed so admirably designed) China about 1650 had, as now, a formidable population in relation to any possible figures that can be applied to other countries.

From the reassessment of the material commented upon above, and a great deal more besides, the situation of the world's population about 1650 now generally quoted, and given in *Determinants & Consequences of Population Trends* published by the United Nations in 1953,[22] are summarized in Table 3.4.

Table 3.4: Estimate of World Population, by Major Regions, 1650 (millions)

Africa	100
North America	1
Latin America	12
Asia (exc. USSR)	327
Europe and Asiatic USSR	103
Oceania	2
Area of European Settlement	118
Area of non-European Settlement	427
World Total	545

We now turn to the factors of growth in these populations from approximately the fifteenth to the seventeenth centuries. From the studies of the growth patterns of modern populations of high fertility and high mortality, as well as of the fertility of sectors of European populations for which sufficient contemporary data are available, three generalizations may be made with reasonable safety.

1 While fertility controls were quite rigidly practised in some areas at specific periods, fertility generally tended to be high, and an average of six pregnancies per married woman by age 49 would not be an unreasonable expectation.

2 The major controls remained the ravages of infectious diseases, and at times wars and invasions, and not inadequate subsistence.

3 There was not any sustained reduction in mortality over large areas, and expectations of life at birth probably seldom exceeded 37 or 38 years over any of the period, and at times fell far below this. Expectations as high as those of many countries of south eastern Asia today (e.g. Malaya, Thailand) were probably unknown until the nineteenth century.

An extensive comparative treatment of life expectations in medieval times by Russell,[23] in an article which elaborates upon his studies of *British Medieval Population*, presents tables based upon tombstone inscriptions of the Roman Empire. These show the highest expectations (up to 42·9 years) in Africa and other dry climates of the Empire least subject to plague, and the lowest in Rome (15·3 years). Most of the expectations lie around 20–24 years. The very low rates for Rome are supported by Durand. After submitting the material of Russell and others to critical analysis, Durand[24] concludes, first, that the expectation of life in Rome probably lay between 15 and 25 years, and secondly, that in the Empire as a whole (assuming mortality to be higher away from the major urban centres than within them, a view which the tables presented by Russell support) a probable life expectation during the first centuries of the Christian era may have been within the range of about 20 to 30 years.

Applying to the Roman data the characteristics of a stable population at given levels of life expectation at birth (e_0^0) Durand shows that a gross reproduction rate of 2·5 and a life expectation at birth of 20 years would have brought about population decline, whereas $e_0^0 = 30$ years would have sustained an increase; and as other evidence suggests that population was slowly increasing, his conclusions of an e_0^0 between 20 and 30 is further supported.

Russell's data for medieval England indicate a 'normal' e_0^0 of between 32 and 35 years; but for the latter half of the fourteenth century, after the Black Death, and the successive visitations of plague which followed it, he concludes that the expectation of life fell to less than 18 years. His estimate for the generation born between 1346 and 1375 was 17·33 years. Russell's figures suggest that an e_0^0 over 30 years was not again achieved until the generation born 1426–1450. The figures he presents of years of life remaining at various ages for males born 1426–1450 offer interesting comparison with a present-day country with very low mortality, in this case Australia, 1953–5. For the former $e_0^0 = 33$, and for the latter $e_0^0 = 67$.

Table 3.5: Expectations of Life at Specific Ages: A Medieval and Modern Comparison

Age	England 1426–50	Age	Australia 1953–5
0	33·0	0	67·1
5–9	36·6	10	59·6
25–29	25·5	30	40·9
35–39	21·7	40	31·7
45–49	18·1	50	22·9
55–59	14·1	60	15·5
65–69	12·3	70	9·6

Russell concludes that under 'normal' medieval conditions of mortality (i.e. when plague was not epidemic) it would require about six children per family to replace those dying. On this basis there was never much margin for growth, for western European society established restrictions upon procreation early on. Probably infanticide and abortion were always practised to some extent, and severely in Rome and the Greek cities, but there were also many more restraints of the 'moral' variety advocated later by Malthus. Some of these restrictive factors were the dominant role of the biological as against the extended family, primogeniture, the custom of the eldest son delaying marriage until the father died, regulations by which peasants often had to seek the manorial lord's permission to marry, edicts (as in some German states) forbidding marriage of paupers. One writer, Lorimer,[25] sees an analogy between the situation of pre-industrial European society and Ireland in the nineteenth century: 'The Irish experience illustrates the restrictive character, as regards fertility, of family structure in pre-industrial western Europe.' However the analogy should not be carried too far, for there is little evidence that either deferred marriage or celibacy was practised in medieval Europe to the extent that it was in Ireland in the late nineteenth century.

Nevertheless the birth rates prevailing in medieval Europe were probably much below those of many Asian countries today. There seems little evidence to suggest that rates would have been substantially above those prevailing in Scandinavia 1735–1800, for which reasonably accurate records are available. These averaged around 33 per 1,000. Probably rates of 40 per 1,000 were exceptional, whereas this level is quite common in the high-fertility countries of the twentieth century.

The main controlling factor of population growth was still infectious disease. Bubonic plague ravaged Europe from the sixth to the fourteenth century. Tuberculosis was also rife, and both diseases spread most readily in urban areas, and in spite of eulogies in history of Roman aqueducts and sewerage, life for the majority of the people was squalid in the extreme. In the warmer climates malaria was a debilitating, as well as a killing disease. The main change in the sixteenth and seventeenth centuries in Europe, compared with earlier times, seems to have been the absence of bubonic plagues.

Russell concludes that the European population probably

54

slowly built up an immunity to tuberculosis, but as this was still the most important single cause of death in Britain as late as the second quarter of the nineteenth century, it probably remained an important killer of *young* adults, and therefore probably had a marked influence upon birth rates, right through the medieval and early modern periods. Plague also tended to attack adults rather than young children, but unlike tuberculosis it was increasingly severe with age. If both tuberculosis and plague were thus age selective, some increased immunity to the former and the disappearance of the latter in the fifteenth century would tend both to reduce death rates and to increase birth rates; the latter by extending the years of fertile life remaining to married women. Herein may lie one explanation of the apparent increase in the rate of growth of many western and northern European countries from approximately the end of the fifteenth century.

Excluding the ravages of the Black Death, the history of medieval population is the story of gradual growth; for most of the time the force of life seems to have been stronger than the force of death. In the Malthusian sense, or in relation to available resources, the restraints upon fertility, among European man at least, were also stronger than they needed to have been, except when plague struck. But medieval Europe inherited the classical notion that population should be kept under control for moral as well as economic reasons, and this view was expressed in the restraints already referred to. Of this aspect, Russell writes:[26]

Roman and medieval society thus determined its own destiny. At any time it could have thrown away its respect for the adjustment of society to subsistence and by rapid procreation have increased its numbers. Only in the time of the two great plagues did loss of life go beyond the limits of potential replacement.

Yet the margin between subsistence and plenty must have been fairly slight most of the time for most of the people, and more improvident procreation may well have reduced population in the long run by introducing periodic famine as well as epidemic disease and, at times, very severe losses through wars, such as the Thirty Years War which may have reduced the populations of the German states by as much as a third.

In the far eastern world of China the upward curve of population was probably continuing for much the same reasons and along much the same lines as in Europe. The role of disease as a controlling factor is less certain but, as in Europe, periods of political instability and warfare, both of which disrupted the ordered pattern of relationship to the land from time to time, were often probably enough to wipe out growth and even to bring decline. Yet if Ping-ti Ho's and Carr Saunders's estimates of 150 million Chinese by 1650 is correct, the upward swing in China after the fourteenth century may have been sharper than in Europe, possibly because then (as now) there were fewer institutional, social and cultural barriers making for fertility restraints than among the European world. One thing seems clear, demographically speaking. If France and the Germanic states were, in quantitative terms, dominating Europe by the seventeenth century, China even then dominated the rest of the world as a single political and demographic unit. Moreover, until western Europe's population 'exploded' in the late nineteenth century as the force of mortality declined, its growth rate was very slight. By contrast China's population appears to have kept up a steady and higher momentum of growth. This fact is often overlooked by Western students who have tended to assume that while European man accelerated his rate of growth, the East remained an inert, over-populated, poverty-stricken mass. As far as China at least is concerned, nothing seems to have been further from the truth. However, it was the people of Europe who first broke away from the Malthusian controls of subsistence, scarcity, famine and disease to establish finally a new demographic balance based upon unique conditions of both mortality and fertility, and for the origins of this story it is necessary to look at the eighteenth and early nineteenth centuries.

Chapter 4

The Growth of the European Nations in the Eighteenth and Nineteenth Centuries

Estimates of the world's population in 1850 ranged between 1,091 and 1,171 millions. There is less conjecture involved in these figures than in earlier times because the habit of census-taking had become fairly common by this period, at least in many European countries. However, it must be admitted that there were still a number of unknown quantities, particularly with regard to the estimated populations of Africa and Asia. But assume for the moment that the figures for 1850 are approximately correct, and assume further that the estimate of the world's population of 545 million in 1650 is also correct, and we are presented with a pattern in which the world's numbers doubled, or more than doubled, in the comparatively short period of 200 years.

These estimates assume that the population of Africa remained approximately stationary.[1] On the other hand there was a very rapid increase in North America from about 1 million in 1650 to 26 million two hundred years later, and a very considerable increase in Latin America from some 7 million to 33 million. Immigration from Europe and the compulsory transfer of some 15 million slaves from Africa were substantial factors in these increases. The estimates of world totals by Carr Saunders, which begin with 545 million people in 1650 and end in 1850 with 1,171 million, as shown above in Table 1.1, are based upon the assumption that the population of Asia rose from 327 million to 741 million, while in the areas inhabited by Europeans population rose from 118 million to 335 million. Thus in a world in which the total population was estimated to have doubled, the European area showed the greatest percentage increase. A discussion of the Asian situation will follow in a later chapter: this chapter will be limited to a consideration of the factors which lay behind this expanding rate of growth in the areas of European settlement, a pattern which is broadly illustrated in Table 1.1.

As already emphasized, the eighteenth century was accompanied by the revival of censuses and the beginnings of reasonably efficient systems of vital registration in European areas. A census of the population was taken in Iceland in 1703, while in French Canada sixteen population counts were made between 1665 and 1754. Before the eighteenth century was out, censuses had also been taken in many German states and in the Scandinavian countries. In Sweden and Denmark parish registers were also reckoned to have attained a high degree of accuracy by the late eighteenth century, and the registration of baptisms and burials by the clergy was well established in England, although the first census did not occur there until 1801.

From such information, and from the principles of 'reverse survival' analysis applied to early nineteenth-century censuses (that is, commencing with the population enumerated at a census and estimating the numbers in each previous year by adding deaths and subtracting births), estimates suggest growth rates throughout the eighteenth century which were almost certainly much above those of earlier periods. As an illustration of possible trends we will consider the case of England and Wales.

The probable trend of population growth of England before the seventeenth century was discussed in Chapter 3, where it was suggested that the upper limit of population at Domesday (1086) was between 1·8 and 2 million. This figure was based upon a multiplier of six persons for each landholder. A figure within this range still implies that very considerable growth occurred over the next 250 years or so. Russell[2] also suggests in his study of British medieval population that the population at the middle of the fourteenth century may have been about 3·7 million, and he supports his estimate of a substantial growth rate around this time from an analysis of the inquisitions post-mortem, and from the evidence of very substantial increases in the numbers of clergy, for whom reasonably accurate figures are available. Russell concludes that the Black Death had a very severe effect on population, probably reducing the total by 20 per cent within a year. Successive attacks of plague thereafter had accumulative effects, and Russell suggests that in the period 1348 to 1400, population may have been reduced by about one half of the level which it could have been expected to attain by the latter date had these catastrophes not intervened. This generalization is based upon the evidence of a commensurate decline in the numbers of clergy. The absence of an increase in clergy until the sixteenth century was taken as further evidence of a lack of marked population increase for almost two centuries after the Black Death; a theory supported by evidence of falling food prices and by the extremely low expectation of life revealed by Russell's life tables which were presented in Chapter 3.

If this evidence of a severe reduction of population after the Black Death, followed by a very slow recovery until the beginnings of the sixteenth century, is to be trusted, there must have been a very rapid increase in population in England and Wales from about 1500 until the end of the seventeenth century, for Gregory King's estimate of 5·5 million for England and Wales in 1695 is now considered to be very close to the true picture. In other words the population in England from the early eleventh century until the end of the seventeenth century seems to have followed the pattern of the logistic curve, with periods of increase being followed by periods of stability and frequently substantial decline after the intervention of catastrophe through plague and other forms of disease; and this only ceased to be the case when the Malthusian controls were finally broken in the nineteenth century. It may well be asked of course why King's figure should be trusted.

Gregory King (1648–1712), a son of a surveyor who, according to a decorous memoir by George Chalmers, practised his profession 'with more attention to good fellowship than mathematical studies generally allow', is best known for his *Estimate of the Comparative Strength of Great Britain* (1695), which was published by George Chalmers[3] long after King's death, in 1802. King had based his estimate on the number of houses subject to tax in 1690, and had used multipliers varying from 5·4 to four persons according to area to get his final estimate for England and Wales of 5·5 million.

This estimate became the subject of lively literary debate,[4] but careful backworking from the early censuses of England and Wales beginning in 1801, especially by John Rickman, appears to have established that Gregory King's estimate of 1695 was not too far off the true mark. Rickman's basic method was to work back from the census of 1801 using constant baptism, burial and marriage rates calculated from data derived from parish records. His estimates for England and Wales in 1700 varied between 5·7 and

6·6 million.[5] Later scholars working further over the data and arguments used by Rickman have tended towards support of the lower rather than the higher figure, thus coming closer to Gregory King's figure of 5·5 million for 1695. But even if the lowest of these estimates, namely that of Professor Glass of 5·2 million, is accepted, this still implies very substantial growth in the fifteenth and sixteenth centuries, and although this growth appears to have been checked for a while in the eighteenth century, it again gathered speed towards the end of that century and at the first census of 1801 the population of England and Wales was enumerated at more than 9 million.

In the eighteenth century, long before the first census was taken, the question of whether the population was increasing or decreasing became the subject of lively controversy. One, Doctor Price, a nonconformist minister of wide interests, who is claimed to be the inventor of the sinking fund as well as the man who preached the sermon which inspired Burke to write his *Reflections,* set out in 1750 to show that population had declined, but he was beaten down by others who argued that baptisms had exceeded burials and that therefore population had been growing. One of the main supporters of the *growth* argument was another parson, the Reverend John Howlett. Dr Price, conveniently for his argument, had used only the London Bills of Mortality; his adversaries went further afield and examined many of the parishes throughout England for the period from approximately 1758 to 1773. These wider researches showed that baptisms had increased more rapidly than had burials, thus establishing the fact of population increase.[6] Subsequent analysis of the records of baptisms and burials and studies which related these to the first census of 1801 confirmed the tendency of population to increase its rate of growth in the later eighteenth century. The pattern of growth between the time of Gregory King and the first census which is now generally accepted, may be summarized as a period of relative stability between about 1700 and 1740 with a population of around 6 million and rapid growth thereafter to about 9·2 million at the date of the first census in 1801.

J. C. Russell's life tables presented in Chapter 3 suggest that the expectation of life at birth in the early medieval period may have been about 33 years. Expectations may have fallen as low as 18 years following the Black Death and levels above 30 years were probably not attained until the fifteenth century. Russell's figures, again as presented in Chapter 3, suggest an expectation at birth of

Table 4.1 : An Estimate of Population Increase, England and Wales, 1700–1801[7]

	Millions	Increase % in immediately previous decade
1700	5·84	—
1710	6·01	3·04
1720	6·05	0·58
1730	6·01	−0·66
1740	6·01	0·08
1750	6·25	3·9
1760	6·66	6·6
1770	7·12	6·9
1780	7·58	6·4
1790	8·22	8·3
1801	9·17	11·5

33 years for England for the period 1426–50. There seems little reason to believe that this situation had greatly altered by the beginning of the eighteenth century. Indeed the estimates of a life expectation just over 30 years for England and Wales at the beginning of the eighteenth century may be compared with Halley's life table of 1694 which was based on population data of the German city of Breslau and which gave an expectation of life at birth of only 27·6 years, with some 43 per cent of children dying before the age of 6. Table 4·1 suggests that after a period of almost stationary population between 1710 and 1740, there was a steady increase in growth rates to the remarkably high figure of 1 per cent a year in the last decade of the century. This pattern suggests that there had almost certainly been some improvement in mortality as the century advanced, unless the whole of the increase in growth rates could be attributed to rising birth rates. But such improvements as there may have been in mortality did not imply a real breakthrough to higher expectations of life, but were rather the reflection of the absence of the great 'killing' diseases, such as plague of previous centuries.

There were, however, some other aspects of population growth at this time that offer interesting comparisons with the high growth of countries in the world as we know it today. It should be emphasized that the growth in European populations was accomplished with marriage and fertility patterns which appear very modest when compared with the situations, for example, in many Asian countries today, where marriages are often almost universal beyond the age of 20 years and where fertility is high enough to produce birth rates of 45 per thousand of population, or even rates above this figure. To illustrate how different the twentieth-century Asian pattern is from that of the eighteenth-century Europe, we consider first the situation which appears to have prevailed in Scandinavian countries, for which the figures of births and deaths are known to be fairly reliable. A summary of the situation with regard to birth rates, death rates and natural increase between 1722 and 1800 in Denmark, Finland, Norway and Sweden is given in Table 4.2.

Table 4.2: Estimated Rates of Births, Deaths and Natural Increase, Scandinavian Countries, 1722–1800[8]

	Denmark			Finland			Norway			Sweden		
	B	D	NI	B	D	NI	B	D	NI	B	D	NI
1722				30·2	23·0	7·2						
1740	30·3	30·5	−0·2	37·9	52·0	−14·1	31·5	27·1	4·4	32·0	35·5	−3·5
1760	31·5	29·0	2·5	46·6	27·9	18·7	36·4	23·3	13·1	35·7	24·8	10·9
1780	33·6	26·1	7·5	41·2	21·0	20·2	33·1	25·8	7·3	35·7	21·7	14·0
1800	29·9	28·5	1·4	37·6	25·5	12·1	31·7	21·2	10·5	28·7	31·4	−2·7

When these figures are examined, it is clear that there were very considerable fluctuations in mortality and fertility during the eighteenth century, but the record of the absence of severe periods of decline after 1740 and the substantial rates of increase that thereafter applied, particularly in the latter half of the eighteenth century, bear a fairly close resemblance to the pattern previously examined in England and Wales. The main cause of these changes of vital rates in these Scandinavian countries in the eighteenth century was related to economic circumstances and not to changes in the patterns of disease.[9] Food conditions affected marriage, birth and death rates, but there was a suggestion of a considerable degree of rationality in the reaction of these populations to the food situation, with marriage rates rising in good times and falling in bad times, and with births reacting likewise. Generally birth rates appeared to reach their highest points by the middle of the century, with a marked fall towards the end of the century. Expectations of life at birth in these countries, although low by today's standards, were high by contemporary standards, or by comparison with the figures estimated by Russell for medieval Europe or by Halley for his figures from Breslau. Consider the following expectations of life at birth estimated for Sweden in the second half of the eighteenth century:[10]

Period	Males	Females
1751–55	36·4	39·2
1771–75	29·1	31·7
1796–1800	37·2	40·0

Other figures available for Scandinavian countries strongly suggest that an important factor limiting birth rates was the relatively low proportion of women who were married. This is in marked contrast to many Asian countries today, or for that matter to the French Canadians of the seventeenth century. In addition the fertility of married women was probably considerably below the high rates of some well-known high-growth areas in the world of the twentieth century. A comparison between the situation in Sweden and Canada in the seventeenth and eighteenth centuries and Turkey and the United States of America in the twentieth century in regard to the proportions of women married is presented in Table 4.3. The next Table, 4.4, then shows the age-specific legitimate fertility rates, that is the births per thousand married women in each age group, in eighteenth-century Sweden and compares this again with Canada in the early eighteenth century and two high-fertility areas of the twentieth-century world.[11]

While the eighteenth-century evidence from England and Wales and other parts of Europe tends to be more conjectural than that of Sweden, firmer evidence of the nineteenth century supports the conclusion that the Swedish patterns illustrated below in

Table 4.3 : Illustrative Figures of Percentages of Women Married

Age Group	Sweden 1750	Sweden 1800	Canada 1681	Turkey 1935	USA c. 1960
20–4	27·0	19·4	76·9	80·8	67·2
25–9	55·5	50·7	91·7	90·8	83·4
30–4	71·3	67·5	94·8	90·8	85·9
35–9	78·9	74·7	89·8	87·5	85·4
40–4	78·6	76·7	93·4	76·6	83·3
45–9	74·6	73·9	89·6	65·2	79·9

Table 4.4: Age-Specific Legitimate Fertility Rates, per 1,000 Married Women

Age Group	Sweden 1776–1800	Hutterites 20th Century	Canada c. 1720	Bengali Areas Rural 1945–6
15–9	522	574	492	118
20–4	467	554	510	323
25–9	382	510	496	288
30–4	323	450	484	282
35–9	224	—	—	—
40–4	121	219	231	100
45–9	29	38	30	33

Tables 4. 3 and 4. 4 may have been fairly typical of the eighteenth-century European situation. If so, a point of great importance to the explanation of the trend towards the expansion of growth rates in European population in the latter part of the eighteenth century is the role that changing patterns of marriage could have played. A comparison of the lines of Table 4.4 shows that the fertility of Swedish women who married approached maximum levels of legitimate fertility which have been revealed in recent studies, particularly at younger ages. Thus one explanation of the relatively low birth rates of Europe in the eighteenth and through much of the nineteenth centuries, probably lies in the considerable proportions of women who did not marry rather than in lower levels of marital fertility, although Table 4. 4 also suggests that there may even then have been amongst European women a tendency to restrict the number of births occurring after the age of about 30 years, compared with the Canadians of the eighteenth century or the Hutterites of the twentieth century.

This reasoning tends to support the argument that the expansion of growth rates of European populations in the late eighteenth century may have had as much, if not more, to do with the changes in marriage patterns and birth rates than with a decline in mortality. If death rates did decline in the later years of the century, this can hardly be attributed to any improvements in medical science, but rather to the fact that the period before 1740 appears to have been a time of excessive mortality. In Great Britain, at least, the early eighteenth century was the period of 'gin mania', accompanied by severe epidemics of fever. The Bills of Mortality show these to have been particularly severe in London between 1701 and 1720, with deaths from fevers averaging 3,000 each year in a total mortality of between 20,000 and 25,000.

Prosperity in Britain in the second quarter of the century did not eliminate fevers and smallpox from the total population, but henceforth these scourges appeared to be less severe amongst the middle classes. That they still seriously afflicted the 'lower orders' is apparent from the Bills of Mortality of such areas as London and Norwich; and a tendency for the high incidence of these diseases to be associated with times of poor harvests suggests that malnutrition was an important factor triggering off their spread. Conversely the relative immunity of the middle classes after about 1750 was again probable evidence that they had at last raised themselves permanently above a Malthusian level of subsistence.[12]

While improvements in medical *science* can have had little effect upon mortality rates throughout the century, there were nevertheless some aspects of medical *practice* and care which may have been of some significance.[13] There was virtually no improvement in diagnosis or in the theories about the transmission of the killing diseases throughout the eighteenth century. The theory of infection was still essentially that of *miasma* – marshes, decaying matter, sick persons gave off a miasma, a subtle gaseous poison which caused disease among those who breathed it. John Graunt had suggested something new when, in commenting upon the results of his study of mortality from the plague in 1636, he concluded that plague spread more from the 'disposition of the air' than from 'the effluvia from the bodies of men'. In attacking smells, however, some check was imposed on infectious diseases; but until the germ theory of the nineteenth century was developed hospitals tended to be sources of infection rather than preventers of disease. The number of hospitals in England increased from two to fifty in the eighteenth century, but apart from segregating some with infectious diseases from the population at large, nothing was done until late in the century to segregate infectious and non-infectious diseases within hospitals. It was believed that infectious and non-infectious diseases could be mixed in the ratio of 1 to 6. Surgery was still sufficiently horrifying in 1825 to frighten Charles Darwin from a medical career. Amputations were still followed by death in almost half the cases. True there were advances in skills and techniques, but these did not produce positive results in lowered mortality until anti-sepsis gained the field in the 1840s.

65

The same argument largely applied to *midwifery*, certainly until the last quarter of the eighteenth century. The first lying-in hospital was founded in London in 1749, and thereafter the practice of institutional delivery became increasingly common. At first these institutions were dangerous sources of infection, but by the last quarter of the century the importance of cleanliness in the labour room had been realized and probably this simple fact was as important in the decline in infant mortality as any improvement in techniques of delivery. The extent of the saving of life in lying-in hospitals in the latter part of the eighteenth century was probably (if figures can be trusted) from about 1 death per 50 deliveries to 1 in 180 or 190 at the end of the century.

Another possible and not altogether implausible explanation why the death rate remained below the birth rate from about 1730 could be a change in the pattern of disease occasioned by increased resistance or by other factors, although knowledge in this field is still very uncertain. Plague, for example, left England in 1666 and an explanation of its disappearance which seems more plausible than the Fire of London (which did not destroy the plague-infested poor suburbs) is an obscure revolution in the animal kingdom which led to the extirpation of the plague-carrying black rat and his replacement by the brown rat.[14]

Such factors tended to eliminate the disastrous *peaks* of mortality, but the basic causes of a continuing high level of mortality remained. Fevers, especially typhus, continued to recur. They were common in the growing industrial towns. Smallpox also continued into the nineteenth century as a significant cause of death. The breakthrough in the control of this disease was greatly assisted by the publication of Edward Jenner's findings in 1798 that an inoculation of cow-pox gave an immunity. But while many of the traditional killing diseases remained and recurred, the significant fact was that the great scourge of plague had gone from Europe, and the new plateau of death, although high, never again threatened to decimate the population.[15] Although high by almost any modern standard, Asian or otherwise, the plateau was nevertheless low enough to enable birth rates to sustain modest levels of increase, and indeed to allow a considerable leap ahead in growth rates when economic conditions were favourable to early marriage.

The 'upsurge' of British population between about 1750 and 1780, which is suggested in Table 4. 1 was not a 'take off' in growth in the sense that is now understood in the demographic processes of so many of today's 'developing' countries; rather was it the sort of comparatively slight and short duration increase that had probably been experienced often enough before and which could be explained by a fluctuation in birth rates followed by a change in age composition, or by a temporary lowering of death rates following a period of ravaging disease which had given the surviving population a high degree of immunity. There was still plenty in the eighteenth-century picture, whether in Great Britain or elsewhere in Europe, to impress Malthus into a theory of despair, for standing thus close to earlier history, an upsurge of growth without a following spasm of decimating disease must have seemed improbable.

Quite probably, therefore, a considerable part of the explanation of increased growth rates in the eighteenth century lies in what Habakkuk[16] described as 'the operation of . . . traditional stimuli in an unusually favourable agricultural environment'. A run of good harvests between 1730 and 1755 and the weakening of the apprenticeship system, which was accompanied by rising wages in skilled and semi-skilled jobs in a relatively fully employed economy, would tend to encourage earlier and more frequent marriage, and therefore an increase in births in a society where there was already a degree of rational control over these matters.[17] Indeed, as will be suggested in later chapters, the situation around the middle of the eighteenth century in England may have been similar to that in the USA, Australia, New Zealand and many western European countries after the Second World War, when marriage and birth rates rose sharply in response to rising wages and full employment.

Thus, while marriage and birth trends almost certainly played an important role in the rising growth rates in the latter part of the eighteenth century, permanently higher growth rates had to depend in the longer run upon the levels of death rates; but not until well into the nineteenth century did there appear to be any assurance that this jaw of the Malthusian vice would not close again. Wherever people crowded together in insanitary conditions, typhus and similar killers raised their heads again, particularly in the new industrial towns. Farr, for example, gave expectations of life in 1841 of 25 years for males and 27 years for females in Liverpool, and only 24 years for males in Manchester. New threats also occurred from the introduction of cholera in 1831. But by then the control over death was extending, although again the controlling factor seems to have been less applied medical science than improvements in the general environment. On the side of medical science the list of developments soon began to look impressive – asepsis associated with the name of Lister, the germ theory of disease developed by Pasteur, the introduction of scientific nursing, the use of anaesthetics in surgery. These had their effect, but in the overcrowded industrial towns they did little to combat the growing scourge of tuberculosis, which was responsible for about half the deaths in England and Wales in the middle of the nineteenth century. The important factors bringing down death rates from around this time were rather public health measures associated with improved sanitation and water supplies, and again more if not better food, better although crowded housing, and a general improvement in living conditions as the 'hungry forties' gave way to the more ample 1850s and 1860s.[18]

From the modern standpoint the vital situation about the middle of the nineteenth century might look rather grim, but compared with the early seventeenth century it denoted a revolutionary change. Consider, for example, Halley's life table of 1694[19] with the official life tables of England and Wales of 1838–54 and also of 1881–90.

Age	Halley 1694	Official life table	
		1838–54	1881–90
0	1,000	1,000	1,000
25	455	624	694
35	392	564	640
45	317	496	564
55	232	409	463

The important victory had however been won by the middle of the nineteenth century. While the vice and misery which Malthus and his contemporaries commented upon in the early nineteenth century were still present, and while conditions in the new industrial towns were at times as bad as anything in the sixteenth century, progress towards a demographic situation new in man's history was under way. As the 'killers' of earlier centuries were beaten, the advocates of birth control were heard; and as Francis Place remarked, to his friend Ensor, rare fellows were the two of them and their contemporaries James Mill and Edward Gibbon Wakefield in being leading advocates of birth control, yet mustering thirty-six children amongst them.

J. T. Krause, in three articles covering the period 1781–1841,[20] subjects to close scholarly argument the conclusions of the traditionalists who sought to explain the expanding growth rates mainly in terms of declining death rates. He concludes, with reference to Britain:

1 That burials and baptisms were generally more inaccurately recorded in the late eighteenth century and early nineteenth century than earlier exponents such as Rickman and Griffith had assumed, and that the 'correction factors' which they had used to convert these rates to birth and death rates were too low.

2 That in the late eighteenth century there was almost certainly a lowering of the age of marriage as a result of relatively good economic conditions before the end of the century, industrialization, the weakening of restrictions regarding apprenticeship, and the weakening of sexual mores during the wars, etc., and that the extension of poor relief did, as Malthus argued, encourage earlier marriage.

3 These factors, plus an increase in illegitimacy in many areas during the Napoleonic wars, tended to raise fertility. Child/women ratios (children aged 0–4 per 1,000 women aged 15–49) were 605 in 1821. These fell to 509 in 1841, but Krause states that the rates of 1810–21, around 600, were almost certainly higher than those for 1780 or earlier in the century.

4 Whereas fertility fluctuated markedly, mortality did not decline until *after 1820*. Economic distress during the period 1793–1820, rapid and unplanned urban growth, and distress and disturbance caused by the wars all encouraged higher death rates; particularly among the poorest classes, and among infants and mothers. Krause suggests that deaths may have increased by over 50 per cent between 1781–90 and 1811–20.

5 Consequently the main factor affecting population growth between 1781 and 1850 was probably changing fertility rather than changing mortality, though more study of detailed parish records is necessary until the case can be proven.

However fascinating may be the search to establish the precise factors which led to the expansion of growth rates of the British, Scandinavian and other populations of Europe in the late eighteenth and early nineteenth centuries, the significant aspects from the point of view of the demographic revolution, which culminated in the controlled fertility patterns of the twentieth century, seem reasonably clear. First, catastrophic onslaughts of killing diseases did not recur after the seventeenth century; a fact which may help to explain the apparently higher fertility of the late eighteenth century since more women were consistently living through a greater proportion of their child-bearing years. Secondly, western Europeans appeared to be reacting with a good deal of rationality along Malthusian lines of restraint long before the long-term decline in birth rates set in during the late nineteenth century; they married relatively late, a considerable proportion did not marry at all, and their marriage patterns appear to have varied in response to such economic factors as wage levels, harvests and the prices of food grains. Thus it was not entirely surprising that people who acted with this degree of rationality in the eighteenth century were followed by descendants who added birth control to marriage control when the latter became inadequate to keep a brake on population growth as mortality rates declined. In the end, the real breakthrough to the demographic revolution was not the likely changes in fertility of the eighteenth century, but the clear and steady downturn of mortality of the nineteenth. As Helleiner concluded, the unprecedented aspect of the demographic development of the eighteenth century was the fact that the secular upward movement started from considerably higher population levels than at earlier times, and that it was able to maintain, and for some time even to increase, its momentum. It was never again reversed by catastrophe, and 'when increase did slow down eventually, it did so owing to the personal decisions of millions of human beings, not to acts of God such as the Black Death of the fourteenth century'.[21]

The nineteenth century undoubtedly witnessed the greatest and most sustained burst of growth in man's history (See Table 4. 5). If we accept the high figures among the many published estimates, that is those of Carr Saunders, the world pattern is a growth from 545 millions in 1750, to 728 millions in 1800, and then to 1,171 millions in 1850 and 1,608 millions in 1900 (See Table 1. 1). With the increasing reliability of census and registration data amongst European nations, the role of these nations in this expansion is relatively certain; and that role includes not only growth in continental Europe but also the outpouring of some 16 million emigrants from Europe in the nineteenth century to make a major contribution to the growth of populations in the New World, and particularly to North America with its increase from 6 to 81 millions and to Latin America with its increase from 10 to 63 millions (See Chapter 5).

Yet by the growth rates prevailing in many parts of the world in the middle of the twentieth century – or even by the estimated average growth of the whole world's population around 1960 of at least 1·7 per cent a year – Europe in the nineteenth century presents a pattern of a slow struggle against odds that still appeared almost overwhelming rather than a population explosion. Nor was the growth trend at all even throughout the century, and as the century advanced, so did the growth differentials. Those with the highest growth rates were the nations which were most successful in both giving most to overseas areas in the way of emigrants and gaining most from international commodity trade. The aspects of the role of imperialism and the access to the resources of a new world as factors in the vital revolution have been too much overlooked by demographic historians. The leaders in the trend towards higher growth rates tended to be the great trading nations of Europe, and these nations were in turn the leaders in the industrial revolution. The industrial revolution brought its blights, especially in the growing industrial cities, but the ever-increasing rows of congested housing into which moved increasing proportions of the populations of the European nations were less menacing to life than the squalor of the pre-industrial rural village. The capacity of these cities to carry more and more people was still not due to any sudden breakthrough in the control of disease (indeed they probably increased the incidence of some of the worst contagious killers, such as tuberculosis) but rather to the capacity of both city and national authorities under the leadership of men like Edwin Chadwick to provide adequate water supplies and waste disposal. However bleak by twentieth century standards might have been the age of which the Hammonds wrote,[22] the occupational opportunities offered in the industrial towns provided the major dynamic of population growth in northern, western and central Europe in the nineteenth century. Public health measures kept disease in check, basic housing conditions gradually improved, as did food supplies and the capacity of the industrial wage earners to purchase these for their dependants. By the middle of the

71

nineteenth century the basic battle had been won for most of north, western and central Europe, and for overseas countries colonized by their emigrants. Death rates which had been 25 and even over 30, at earlier times, began to approach and then to fall below, 20 per 1,000 of population. As medical science came to supplement improving physical environments as the century closed, the decline in general death rates began to accelerate, from around 15 per 1,000 about the turn of the century in many areas to 12 and lower by the outbreak of the Second World War (Table 4·6).

As already emphasized, the pattern generalized above applied on the whole to the industrializing nations. There were however considerable variations on this general theme.[23] Ireland decreased in population in the nineteenth century from about 8·2 millions in 1843, to 5·7 millions in 1863, primarily as a result of the great emigrations following the potato famines. Continued emigration and a relatively low birth rate and high death rate combined to reduce the Irish population to less than 4·5 millions by the end of the century.[24]

Another important exception in western Europe was France, whose population increased from about 35 millions in 1840 to only 40 millions by the end of the century, basically as a result of a low birth rate (which had been steadily declining even in the first half of the century) and a relatively high death rate.[25] While the French population was almost stationary by 1875, growth rates in England and Wales, Holland, Germany and the Scandinavian countries were at their peaks, generally between 1·0 and 1·5 per cent a year. In eastern European countries birth rates tended to be higher than in the West. But death rates were also generally higher with growth rates consequently held down below 1 per cent. In Russia, however, the estimated birth rate 1878–82 was 48 per 1,000 of population, and an estimated high death rate of almost 35 per 1,000 still therefore left a growth rate of 1·3 per cent, one of the highest of all European countries.[26] Generally, the expansion in growth rates in eastern and southern Europe did not occur until the twentieth century when their death rates began to follow the downward course which had so clearly become apparent in the West by the third quarter of the nineteenth century.

There were sufficient variations in the demographic patterns and trends of Western nations in the late nineteenth, and into the twentieth centuries, to cast doubt upon the validity of any single theory

Table 4.5 : Mean Populations (in thousands)

	England & Wales	Ireland (all)	France	Germany	Holland	Norway	Sweden	Denmark	Italy	Spain	European Russia
1841–45	16,333	8,246	35,273	29,474	2,972	1,286	3,224	1,329	—	—	—
1861–65	20,629	5,703	37,700	34,091	3,432	1,649	3,993	1,670	—	—	—
1881–85	26,630	5,037	39,426	40,974	4,198	1,927	4,605	2,033	28,779	17,137	76,769
1901–05	33,297	4,421	40,884	52,798	5,387	2,285	5,214	2,518	32,856	18,936	103,610
1921	37,887	4,364	39,240	61,328	6,921	2,668	5,929	3,285	37,709	21,421	—
1931	39,988	4,208	41,860	65,441	7,999	2,822	6,152	3,570	41,254	23,298	121,455 (1929)

Table 4.6 : Vital Rates, Selected European Countries[27] (In some cases dates are approximate only)

	England and Wales			France			Sweden			Ireland		
	BR	DR	NI	BR	DR	NI	BR	DR	NI	BR	DR	NI
1808–12				31·4	25·7	5·7	31·8	33·1	–1·3			
1828–32				29·9	25·9	4·0	32·5	25·8	6·7			
1848–52	33·4	22·6	10·8	27·0	23·5	3·5	31·5	20·6	10·9			
1878–82	34·4	20·3	14·1	24·9	22·4	2·5	29·6	17·6	12·0	24·8	18·6	6·2
1908–12	25·2	14·2	11·0	19·4	18·5	0·9	24·7	14·1	10·6	23·3	17·0	6·3
1918–22	20·9	13·7	7·2	17·3	20·0	–2·7	21·0	14·2	6·8	20·6	15·9	4·7
1928–32	16·1	12·2	3·9	17·7	16·4	1·3	15·2	12·0	3·2	19·6	14·4	5·2
1935–39	15·0	12·0	3·0	14·9	15·6	–0·7	14·5	11·7	2·8	19·4	14·3	5·1

	Italy			Russia			USA			Australia		
	BR	DR	NI	BR	DR	NI	BR	DR	NI	BR	DR	NI
1808–12												
1828–32												
1848–52												
1878–82	36·7	29·0	7·7	48·4	34·9	13·5	33·1			35·2	15·2	20·0
1908–12	32·7	20·8	11·9	45·6	28·9	16·7	27·0			27·2	10·7	16·5
1918–22	26·4	21·1	5·3	40·9	21·7	19·2	23·4	13·5	9·9	24·7	10·5	14·2
1928–32	25·5	15·2	10·3	43·8	18·9	24·9	18·6	11·5	7·1	19·3	9·0	10·3
1935–39	23·2	13·8	9·4	44·2	20·8	23·4	17·1	11·0	6·1	17·3	9·6	7·7

about demographic transition from uncontrolled to controlled fertility. The cases of France and Ireland have already been mentioned and deserve further consideration, as does the situation of the Netherlands.

The population of France increased between 1801 and 1936 by 52 per cent from 27·5 to 41·2 million. Of this increase 77 per cent took place before 1866, so that thereafter the population was relatively stationary, increasing by only 10 per cent between 1872 and 1911. After the return of Alsace-Lorraine after the First World War, the French population of 38·8 million was only 2 per cent larger than in 1866. Heavy war losses, estimated at 2·85 million in 1914–18 helped to hold down the population growth, but the slow increase was basically the result of many decades of low fertility.

Landry estimates[28] that the increase of 14 million between 1801 and 1936 was made up on the credit and debit sides, roughly as follows:

Immigrants and their children	+ 5·5 million
Prolongation of life	+ 16·8 million
War losses and their offspring	− 3·3 million

leaving apparently a 5·3 million loss through inadequate reproduction. In eleven out of the sixty-four years, 1850–1913, deaths exceeded births. The net reproduction rate, Spengler[29] states, was only 1·08 in 1806–20, 1·01 in 1841–50, and 1·04 in 1861–90, and thereafter it gradually declined to 0·89 in 1936–9. The result was that the power that was numerically dominant in western and central Europe before the mid-nineteenth century, had been outstripped by the twentieth century by Germany. Whereas France comprised 15 per cent of Europe's population in 1750, the proportion had fallen to 7·9 per cent by 1939.

The explanation for France's stability has often been expressed in social terms. French mores and folk-ways have long emphasized the advantages of the small family; as a result of wars and revolutions social customs were disrupted; and the Civil Code required parents to bequeath at least a specified portion of their property to each child. Spengler[30] has emphasized the problems of pinning down specific economic factors that may have been important. Trade cycle movements did not suggest any marked difference from other rapidly growing countries. France was less industrialized than other European areas; a factor that might have been

75

expected to support higher rather than lower fertility. But savings were lower even though theoretically, Spengler argues, they might have been expected to be higher in a stationary rather than in a rapidly growing population. The exceptional and paradoxical in France may be explained by the fact that there was never a dynamic phase of technical innovation as there was in Germany and England. Admittedly the resource potential was smaller in France than in Germany or the United Kingdom, but even so, available resources were used with less efficiency with the result that real incomes lagged below their potential, and the savings advantages that may have emanated from a near stationary population never became apparent. But such economic factors, summarized by Spengler as 'the unenterprising character of so much entrepreneurial behaviour', were probably less important as determinants of demographic behaviour than French value-patterns, the reactions to a past age of splendour, political and national instability far into the nineteenth century, and the highly rational attitude of French peasantry to the balance between the land and its occupants.

In France, the essential features of the low rate of natural increase throughout the latter part of the nineteenth century and into the twentieth century, were as follows:

1 The relatively low birth rates, cf. England and Wales 1878–82: 34·4; and France 1878–82: 22·6.

2 The relatively high death rates, which became increasingly apparent as the century advanced until by 1928–32 the French death rate of 16·4 was well above that of England and Wales (12·2), Sweden (12·0), or Ireland (14·4), and also above Italy (15·2).

3 The small families when couples were fertile. The most important family sizes in France throughout the latter part of the nineteenth century and well into the twentieth century were those of one and two children. Consider the following distribution of average family sizes for each 1,000 married women:[31]

	1901	1911	1926
0	160	156	161
1	262	279	314
2	235	237	240
3	145	141	130
4+	198	187	155

In other ways, the low French fertility had many of the characteristics of the low fertility patterns that emerged later in other
western European countries, with the highest fertility in manual
and low-income occupations and lowest fertility amongst the
professional and upper income groups. The mean number of
children born per 1,000 families of all ages for selected groups in
1911 were as follows:

Mining workers	289
Fishermen	256
Metal workers	253
Liberal professions	153
Commerce and Banking	168
Domestic service	144
Total average	213

Compared with France, the Irish situation had more unique
features. Here, firstly, was the unusual case of a European population decrease in the nineteenth century from a mean of 8,246,000 in
1841–5 to 5,037,000 in 1881–5 and again to 4,208,000 in 1931.
Initially, of course, the decrease was due to overseas emigration,
which exceeded one million in the decades 1841–50 and 1851–60,
and which continued to remove well over half a million people
during most of the following decades until the end of the century.
(Table 4. 7.)

Table 4.7 : Emigration from 32 Counties of Ireland 1825–1925[32]

1825–30	111,394	1881–90	734,475
1831–40	395,481	1891–1900	460,917
1841–50	1,179,360	1901–10	485,461
1851–60	1,216,265	1911–20	229,239
1861–70	818,582	1921–25	146,834
1871–80	542,703		

Even more remarkable was the very low level of the birth rate of
Ireland in the latter part of the nineteenth century. The recorded
rate in 1846–70 was only 25·8. It rose slightly to 26·3 in the next
decade 1871–80, and thereafter fell away sharply to 22·2 in 1900
and 19·34 in 1931–40.

Table 4.8 : Irish Marriage and Vital Statistics

	Marriages per 1,000	Births per 1,000	Deaths per 1,000	Infant Mortality per 1,000 live births	Natural Increase per 1,000
1864–70	5·10	25·79	16·23	95·61	9·56
1871–80	4·54	26·31	18·06	96·80	8·25
1881–90	4·02	22·88	17·56	93·06	5·32
1891–1900	4·45	22·20	17·70	99·42	4·50
1901–10	4·84	22·54	16·91	91·37	5·62
1911–20	5·11	21·50	16·64	84·06	4·86
1921–30	4·76	20·23	14·45	69·90	5·78
1931–40	4·86	19·34	14·17	68·41	5·17

Behind this low birth rate was the classic example of the Malthusian virtue of restraint from marriage. Marriage rates averaged only 5·10 per 1,000 of population 1864–70 and 4·45 1871–80. It remained below an average of 5 per 1,000 each following decade until 1910. This propensity to celibacy runs well back into Irish history. In the latter part of the nineteenth century census figures indicate that about four out of ten women aged 25–35 and two out of ten women aged 35–45 were unmarried. In the first quarter of the twentieth century the figures rose sharply to even higher levels – five unmarried out of ten aged 25–35, and three out of ten aged 35–45.

Herein lies one of the major causes of the comparatively low birth rates of Ireland. On the other hand the average number of children per woman who did marry remained high even into the twentieth century. Among women married before age 45 whose marriage had lasted 30–34 years by the census date, the average number of children was 6·77 in 1911 and was still 4·94 in 1946.[33] Again, the number of children aged 0–4 per 1,000 married women under the age of 45 years remained around 131 in Ireland between 1861 and 1926, whereas in England and Wales it was less than 120 between 1861 and 1881 and had declined to 90 in 1901 and to 71 by 1926.

This relatively high marital fertility kept the Irish birth rate much above that of France, and a lower death rate gave Ireland a further advantage in terms of natural increase. This low general death rate seems to have been marked by a low infant death rate per 1,000 live births. The Irish rate was below 100 between 1861 and 1901, compared with 157 (1864–70) and 128 (1901–10) in England and Wales. Not until the twentieth century did England and Wales take a lead over Ireland in this respect.

Generally the Irish pattern both rejects and fits different aspects of Malthusian theory. Mass migration was not followed by higher domestic growth rates, as Malthusian theory would have led one to expect. Instead, but as a supplement to emigration, the Irish practised postponement and avoidance of marriage as a further check to population growth. As will be shown later, other countries of western Europe also displayed restraints from marriage, but Ireland remained the supreme example in this regard. The recurrent threat of famine probably remained a more potent force encouraging celibacy in Ireland than in almost any other Western country. In addition the right to livelihood from the family's land, already in most cases a mere plot of soil, was limited to one son, and his opportunity to marry had generally to await the death of his father or the vacation of the ancestral cottage by his parents. As Arensberg and Kimball have written:[34]

The Irish experience illustrates the restrictive character, as regards fertility, of family structure in pre-industrial western Europe in association with sanctions against extra-marital fertility, though such restriction of marriage was not enforced with equal intensity in any other situation.

There was, of course, some restriction of fertility within marriage in medieval society. This might be achieved either by avoidance of sexual relations between spouses after several children had been born or by the practice of coitus interruptus or, occasionally, by abortion. Such practices were apparently present, but were certainly not widespread.

William Petersen,[35] writing of 'The Demographic Transition in the Netherlands' also draws attention to features of the Dutch demographic history which do not fit into the generalized pattern of European demographic transition based upon the stable fertility-declining mortality hypothesis. In support of McKeown and Brown,[36] he also emphasized that for the first half of the nineteenth century at least mortality did not fall significantly, and indeed tended to rise in the growing industrial towns, but the majority of the population was still rural, and better farming methods and the cultivation of new land improved the general health of the rural areas. When the shift to the towns did begin to take hold as industrialization increased, it tended to lead to the disintegration of the extended family system, which had meant in Holland in effect that two biological families lived under one roof, and that one member of the family married in each generation. Thus while the joint household provided strong checks to marriage and fertility, nevertheless the unmarried had a definite function in the household as servants, farm workers, etc. As this joint household began to disintegrate with consequent emphasis upon the nuclear family, and as the appendages of the joint household system found an opportunity to escape from what they began to perceive as sexual and social frustration, fertility began to rise. Petersen quotes studies to show that the highest fertility was in fact, not in the rural areas, but in the cities. In addition some restraint from marriage was not, as in Ireland, also accompanied by low illegitimacy, pre-marital intercourse being an accepted phenomenon, though unmarried pregnancy was usually followed by marriage.

Petersen concludes:

In the *traditional family* typical of the pre-industrial period, the postponement of marriage plus the non-marriage of a portion of the population, constituted an onerous but efficient means of holding fertility in check. In the *proletarian family,* typical of the mass of either rural or urban workers released from the prior institutional and normative restrictions, there was no effective ban either to early marriage or to procreation. Indeed, social control was often barely strong enough to compel marriage once a child had been conceived. In the *rational family* type, which arose among the middle classes during the nineteenth century and then gradually spread to the rest of society, a sense of parental responsibility is apparent, and with it a limitation of family size. The average age at marriage rose again, and later the same end was achieved with less privation by the use of contraceptives.

Too much should not be read into Dr Petersen's theory. While social changes accompanying the industrial revolution may have tended to encourage earlier marriage in Holland and in other countries as well, the rise of the *proletarian family* was certainly not accompanied by universal marriage. An important contribution to the control of population growth in western Europe throughout the nineteenth century continued to be restraint from marriage. The significant variant to the general western European pattern was the low fertility of marriages in France, rather than the high proportions of Irish who did not marry. The marked difference in marriage patterns at the end of the nineteenth century between western and central Europe on the one hand and southern and eastern Europe on the other is apparent in Table 4·9, which gives the percentage proportions of single women, ranked by those proportions at age 25–9. The ranking would be much the same for males. In other words, the differences are not due to marked differences in sex ratios which would reduce the 'risk' of marriage of women in monogamous societies.

Table 4.9: Proportions per cent of Single Women around 1900, by ages 25–29 and 45–49. Ranked by proportions single by age 25–29[37]

Country	25–29	45–49
Ireland	59	17
Sweden	52	19
Norway	48	18
Switzerland	45	17
Holland	44	14
Great Britain	42	15
Denmark	42	13
Portugal	41	20
Finland	40	15
Austria	38	13
Germany	34	10
France	30	12
Italy	30	11
Spain	26	10
Hungary	15	4
Greece (1907)	13	4
USSR (1926)	9	4

Clearly by the twentieth century a considerable number of Western countries were achieving, albeit by slightly different routes and with different time perspectives, a new demographic balance in which restraint from marriage still remained, as it seems to have been for almost three centuries, one major element, while the other major element was to become increasingly widespread application of fertility control within marriage. Many explanations have been offered for the decline in marital fertility which became apparent in most Western countries during the last quarter of the nineteenth century; the increased cost of rearing children with the introduction of compulsory education, the increasing affluence of society, the weakening of religious beliefs, the cult of hedonism, and so on. Probably all were involved; but one of the major pressures for increased efficiency in birth control, especially in societies where marriage control was already well established, was probably the trend in mortality and the facts that increasing proportions of the children conceived were born alive and lived to adult life, and that with the reductions in adult death rates married women were living through more of their reproductive years, and, as a further consequence of this, within those reproductive years fewer marriages were rendered infertile by the death of a spouse.

The trend towards declining birth rates, closely associated with the decline in death rates, was summarized in Table 4.6. For the most part these declines in fertility were due to reductions in family size, first among the higher income and social classes, who were at that time also the best educated, and among the new urban rather than among the traditional rural classes. But as the decline continued into the twentieth century these differences tended to narrow towards lower national averages, and in some instances (as in Sweden in the 1920s) positive relationships began to appear between income and family size. Significantly these declines gathered pace as life expectancies attained unprecedentedly high levels. Infant death rates per 1,000 live births had fallen in England and Wales from 157 in 1864–70 to 128 in 1901–10, and by 1921–30 were down to 72. This was a fairly typical pattern. Life expectations at birth which were between approximately 45 and 50 years in the late nineteenth century in western Europe had advanced to 60 years and over by about 1930. The significance of these trends for fertility is seen in the fact that whereas only about 60 per cent of female infants born in the 1840s were living to marriageable age, three-quarters of those born in the 1880s were doing so, and among those born about the beginning of the First World War, over 90 per cent were living to marriageable age. Similarly, increasing proportions were living through to age 50, that is the end of the reproductive period, the increase being from less than half at the middle of the nineteenth century to more than three-quarters by 1914 (Table 4.10).

In these conditions, those who did marry had either to reduce the number of pregnancies or carry the burden of a minor population explosion. For the most part the parents of the later Victorian and Edwardian era were choosing the former, not with any great degree of sophistication but by more rigorous application of fairly

Table 4.10: Female Survivors and Years Lived in Child-bearing Age in Life Table Populations[38]

England and Wales		Years lived		Sweden			Years lived
	At 15	At 50	15–50		At 15	At 50	15–50
1838–54	697	473	20·77	1816–40	719	513	22·08
1871–80	725	521	22·31	1871–80	749	580	23·57
1891–1900	755	580	23·99	1891–1900	809	640	25·56
1910–12	828	689	27·08	1911–15	878	713	28·04
1933	907	788	30·03	1926–30	916	779	29·89

France		Years lived		Italy			Years lived
	At 15	At 50	15–50		At 15	At 50	15–50
1840–59	676	477	20·27	1876–87	588	409	17·66
1908–13	816	636	25·71	1910–12	744	582	23·35
1925–27	868	702	27·69	1930–32	822	693	26·80

Germany		Years lived		USA (Massachusetts)			Years lived
	At 15	At 50	15–50		At 15	At 50	15–50
1871/2–80/1	639	452	19·48	1889–90	723	506	21·81
1910–11	779	632	25·07	1909–11	822	651	26·35
1931	901	788	29·93				

Australia		Years lived	
	At 15	At 50	15–50
1881–90	807	600	25·12
1901–10	876	719	28·40
1932–33	942	840	31·60

traditional methods, such as condoms and *coitus interruptus*, applied not to space families but to reduce ultimate family size. The degree of their success was seen in western European birth rates of around 20 per 1,000 as shown in Table 4.6, about the time of the First World War. It took the great depression of the 1930s to tighten control to the point that birth rates fell to levels at which the implied level of reproduction presaged eventual population decline. Whereas western Europe recovered sufficiently after the Second World War, partly as a result of a marked change in marriage trends, to avoid that prospect, the east and south followed the earlier pattern of the west, downwards to birth rates which in some cases resembled the minimum levels of western Europe in the 1930s.

Figure 4.1 : Birth and Death Rates, Selected Countries of Europe c. *1820–1930*

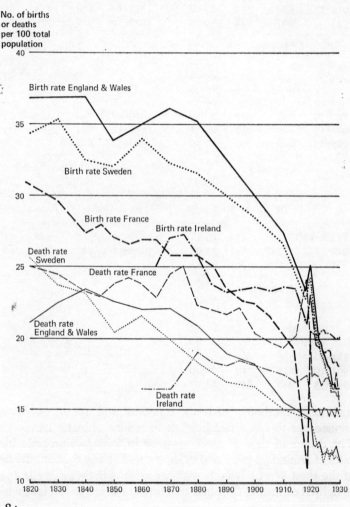

Chapter 5

The Great Migrations

Mass movements of people across land areas and over short sea routes, and at times over quite extensive stretches of the world's major oceans, go far back into history. In the centuries before Christ, the Huns invaded Europe, India and China. In the ninth century Europe was invaded by Vikings and Magyars. In the thirteenth century Genghis Khan extended the Mongol Empire through Russia and China. Such invasions took heavy tolls of life, but they also assisted the spread of settlement. By the seventeenth century the land masses of Asia and Europe probably carried over 400 million people. The other major areas of settlement were Africa with possibly up to 100 million (although some estimates go as low as 60 million) and Central and South America with perhaps 10 to 12 million (Table 1.1).

The voyages of discovery by Europeans in the fifteenth and sixteenth centuries paved the way for a new type of migration: the extensive movement of Europeans over the long sea routes, where they conquered and decimated the sparse indigenous population and began that long history of settlement which has given rise to the great and populous nations of North and Latin America and to the relatively new nations of European stock in Oceania. Since the sixteenth century over 60 million Europeans appear to have moved overseas. The greatest exodus occurred in the fifty years after about 1875. The movement appeared to be a spent force by the 1930s, both because of the low reproductivity of most of the European zones of origin of the emigrants and because of the apparent incapacity of the New World countries to develop their vast resources at a pace which could absorb more than their own natural increase; but there was a considerable revival after the Second World War with an exodus of over 10 million people in the two post-war decades.

Exact measurement of this emigration from Europe over short periods of time is difficult even today because of inadequacies in the statistical records of many of both the sending and receiving countries, and there are few statistical records of any kind before the nineteenth century. Before 1800 the volume of voluntary emigration was clearly relatively small, for by then the populations of Northern America and Latin America were estimated to be only about 6 and 23 millions respectively. Hansen[1] emphasizes that up to 1800, when the Atlantic crossing was still a serious risk to life, health and property, many who did emigrate were military and commercial adventurers, deported criminals, political and religious refugees and other persons with compelling reasons for leaving their home countries. Some, on the other hand, had set out as recruits in organized schemes of colonization. But in addition to these free immigrants to the American zone there were the millions who were introduced as slaves, mainly from the west of Africa, recruited as labour for the cotton plantations of the American colonies and the sugar and coffee plantations of Central America, the Caribbean, and of Venezuela and Brazil.

One estimate[2] puts the total number of slaves taken to the Americas at 15 million, transported by some 50,000 voyages, with the British (including the USA to 1783) and Portuguese heading the list, each having transported 4·5 million followed by the French (2·0 million), Dutch (1·8 million), Spaniards (1·0 million), and the USA after 1783 (1·0 million). The trade began in the sixteenth century with the shipment of an estimated 900,000 slaves. This rose to 2,750,000 in the seventeenth century, and then to the massive total of 7,000,000 in the hey-day of the eighteenth century, followed by a further 4,000,000 until the final abolition of the trade in 1865. The slaves were required primarily as labour units, and among them males far outnumbered females, and females who were pregnant or who had small children were not wanted. Nevertheless, through their high reproduction in the Americas, assisted by quite extensive intermarriage with the non-Negro population, the numbers sprung from Negro stock grew, until today it is estimated that over 40 million persons in the Americas and the Caribbean are descended from slaves. In some of the Caribbean Islands hundreds of thousands of Negroes, faced with a situation of overpopulation about a century after the trade was finally banished, migrated back to one of the countries in which the slave traders had once descended upon their African forebears.

As the slave trade declined, the pace of free emigration from Europe quickened.[3] Until about 1890 by far the greatest contribution came from the British Isles, with a gross outward movement between 1846 and 1890 of over 8 million in a total emigration from all European areas of some 17 million. One of the major elements in the exodus from British territory was the outpouring of 1·6 million Irish in the eight years following the potato famine of 1845–7. Rural poverty and periodical crop failures were also major factors behind the emigration of almost 3·5 million persons from German territories between 1846 and 1890. Almost the whole of this movement from central and northern Europe and about three-quarters of the emigration from the British Isles went to North America. At first the attraction was cheap land and the westward-moving American frontier, but by the final quarter of the century the attractions for immigrants were increasingly associated with non-rural employment. For the most part this great exodus before about 1890 was a voluntary movement operating on *laissez-faire* principles and financed by personal savings or by assistance from relatives who had moved across the Atlantic and started a 'migration chain', that is drawing out members of their own kith or community. As far as Britain was concerned, the 'systematic colonizers' as they became known, headed by Lord Durham and advertised by Edward Gibbon Wakefield, attempted to evolve a self-regulating system of planned colonization whereby the revenue from the sale of land in the developing country would be used to bring out and settle new emigrants, whose labour in the essential tasks of building a new nation would be guaranteed by keeping land at a price sufficient to ensure that they could not afford to buy it for a considerable time. The Wakefield system, as it became known, was never effective in North America, but many of its basic ideas became the foundations of schemes of planned and assisted immigration which made a significant contribution to the settlement of Australia and New Zealand. For example, assisted immigrants comprised about half the net gain through immigration to the Australian colonies before 1890;[4] and in New Zealand after the assumption of British Sovereignty in 1840, new settlements south of the Auckland province began as planned systems of colonization.[5]

There was a temporary and marked reduction of emigration from the British Isles for twenty years after 1890, but then a swing upwards to a record annual average of 265,700 for the five years 1911–15. For the thirty years 1891–1920 a further 4·8 million people left the British Isles, with about three-quarters of them again going to North America. This emigration during the period 1891–1920 was, however, greatly exceeded by the outpouring from southern and eastern Europe. An annual average of 246,000 people left Italy, 145,000 left the group of Austria, Hungary and Czechoslovakia, 118,000 left Russia, Poland, Lithuania, Estonia and Finland, and 139,000 left Spain and Portugal. The Spanish and Portuguese flowed mainly to Latin America, but most of the rest went to North America, particularly to the USA.[6]

These thirty years, 1891–1920, marked by far the greatest outflow from Europe – a total of about 27 million people or an annual average of over 910,000. The First World War put an end to this vast emigration, and after the war the flow from southern and eastern Europe was held down by the American immigration quota laws. Nevertheless significant numbers continued to move in the 1920s from Italy, Spain and Portugal, particularly to Latin America; but again the British Isles were by far the most important source of emigrants. The great recession of the 1930s reduced European emigration to very low levels, and the Second World War then brought it to a halt.

Table 5.1 : *Annual Average Overseas Emigration from Europe: Gross Movement in thousands*[7]

Area	1846–90	1891–1920	1921–39	1940–45	1946–63
All Europe	376	910	366		585
Major Areas:					
1 British Isles	180	161	106		162
2 Germany	76	30	36		92
3 Sweden, Denmark, Norway	26	35	14	SECOND WORLD WAR	12
4 France, Switzerland, Netherlands	16	14	9		87
5 Italy	31	246	68		111
6 Austria, Hungary, Czechoslovakia	14	145	15		—
7 Russia, Poland, Lithuania, Estonia, Finland	8	118	44		—
8 Spain, Portugal	26	139	55		71

For the whole period 1846–1939, of some 51 million people who left Europe, about 38 million went to the USA, 7 million to Canada, 7 million to Argentina, 4·6 million to Brazil (with the greater part arriving between 1880 and 1930) and about 2·5 million to Australia, New Zealand and South Africa. British (including the Irish) predominated in the flows to Canada, Australia, New Zealand and South Africa; Spaniards in the flow to Argentina; and Portuguese in the flow to Brazil. The flow to the United States could scarcely have been more cosmopolitan, with Germany accounting for 6 million, Great Britain, Ireland, Austria-Hungary and Italy each around 4·5 million, Russia 3·3 million and the Scandinavian countries about 2·4 million. The manner in which this vast input changed between northern and southern areas of Europe is illustrated in Table 5.2.

Table 5.2: Immigration to United States of America 1819–1940 (in thousands)[8]

Source	1819–80	1881–1940	1819–1940
1 *Selected Areas*			
Great Britain	1,949	2,305	4,254
Ireland	2,830	1,762	4,592
Germany	3,052	2,969	6,021
Denmark, Norway, Sweden	410	1,945	2,355
Austria-Hungary	81	4,063	4,144
Russia	42	3,299	3,341
Italy	81	4,638	4,719
Total	8,445	20,981	29,426
2 *All Areas*	10,188	28,101	38,289

Throughout much of the nineteenth century there was a high degree of complementarity between the sending and receiving countries. In the early part of the century most of the immigrants were settled on the land, their establishment being facilitated by land grants, and in the cases of Australia and New Zealand frequently by assisted passage schemes. At the same time a variety of factors, such as the decrease of the size of farms through inheritance to almost subsistence holdings as in southern Germany, Austria and Norway, the consolidation of small holdings as in England, and increasing productivity, all tended to create surpluses of rural labour within Europe. The most acute pressures occurred in Ireland where absentee landholding, the lack of investment within the country and rapid population increase, brought the people practically to subsistence levels, and the potato famine of 1847 was considered the most important factor contributing to the subsequent mass emigration of 1·6 million persons over the next eight years.

Thus, until about the 1860s the 'push' of land scarcity in Europe was strongly reinforced by the 'pull' of cheap land in the New World, especially in North America and in the British overseas colonies. The cheapness of land also helped to sustain a labour scarcity in the immigrant countries, thus attracting new flows of immigrant labourers. In addition there were few restrictions upon emigration, the basic problem being only the passage cost, which in some cases was solved, as already indicated, by subsidy and in others by the rigours of a minimum steerage Atlantic crossing.

By the 1870s the hey-day of land settlement was over. Investments in North America and the British colonies in particular, both from domestic capital and from foreign lending, especially from Britain, were going increasingly into railroads, manufacturing and urban housing. In addition, the high productivity of overseas farming, especially in the USA, was outstripping that of the European farmer, thus bringing a crisis to agriculture throughout Europe and thereby creating a further 'push' factor making for increased emigration. These economic factors were operating at a time when many of the European populations were reaching their maximum growth rates, around 1 per cent or slightly more each year. There were temporary set-backs in the immigrant countries following excessive borrowings or withdrawals of overseas investments, but generally the economic factors favouring the New World were overwhelming.[9]

These were the conditions behind the great outflows of the 1880s up until almost the outbreak of the First World War. The great bulk of the immigrants, especially from continental Europe, continued to come from the peasantry, but they now found employment in railroad construction, in mines and in the growing urban industries, rather than in rural occupations.

As already indicated, the First World War ushered in many changes which were to militate against international emigration. The US Quota Acts of 1921 and the Immigration Restriction Act of 1924 cut the permitted immigration to about 162,000 a year with particularly severe consequences for southern European immigration. These restrictions helped to turn an increased flow of British emigration to the British Dominions. Following the Report of 1917 of the Dominions Royal Commission, which aimed to expedite the development of the Empire, partly through a redistribution of its European population from the heartland to the periphery, Britain passed the *Empire Settlement Act* in 1922 as the basis of a grand scheme of planned emigration.[10] In the ten years 1922–31, 400,000 emigrants were assisted under the scheme, most of them to Australia and New Zealand, but the grand scheme of a major 'redistribution' of population never looked like succeeding. The main attraction for British emigrants continued to be North America, but the flow was less than half that of the 1880s.

Southern Europeans, deflected from the USA after 1924, continued to find some outlet to Latin America, but opportunities were restricted by systems of land tenure which prevented most of the settlers from acquiring cheap land and by the inadequacy of domestic capital for the development of transport and productive plant. Many of the immigrants went to urban areas, where again the attractions were limited because of low wages, inadequate housing, and, frequently, political instability.

The First World War had also brought a marked change in the pattern of international investments, with capital now flowing from the USA into Europe and particularly Germany, thus tending to decrease the incentives for emigration overseas. The collapse of the boom in this American private investment in Europe and the onset of the world depression by 1930 virtually brought European overseas immigration to a halt until after the Second World War. Economic factors were undoubtedly the most important determinants operating in the 1930s to damp down the flows of international migration, but these were backed by increasing controls of a political character, associated substantially with the rise of totalitarian states within Europe, which prevented the free movement of people.

The majority of studies produced throughout the 1930s, and also into the 1940s, tended to conclude that there could be no revival of emigration from northern and central Europe, for population decline was projected as the inevitable result of the prevailing fertility levels.[11] The response in some European countries to this new demographic situation was to institute pro-natalist social and economic policies,[12] and in others to issue warnings that any desire on the part of the receiving countries to continue large-scale immigration would require major changes in traditional policies, with a shift in favour of immigration from southern and eastern Europe where population growth rates were still relatively high and economic growth rates still relatively low.[13] But the warnings were scarcely necessary since few immigrant countries, still struggling to achieve reasonably full employment of their existing populations, were willing to encourage new inflows.

Thus, by the 1930s the complementarity of the *emigration* needs of European countries and the *immigration* needs of the New World had been broken, and new theories were formed from the evidence of the depression years to prove that the demographic, economic and social factors were interrelated to prevent a recurrence of large-scale international movements. How far have subsequent events supported these conclusions?

The Second World War, however, was accompanied and followed by unexpected changes in demographic and economic patterns. First, war casualties, although less age and sex selective in many countries than had been the case in the First World War, cut severely into the numbers in the younger working age groups. The loss of life due to this war has been estimated at about 7·8 million persons in western Europe, and 5·6 million in eastern Europe excluding the Soviet Union.[14] For the Soviet Union the estimated loss has been placed as high as 17 million.[15] Next to the Soviet Union, the highest losses were sustained by Poland (4·3 million), Germany (4·2 million) and Yugoslavia (1·7 million).

Secondly, the war had brought about major transfers of population as a result of the use of forced labour during the war and of boundary changes. Millions of the persons so uprooted by the war eventually returned to their original countries through their own efforts or with the assistance of the United Nations Relief and Rehabilitation Administration (UNRRA) and other international agencies, but few European countries showed any substantial increase in the population of working age between the immediate pre- and post-war years, and in some cases, notably in the Soviet Union, West Germany and Poland, age and sex structures had been changed in a manner which left severe deficits of manpower. Belgium, Denmark, Finland, France, Italy, Netherlands, Norway,

Sweden, Switzerland and the United Kingdom all finished the war with populations of working age equal to or slightly above the pre-war level.[16]

The third factor of the post-war European scene was the change in birth and natural increase rates compared with pre-war years, which will be discussed in more detail in Chapter 6. Here it is sufficient to note that in the traditional low fertility areas of north-western Europe there was a sharp rise in birth rates, for example, in England and Wales from an average of 14·9 in 1935–9 to 18·0 in 1945–9, and in France from 15·1 to 20·1 over the same period. By contrast, the rates of many southern and eastern European countries declined over this period, as in Italy from 23·2 to 21·2 and in Portugal from 27·1 to 25·4. The higher post-war birth rates in the north and west presaged higher increments to their populations of working age by about 1960 but of course provided no relief for the immediate deficits arising from war casualties and low birth rates in the 1930s. Conversely, the falling birth rates of southern and eastern countries offered no prospects of immediate reduction in growth rates of the working populations.

The general pattern within Europe *immediately* after the Second World War was, therefore, one of relatively slow increases in the work forces of many of the countries of central, northern and western Europe, and of relatively rapid increases in the south and east. This demographic profile, therefore, appeared to confirm pre-war judgement that the most likely source of emigration would remain the south and east. In central and northern Europe the prospect of mass emigration was on the whole feared rather than welcomed, an exception here being the Netherlands.[17] Generally, however, the problem of post-war Europe was felt to be increasing productivity and the redistribution of manpower within Europe as a related factor, rather than the export of manpower abroad.[18]

At the conclusion of the war, overseas opinion was equally cautious. The first concern of such countries as the USA, Canada, Australia and New Zealand was the successful re-employment of their armed forces; only then would a resumption of large-scale emigration be welcomed, when it could help to supplement the deficits in work forces which were the products of the low birth rates of the 1930s. The one area in which these overseas countries felt morally bound to act concerned the resettlement of displaced persons who were unable to return to their native lands.

The resettlement of these displaced persons had the unexpected result of reopening the channels of international migration. In practically all the traditional receiving countries which had participated in the war, demobilization was in fact quickly and painlessly handled and was accomplished without satisfying the demand for labour. But labour-hungry economies were not the prerogative of the traditionally immigrant or developing countries, such as Australia, New Zealand, or Canada. Many of the countries of northern and western Europe were also to remain short of labour for the work of reconstruction. Here was the clash of interests between traditionally emigrant and immigrant countries of which the Overseas Settlement Board of the United Kingdom had written in 1938. What then was the role of population transfers and refugee movements after the war?[19]

At the end of the war, some 15 million people in Europe awaited transfer from one country to another. In western Europe there were two major categories; German nationals living outside post-war German territory who had to return to within the new German boundaries in accordance with Article XIII of the Potsdam Agreement of August 1945, and the non-German refugees who had been uprooted from their homes during the war. In addition, several million people were to be transferred across international boundaries in southern and eastern Europe.

By October 1946 about 9·7 million German nationals had been transferred, over two-thirds to the three western occupation zones which were also to receive a continuous stream of settlers from East Germany. By September 1950 there were 9·4 million national refugees in West Germany (with a total population then of 31·8 million) and by 1957 this had increased to 12·2 million. Of the total estimated net immigration of 2·4 million between 1950 and 1957, approximately 1·6 million appear to have come from East Germany. This massive inflow of refugees to West Germany must be considered to some extent as a demographic replacement of war losses. The refugees transferred by 1950 were heavily weighted in the young and working age groups; 25 per cent were under age 15 and 68 per cent were of working age (15–64). In 1950, however, the population structure of West Germany was still far from 'normal', with females exceeding males in the age group 25–45 in the ratio of 100 : 77, or by 1·7 million. Over the whole population the excess of females was about 3 million.

In the case of East Germany, the 3·6 million German nationals transferred by October 1946 represented a similar proportion of the total population of 17·3 millions to that in West Germany. Again, the majority were either children (26 per cent) or of working age (66 per cent). Thereafter, the refugee influx to East Germany was offset by emigration and the imbalance of the sexes has remained even more marked in the East than in the West. For example, in East Germany, females exceeded males in the ratio of almost 2 to 1 between ages 30 and 45 years.

Quite massive movements also occurred elsewhere. Poland lost 70,000 square miles to the Soviet Union and gained 45,000 square miles of former German territory. The cession to the Soviet Union led to the transfer in 1945 and 1946 of 50,000 Lithuanians, 30,000 Byelorussians and 420,000 Ukrainians from the new Poland, and the transfer into Poland of 1·5 million Poles and Jews. In addition, between 1945 and 1948 at least 500,000 Poles returned to Poland from the Soviet Union. A further 1·5 million Poles were repatriated between 1946 and 1948, mostly from Germany. These transfers and the expulsion of Germans gave the new Poland both a homogeneous population and a net gain of immigrants over emigrants of about one million persons, but the new Poland was made up of only 24·8 million people in 1950 compared with 32·1 million in 1939.

Other substantial movements in central, eastern and southern Europe included the transfer of 100,000 persons from Czechoslovakia to Hungary, the repatriation of about 100,000 persons from Germany and the Soviet Union to Czechoslovakia, the repatriation of about 130,000 Hungarian displaced persons, and in 1950 and 1951 the expulsion of 154,000 persons from Bulgaria and their resettlement in Turkey, mainly on land abandoned by the Greeks between 1922 and 1928.

The countries most affected by these post-war transfers were Poland, Czechoslovakia and Germany. As a result of both war casualties and transfers of population and land, Poland and Czechoslovakia lost population, much of it highly skilled, which hampered reconstruction after the war. By contrast, the mass transfer of German 'expellees' into Germany created at first acute problems of labour surpluses at a time when there was little capital to stimulate investment. The problem was particularly severe in West Germany. Yet by 1950 the unemployment rate among expellees was down to 6·9 per cent and over 1·1 million expellees were then employed in metallurgy, engineering manufacturing and construction – all industries vital to Germany's long-term economic revival. By that stage one-fifth of all employed workers in West Germany were 'expellees'. While this influx had caused great initial hardship, it also gave the country the work-force essential for economic reconstruction.

Compared with this massive movement of German nationals, the resettlement of displaced persons by the International Refugees Organization was a small affair.[20] Between 1947 and 1951 the IRO resettled 1,038,700 displaced persons. Of these 720,000 originated from West Germany, 145,000 from Austria, 24,000 from the Middle East, and 20,000 from the Far East. The main areas of resettlement were:

USA	328,900
Australia	182,200
Israel	132,100
Canada	123,500
United Kingdom	86,300
France	38,500
Argentina	32,700
Brazil	28,800
All others	85,700
Total	1,038,700

As was previously indicated, this displaced person resettlement, undertaken primarily for humanitarian reasons, set the immigration flow in motion again in some of the traditional receiving countries at a time when there was still considerable scepticism concerning the absorptive capacities of their economies. The Australian government, for example, began by a cautious target of 12,000 displaced persons a year, but the economy soon proved hungry for new workers, and the target was raised to 20,000. The flow then became a flood, and between 1949 and 1951 some 182,000 displaced persons entered the country. In Canada, too, and to a smaller extent in Latin American countries, the displaced persons primed the immigrant pump for larger flows of non-refugee immigrants.

In terms of gross emigration, non-refugee movements from Europe after 1945 appear at first as a modest revival of traditional patterns, with the United Kingdom again as the most important contributor, with Italy a close second, followed by the Netherlands and the Federal Republic of Germany; but when these outflows are considered against inflows from all sources to give an overall net balance, the important sending area is still southern Europe (see Table 5.1). However, when only the *balance* of *overseas* movement is considered, the United Kingdom continues to remain an important emigrant country, second only to Italy. Overall, the total movement out of Europe between 1945 and 1963 seems to have exceeded 10 million persons, with a movement from overseas into Europe of some 3 million, leaving a *net* loss of some 7 million.

Figure 5.1 : Gross Overseas Emigration from Europe, 1946–63

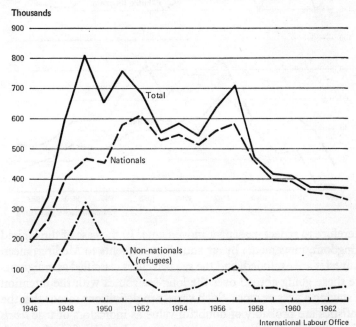

International Labour Office

The gross movement from Europe after 1946 is summarized in absolute numbers in Table 5.1 and in Figures 5·1, 5·2 and 5·3. These figures and charts can only be taken as rough guides to total movements, for the statistics on which they are based are often not strictly comparable. Few relate strictly to persons intending to settle, or even to remain abroad for a year or more, and tend

Figure 5.2: Gross Overseas Emigration of Nationals from the Federal Republic of Germany, the Netherlands and the United Kingdom, 1946–63

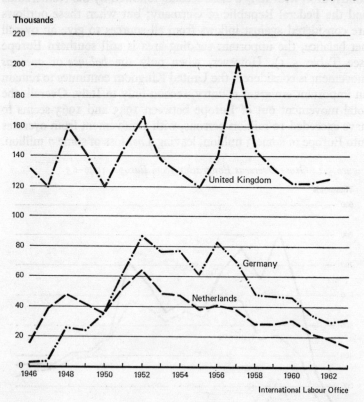

International Labour Office

therefore to reflect passenger movements. In the case of the United Kingdom, movements by air and all movements to Mediterranean countries are excluded, and the sea travellers classified as emigrants are those going abroad over the long sea routes with the intention of staying a year or more. Such variety in definitions means that the statistics are probably of doubtful value as indicators of true *levels* of emigration for permanent settlement; but the fact that each country's series is consistent over the period 1947–63 means that they can serve as a useful guide of *trends*.[21]

In terms of levels, the statistics covering the period 1946–63 suggest an annual average outflow from Europe to overseas countries of some 585,000 persons a year, an average only exceeded during the great exoduses of 1891–1920. (See Table 5·1.) Refugees formed a substantial part of the movement out of Europe up to 1950, but thereafter the ordinary emigrant dominated the pattern, with numbers large enough from 1950 until 1957 to appear to belie that pre-war opinion which foresaw the end of European emigration, particularly from north-western Europe. In fact, between 1946 and 1957 north-western Europe (British Isles, Belgium,

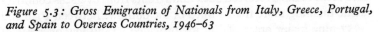

Figure 5.3: Gross Emigration of Nationals from Italy, Greece, Portugal, and Spain to Overseas Countries, 1946–63

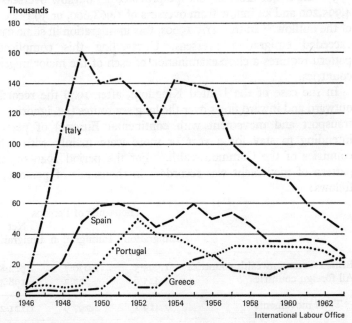

International Labour Office

Netherlands, Scandinavian countries) appears to have provided 41 per cent of European overseas emigration, compared with 21 per cent from central Europe (West Germany, Austria and Switzerland) and 38 per cent from southern Europe (Portugal, Spain, Italy, Malta, Greece). Of this outward movement, about 70 per cent went to North America and almost 20 per cent to Oceania, with the remainder to Africa and Asia. After 1957 there was a marked decline in emigration overseas from all these countries (Figures 5·2 and 5.3). Why did this decline occur? The argument so far, based only upon overseas movement, excludes the important fact that by the 1960s north-western Europe had itself become an important magnet for *immigrants*, particularly from southern Europe, which largely replaced the net loss over the long sea routes to the Americas, Oceania and elsewhere. When these *intra*-continental and overseas movements are considered together, the pattern is much more in keeping with the prognostications of the 1930s. Indeed, in terms of overseas movement alone, the major sending countries also seem to have received back immigrants from overseas countries alone totalling more than a third of the outflow. Between 1946 and 1957 nine major areas of Europe provided an outflow overseas of 4,995,200 and an inflow from overseas of 1,968,600, or 39 per cent of the outflow.[22] In the early 1960s, this immigration in some cases exceeded emigration overseas. Unravelling this complicated pattern requires a close examination of each of the major migrant countries.

In the case of the United Kingdom, after 1946 the recorded outward and inward flows over the long sea routes (i.e. ignoring air transport and movement with continental Europe) of persons intending to stay for a year or more were mainly with other countries of the Commonwealth.[23] For the period 1946–63, the pattern of movement was recorded, in thousands of persons, as follows:

	Thousands of Persons		
	Emigration	Immigration	Net Emigration
British Commonwealth countries	1,993·5	1,070·7	922·8
All foreign countries	425·6	227·2	198·4
Total movements	2,419·1	1,297·9	1,121·2

Within the Commonwealth the main net loss was to Australia (504,000), Canada (364,000), New Zealand (118,000); and the main net gain was from the West Indies and the Indian subcontinent.

The inclusion of air transport statistics would increase the number of recorded emigrants, especially to Canada, but it would also increase the number of immigrants, particularly from the West Indies and the Indian sub-continent. The statistics based on the long sea routes indicate a net gain in 1946–63 from the West Indies, India and Pakistan of fewer than 250,000 persons. By contrast, the government's White Paper on 'Immigration from the Commonwealth' of August 1965[24] estimated the net gain in 1955–62 from the Caribbean, Asia, East and West Africa and the Mediterranean to have been 472,350. Nine months earlier the Home Secretary had informed the House of Commons that there were then in the United Kingdom some 800,000 immigrants from the new Commonwealth countries, that is excluding Australia, Canada and New Zealand. The latter figure probably included the children born in the United Kingdom to these immigrants. It appears to have been the variety of this inflow, and both its actual and potentially rapid increase that led to the drastic revision of the United Kingdom immigration law in April 1962, which required Commonwealth citizens seeking entry to the United Kingdom for purposes of employment to hold a Ministry of Labour employment voucher and also restricted a worker's dependants to his immediate family or spouse, dependent children, and parents beyond working age. The White Paper of August 1965 proposed tightening entry controls even further by reducing entry vouchers from an estimated 20,800 a year to 8,500 limited to those with specific jobs to go to and to others with skills particularly required in the United Kingdom (e.g. doctors, dentists, trained nurses, teachers and graduates in science and technology). Persons thus admitted could also bring their wives and children under the age of 16 years with them.[25]

The White Paper of 1965, with its tightening of entry controls, its frank statement that 'the United Kingdom is already a multiracial society', and its positive measures to promote integration clearly recognized the new role of Britain as an immigrant country receiving settlers from distant parts of the Commonwealth; but over these long sea routes the United Kingdom still remained the loser, by about a million between 1946 and 1963. However, this is only part of the complicated pattern of movement centred on the United Kingdom, for, as will be shown in more detail later, there were substantial gains after 1946 from short sea and air routes, especially from the Republic of Ireland and continental Europe, which appear to have given the United Kingdom an overall net balance of immigration until 1963. Official figures of total movements indicate a net emigration in 1953–7 of 205,000 and a net immigration in 1958–63 of 487,000, leaving a net *gain* in 1953–63 of 282,000.[26] Thus the United Kingdom was involved substantially both in the overseas and in the intra-continental migrations, and this combination was also a marked feature of other countries in the post-war period.

The other two most significant areas of *overseas* emigration from Northern and Central Europe after 1947 were the Netherlands and the Federal Republic of Germany, which, like the United Kingdom, have been both emigrant and immigrant areas. In each case the inward and outward movements have been from quite different areas.

The Netherlands was one of the few countries of northern Europe which actively encouraged emigration after the war, when the government felt that both industrialization and land reclamation would not be sufficient to absorb the expected supply of Dutch labour. Through state and voluntary agencies, emigrants were able to secure passage assistance, pre-training and assistance to adjust to the area of emigration. The objective, as laid down in 1952, was the removal each year of about half the increment to the working population, or about 60,000 emigrants. In terms of gross emigration this figure was reached, but in terms of net migration the pattern was very different. Moreover, whereas the initial emphasis was upon the emigration of surplus rural workers, these became a relatively minor part of the outflow, accounting for only 26,100 emigrants in the whole period 1945–62.

The balance sheet of Netherlands migration since the Second World War until 1963 may be summarized as follows:[27]

	Numbers in thousands
Emigration	
Sponsored	409·6
Unsponsored:	
To Netherlands Territory	218·4
To Other Countries	452·3
Total Emigration	1,080·3
Immigration	
From Netherlands Territory	471·5
From Other Countries	482·9
Total Immigration	954·4
Net Emigration	125·9

It should be emphasized, however, that the whole of the loss was incurred in the ten years 1951–60, and that in the following three years the Netherlands gained, in the movement to and from all sources, a net balance of 34,000 people.

An interesting aspect of the Netherlands story summarized above was the *sponsored* emigration, which gathered pace quickly after the war. Between 1951 and 1960 some 320,700 sponsored emigrants left Holland, most of them for North America (156,000), Oceania (107,000) and South Africa (28,000). How far this movement might have occurred in any case in the climate favouring emigration in the post-war years, is a matter of conjecture. The policy seems to have encouraged a psychological atmosphere in favour of emigration, which became for a time a more powerful 'push' factor than economic motivations. For the emigrants themselves, the sponsored movement was particularly important because they had available a degree of assistance through all phases, from pre-migration preparation to after-assistance, which has seldom been accorded. This, together with the religious character of Dutch emigration, gave the sponsored movement a very strong group character.

In the case of West Germany, emigration overseas from 1946 to 1963,[28] although exceeding 1,500,000, was only a fraction of the massive gains through post-war refugee immigration and population transfers into Germany which have already been discussed. In the first seven or eight years a considerable part of the movement from West Germany was of non-nationals, with most of the flow going to the USA, Canada and Australia. After about 1950 most of the emigrants were German nationals, but the flow decreased markedly by 1960, that is at the time when labour shortages were beginning to attract large numbers of immigrants from other parts of Europe into West Germany. In a total outflow overseas between 1946 and 1963 of 1,603,000, of whom 858,000 were German nationals, by far the greatest number went to the United States (788,000), the other two most important areas being Canada (345,000) and Australia (229,000).

Among southern European countries, Italy had been by far the most important source of overseas emigration since the war.[29] Italy's pattern has differed from that of the United Kingdom or of the Netherlands in that she has also been the main emigrant country to continental Europe, thus yielding a net loss to all areas.

Italy ended the war with a high emigration potential; war casualties had been light, the labour force was increasing rapidly and internal investment was still at a low ebb, particularly in southern Italy. Consequently, Italian emigration revived quickly, with the net loss of Italian nationals to overseas countries exceeding 400,000 between 1946 and 1950. At the same time, almost 168,000 Italian workers and their families moved into France as permanent settlers. The pull of Europe did not immediately diminish the overseas flow, for the net loss overseas was 522,000 between 1951 and 1955 and again 330,000 between 1956 and 1960. But the tide was turning, and, as Figure 5. 3 shows, there was a steady decline in the overseas outflow from Italy from 1956 until 1963. Nevertheless, over the whole period 1946–63 Italy's net loss overseas, estimated at 1,347,000, exceeded that of the United Kingdom. But, whereas UK overseas emigration was again on the up-turn in 1963, Italian emigration was still declining.

The spread of Italian settlers since 1945 to almost all of the main immigrant countries outside Europe is seen in the following summary of the emigration *overseas* of Italian nationals between 1946 and 1963.

	Total Emigration (000's)	Net Emigration (000's)
Selected Areas:		
Canada	283·7	271·1
USA	304·7	254·2
Argentina	489·2	389·1
Brazil	114·7	78·7
Venezuela	241·8	138·4
Australia	259·4	237·3
All Areas	1,808·6	1,346·9

The most striking features of the Italian emigration pattern is perhaps the sharp decline, after about 1958, in gross emigration to Latin America, and also the rising immigration from the same area (particularly from Brazil); an immigration which left Italy a net *gain* with Latin America between 1961 and 1963 (See Figure 5. 4). This decline in Italian emigration suggests that it may be associated with major economic and demographic changes in Italy. Firstly, the decline coincides with rising *per capita* incomes in Italy, and a marked reduction of unemployment and underemployment

Figure 5.4: Net Migration from Southern Europe to Latin America, 1958-63

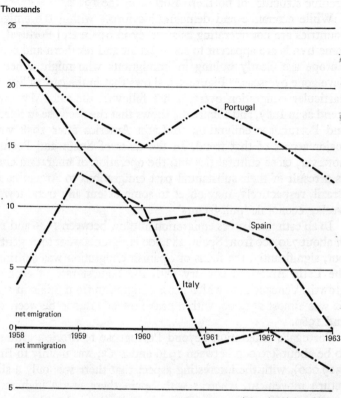

Thousands

International Labour Office

following the adoption of a development plan covering 1954-64 which aimed at finding 400,000 additional jobs a year, of which 80,000 were to be provided through emigration. Secondly, these factors tend to leave only the high income countries of the USA, Canada, Australia, and of northern and central Europe, as the areas with any economic attraction for the prospective Italian emigrant. Thirdly, as a result of falling fertility since about 1940 and a birth rate consistently below 20 since 1945, there will be only a slow increase in the Italian work force in the future. The 4·1 million persons aged 20-24 in 1961 (who would already have been depleted by emigration, may be compared with the 3·8 million aged

15–19, the 4·2 million aged 10–14 and the 4·0 million aged 5–9. In this regard, Italy in the mid-1960s was approaching the demographic structure of northern Europe of the 1930s.

While economic and demographic forces within the emigrant countries are not operating as strongly in Spain and Portugal, the same trends are apparent to some extent and northern and central Europe are clearly pulling in immigrants who might otherwise have gone overseas.[30] Figure 5. 3 shows that in the case of Spain in particular emigration overseas has followed the same downward trend as in Italy, and Figure 5·4 shows that the decrease in Spanish and Portuguese emigration to Latin America after 1958 was a major aspect of that trend. In the cases of Spain and Portugal, however, close cultural ties and the operation of migration chains as a result of their substantial past emigrations to Argentina and Brazil, respectively, may offset to some extent any trend towards weaker economic 'pull factors'.

In an estimated gross emigration outflow between 1946 and 1962 of about 740,000 from Spain, 282,000 emigrants went to Argentina, but, significantly, the focus of Spanish emigration was shifting to the Latin American country with the highest rate of economic growth, Venezuela, to which gross emigration from Spain in 1946–62 was almost 231,000, with a peak flow of 114,000 between 1956 and 1960.

Portugal's emigration beyond Portuguese territories, estimated to be about 470,000 between 1946 and 1963, was mainly to Brazil (329,000), with the interesting aspect that there was only a slight return movement, whereas with Spain there was a high return movement (See Figures 5· 3 and 5. 4). Over the whole period 1946–63, the immigration from Latin America to Spain probably exceeded 280,000 persons, compared with fewer than 100,000 to Portugal.

Two other southern European areas of emigration deserve comment; Greece[31] and Malta.[32] At least 250,000 Greeks emigrated from 1946 to 1963. One study estimates the total Greek emigration in 1950–9 to be 188,100 which, with a further 107,000 emigrating in 1959–62 and 16,000 emigrating in 1946–9, would put the total for the period 1946–62 at 311,000. About 48,000 Greeks entered the USA. The most interesting receiver, however, was Australia. About 33,000 Greeks had settled there before 1939, but this nucleus was augmented by 112,000 Greek nationals who entered

Australia as 'permanent and long-term arrivals' (i.e. intending to stay a year or more) between 1945 and 1962. Several thousand of these would be Greeks returning again after a visit to their homeland, but the flow puts Greeks next to Italians in the immigration of southern Europeans to Australia.

Finally, Malta has sent a large number of settlers abroad in relation to its total population of 328,000 in 1962. Indeed, with restricted resources and employment opportunities, and a high rate of growth, emigration has been regarded as an essential outlet to prevent overpopulation. Between 1946 and 1963 gross emigration amounted to 87,000, or over a quarter of the 1963 population, with the largest flows to Australia (49,000) and the United Kingdom (20,000). Since 1956, as in the cases of Greece and Italy, emigration has declined.

The discussion of emigration has already indicated the major receiving areas with the important exception of Israel, which, with almost two-thirds of its population still foreign born in 1963, was the classic example in the contemporary world of an immigrant country.[33] The greatest movement into Israel occurred between 1948 and 1951, the period of 'the ingathering of the exiles', when 693,800 persons, most of them from Europe (338,400), Asia (237,000) and Africa (93,800), moved into the country. By 1960 the total immigration had exceeded one million.

This rapid influx was largely made possible by three factors; the dedication and skills of the Jewish population, substantial foreign aid, and the departure of the Arabs in numbers which probably exceeded Jewish immigration between 1948 and 1951. In terms of economic, social or cultural factors, the Israeli situation has been unique compared with other contemporary immigrant countries, for it involved the building of a new nation rather than the growth of an established country, and the problems of assimilation were not those of merging an established and new cultures but of moulding a new nation out of diverse elements in which the only common bond was their faith and, for a great many of the settlers, previous persecution. The parallel is rather with frontier development of the USA, Australia or New Zealand in the early nineteenth century than with other immigration movements of the twentieth century.

In terms of the numbers of new settlers absorbed, the United States of America[34] retained its role as the premier immigrant country, receiving between 1946 and 1963 approximately 4·3 million immigrants, of whom some 2·3 million were from Europe, with other substantial gains from Canada, Mexico, the West Indies and Latin America, and with apparently little loss through emigration. Substantial as this inflow was, it constituted a mere fraction of the total annual natural increase of between 2·8 and 2·9 million in the USA. Economically, the impact of immigration has therefore been relatively less than in smaller countries, but from the humanitarian angle the role of the USA has been substantial, for among the 1·4 million immigrants received between 1946 and 1952, almost half a million were refugees from Europe. In addition, the USA has been the major contributor to funds for the resettlement of refugees in other countries.

While Canada[35] appears to have continued its traditional role of supplying emigrants across its land frontier with the United States, it has itself been a major immigrant area, having received between 1946 and 1962 some 2,151,000 immigrants, of whom 1,849,000 came from Europe. In the immediate post-war years refugees, including 123,000 IRO displaced persons, were important elements of the flow, but since then the main contributors have been nationals of the United Kingdom, Italy, West Germany, and the Netherlands. The lowest annual intake from Europe was 62,000 in 1950, and the highest 257,000 in 1957, which included a flood of 109,000 British immigrants following the Suez crisis. As Canada does not keep statistics of emigrants, it is difficult to determine the net migration for Canada. One estimate suggests that up to 1957, with a total immigration from Europe of 1,466,000, the number of emigrants to Europe probably did not exceed 150,000. To this should be added the emigration of some 320,000 to the USA, which would, however, still leave Canada a substantial immigrant country with a net gain in 1946–57 of around a million.[36]

This immigration was in the Canadian tradition. The variations that could occur were limited by Canada's immigration regulations, which restricted unsponsored immigrants to two categories: British subjects by birth or naturalization, and citizens by birth or naturalization of France, Ireland and the United States; and secondly, citizens from western European countries and refugees from Europe selected by the Department of Immigration for placement in employment or self-establishment in agriculture, business or industry in Canada. New regulations in 1962 made sweeping changes in regard to unsponsored immigrants, specifying only that an applicant must possess a skill or training that will enable the immigrant to fit into the Canadian economic and social structure.[37] The basic objective of the new regulations was to remove any suggestion of discrimination on grounds of race or citizenship and to ensure that the new immigrants would have the skills required by the Canadian economy. However the new regulations, with their emphasis upon skilled immigrants, are not likely to alter quickly the ethnic balance of Canada's settlers.

In Australia, the third major immigrant country of the post-war period, policy has restricted immigration for permanent settlement almost wholly to Europeans, but within this European flow there has been a marked change since 1946 compared with pre-war immigration. State-assisted immigration has a long history in Australia, but this assistance was almost wholly restricted before 1946 to British subjects. Since then, beginning with the displaced person immigration in 1948–50, and as a result of agreements with European governments, assisted schemes have operated widely throughout Europe. Of all the receiving countries, Australia has been by far the most active in seeking out and recruiting new settlers in the post-war period.

From October 1945 to March 1964, immigrants introduced under government-assisted schemes, and their relation to unassisted 'permanent and long term' arrivals, were:[38]

	Assisted	Non-Assisted	Total
British	546,400	510,400	1,056,800
Non-British	492,800	540,600	1,033,400
Total	1,039,200	1,051,000	2,090,200

Assuming that the 'non-assisted' category carries a higher proportion than the 'assisted' of long-term visitors, as opposed to 'permanent settlers', it seems clear that assisted schemes have helped more than half Australia's post-war settlers, and that among the 'assisted' approximately one-half have been non-British, and that about a half of the non-British have been assisted. There seems little doubt that these assisted schemes were substantially responsible to 1964 for the large influx from non-British settlers, but once the flow was started the factor of chain migration helped to sustain it. This has been particularly important in the case of southern Europeans.

The use of 'permanent and long-term arrivals' as the definition of an immigrant to Australia inflates the role of British settlers as it covers all persons entering the country for a year or more and therefore includes a considerable number of long-term visitors.[39] Even so, the British, with a little more than a third of the *net* gain since 1945, have been the largest national group. Historically considered, however, the unusual feature of Australian post-war immigration has been the important role of non-British immigrants, dominated by the Italians, with 271,600 persons of Italian birthplace entering Australia as permanent and long-term arrivals from 1945 to March 1964, all but 43,700 of them without any assistance from Australia. Greeks numbered 111,800, of whom 35,300 were assisted. By contrast, much higher proportions of the northern European immigrants came under assisted schemes: of 134,600 Dutch, 83,600 were assisted, and of 98,000 Germans, 71,800 were assisted.

However, the Australian pattern has not been all gain. From statistics of permanent and long-term arrivals less departures, a reasonably accurate estimate can be made of net gains over a number of years. For 1946–63 these indicate that 2,040,000 long-term and permanent arrivals were offset by 659,100 long-term and permanent departures. The net gain of 1,381,300 thus probably provides a fairly accurate picture of the 'settler' content of Australian immigration throughout this period.[40]

In the case of New Zealand the post-war pattern has been much more in the tradition of British immigration which has always dominated New Zealand's intake. There was less emphasis upon recruitment and sponsorship than in the case of Australia, and the only substantial supply of non-British immigrants has been from the Netherlands. It is a tribute to New Zealand's 'pull' factor that in an essentially *laissez-faire* situation, and remote from Europe, some 400,000 immigrants entered the country between 1946 and 1963, and that the net gain was about 230,000.

United Kingdom immigrants also dominated the post-war movement to the Union (now Republic) of South Africa.[41] In a total immigration from Europe in 1946–63 of 230,000, about 58 per cent were from the United Kingdom, the other main European elements being the Dutch and the Germans. The overall pattern was the arrival of 327,700 immigrants and the departure of 192,500 emigrants, leaving a net gain of 135,200. A quick flow of immigration immediately after the war was to some extent the result of active encouragement by the government, including missions in various European countries, but when much stricter screening of immigrants was instituted after 1948, immigration fell away and was accompanied by an increase in emigration, especially to the Rhodesias. After 1950, a less stringent policy was adopted, partly to alleviate the scarcity of skilled workers, and special efforts were made to attract workers from the Netherlands and West Germany. In 1961, new measures were taken to recruit new settlers: a separate Department of Immigration was established; financial assistance was offered to immigrants; and assistance was provided to find employment. The sharp upward trend in immigration in 1962 and 1963 seems to have been associated with these positive measures.

These six countries (USA, Canada, Australia, New Zealand, South Africa and Israel) were the main recipients of emigrants from Europe. The one remaining immigrant area of major importance is South America. Statistics compiled from the countries from which emigrants moved to South America indicate a total inflow from Europe between 1946 and 1963 of about 1,522,000, with a backflow to Europe of 494,000, thus leaving a net gain to all South American countries of 1,028,000.[42] The tendency for immigration to these countries to decline sharply after about 1958 has already been stressed (See Figure 5.4). Generally immigration has been a much smaller component of growth in Latin America (with the possible exception of Argentina) than in the cases of Canada, Australia or New Zealand. For one thing Latin America contains countries with some of the highest natural growth rates in the world. From natural increase alone Venezuela's population is expected to increase from 7,331,000 in 1960 to over 13,000,000 in 1980. Estimates for Brazil over the same period show population rising from 70,600,000 to almost 127,000,000, an increase of 75 per cent. The prospect of most other Latin American countries is in keeping with, or above, this percentage change. Thus, while selective immigration may be important in the short run to supply necessary skills, the longer term outlook is unfavourable to international immigration. In this regard the prospect in Latin America, with the possible exception of Argentina, is quite different from that of Australia, or even of Canada, where rapid industrialization and the development of new resources and lower rates of natural increase leave a wider margin for continued immigration, if the immigrants can be found. This last question of the 'immigrant market' is becoming increasingly a function of Europe's own capacity to absorb immigrants, but from 1946 until 1963 the contribution of Europe to overseas emigration has been very considerable, as Table 5·3 shows. In all these seven major overseas

Table 5.3: The Main Receiving Areas of European Emigrants 1946–63

Country or Area	Estimated Total from European Countries	Immigration from all Countries	Net Migration
USA	2,267,000	4,343,000	—
Canada	1,918,000	2,245,000	—
Australia		2,040,000	1,381,000
Israel		1,100,000	—
New Zealand		387,000	226,000
South Africa	230,000	328,000	135,000
South America		1,552,000	1,028,000

areas the greater part of the immigration flows, although not always measurable because of the inadequacies of official statistics, have come from Europe, where growth rates have continued to be relatively low.

There now remains the third part of the equation to be considered. So far the major areas of outflow from Europe overseas and the main overseas receiving areas have been discussed; but there remains the pattern of international movement within Europe. Did this also flow from the traditional countries of *emigration*, such as the United Kingdom and Italy, or, if not, how did it affect their overall net losses through movements to and from all overseas sources? It has already been noted that the United Kingdom and Italy each lost over a million persons in terms of net emigrants *overseas*.

Once the great refugee readjustments after 1945 were completed, Europe began to move closer to the ideal of a free labour market, with a considerable volume of movement for purposes of both permanent settlement and temporary employment. In international movements within Europe up to the Second World War, France stood out as the main immigrant country, reaching a maximum of 200,000 persons annually between 1926 and 1930.[43] Twice, however, Germany appears to have replaced France as the chief *immigrant* country of Europe – during Germany's rapid phase of industrial development from the 1880s until approximately 1905; and between 1933 and 1939, a period of industrial expansion associated with rearmament, when there was a net gain of 500,000 immigrants, many of whom were ethnic Germans from Austria, Sudetenland and other areas of central and eastern Europe.[44] With the exception of the ethnic Germans, the main sources of these European immigrants were Italy, Poland and Spain.

European international movements after 1945 followed a broadly similar although more complicated pattern. Until 1957, the most important cross currents converged on five countries (Sweden, United Kingdom, Belgium, France and Switzerland) and branched out again from these countries in the form of return movements since much of the initial immigration had been for limited periods of employment. In Sweden most of the immigrants came from neighbouring countries, particularly from Finland. In the United Kingdom they came from Ireland and, indirectly, from eastern Europe. In Belgium, France and Switzerland, the main source continued to be Italy. In terms of net gain, France and the United Kingdom dominated the scene among these five countries. One estimate puts the net gain of aliens in 1946–57 to Sweden at 101,200 and to Belgium at 184,200, and the number of foreign workers subject to employment restrictions in Switzerland in 1957 at 237,000.[45] Over the same period 367,000 European workers were granted entry permits to the United Kingdom, which at the same time received a net gain of 318,000 immigrants from the Republic of Ireland. These sources thus substantially offset the United Kingdom's net loss over the long sea routes during this period.

In France the net permanent gain was similar to that of the United Kingdom. The permanent immigration of workers and their families in 1946–57 was about 604,000, of whom 418,000 were Italians. As France was not an emigrant country, these European immigrants represented a direct supplement to the French labour force, to which must be added a considerable volume of seasonal workers (again mainly Italians) who were estimated to number around 50,000 in 1956 and 1957.[46]

After 1957 the immigration movement within Europe increased markedly, particularly as a result of the re-entry of West Germany into the European labour market. The immediate post-war influx of 9·4 million refugees into West Germany by September 1950 was followed by a continual and substantial movement from East Germany and from the former east German provinces. The net gain in 1950-7 of about 2·4 million persons, mainly from these sources, constituted by far the largest migratory movement within Europe during this time, but since it concerned essentially ethnic Germans it is not strictly comparable with the movements discussed above into the five north-western European countries. Nevertheless, even allowing for the political aspects involved, it demonstrates the drawing power of the West German economy, a power which was again clearly demonstrated in the rapidly growing non-German immigration to West Germany after 1957.[47]

Central and north-western Europe have thus become important immigrant receiving countries, competing with the overseas countries for workers from southern and eastern Europe. As a considerable proportion of this intra-European movement has been of a seasonal and temporary character, a direct comparison between it and movement overseas is difficult. Figure 5·5 can therefore be taken only as an approximate picture of the trend in intra-continental Europe and of its level compared with the flow of emigration overseas from those same areas.

As emphasized earlier, the pace of *overseas* emigration from southern European countries began to slow down after about 1958, and in some instances gave rise to a net immigration (See Figure 5.4.) This was particularly true of the movement from southern Europe to Latin America. A particularly interesting point now to be observed is that the pace of Italian emigration into other parts of Europe seems also to have slowed down after 1961. This decline was offset by a continued sharp rise in emigration from Greece, Portugal and Spain into Europe (Figure 5.5). Spain, with 58,000 foreign workers admitted in 1963, replaced Italy (13,000) as the main source of immigrants to France. The Italians were still the main source of immigrants in Switzerland and Germany, but the general weakening of Italian emigration to Europe, as abroad, may again be associated with rising *per capita* incomes and the relative stability of the age cohorts now entering the Italian labour force.

Finally, further evidence of the 'pull' of the now rich but

Figure 5.5: Gross Emigration from southern Europe to Overseas and to Europe, 1956–63

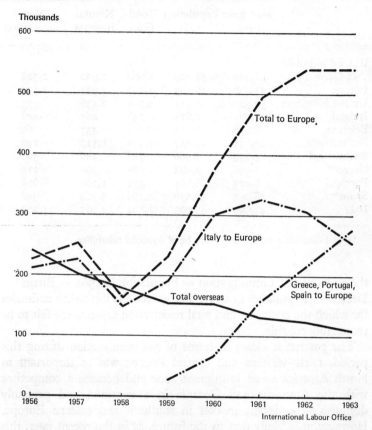

Thousands

International Labour Office

relatively slowly growing countries comes from the United Kingdom, where immigration *from all sources* appears to have exceeded emigration *to all sources* each year, from 1958 to 1963, with a total net gain of 487,000, which exceeded the estimated net loss of 205,000 from 1953 to 1957. The increasing extent to which northwestern and central Europe competed with overseas countries for European immigrants is indicated in Table 5·4 which attempts to provide a final summary of the overall position resulting from movements to and from all sources between 1951 and 1961 by taking the estimates of population (in most cases close to census years) at these two terminal points and estimating net migration by

115

Table 5.4: Net Immigration 1951–61 as derived from Population Estimates and Vital Data: Selected countries of Europe (in thousands)[48]

	Mid Year Population 1951	Mid Year Population 1961	Total Gain	Natural Increase	Net Immigration
Federal Republic of Germany	48,369	54,029	5,660	2,932	2,728
France	42,056	46,163	4,107	2,933	1,174
United Kingdom	50,562	52,925	2,363	2,436	−73
Ireland	2,961	2,818	−143	265	−408
Belgium	8,678	9,184	506	437	69
Netherlands	10,264	11,637	1,373	1,512	−139
Switzerland	4,749	5,496	747	387	360
Greece*	7,646	8,402	756	968	−212
Portugal	8,463	8,894	431	1,109	−678
Spain*	28,095	30,559	2,464	3,404	−940
Italy	47,099	49,903	2,804	4,067	−1,263

*Population estimate considered to be of doubtful reliability.

the equation: Net immigration = Population in 1961 − Births + Deaths − Population in 1951. The exercise is limited to countries for which the estimates and vital registration systems are felt to be reasonably reliable.

The pattern is clear; in terms of net immigration during this period, north-western and central Europe was as important as North America as an immigrant zone and became a competitor with the Americas and Oceania in a common and probably diminishing emigrant market in southern and eastern Europe. However, it is likely that in the future, as in the recent past, this *net* pattern in Europe will continue to be the product of those complicated flows of which the United Kingdom provides the best examples.

On the American continent a significant intra-continental movement has also developed since the Second World War, particularly into the USA. The Canadian situation has already been discussed. Another major movement, some of it illegal, has been from Mexico to the USA. In 1957 there were 452,000 Mexican farm labourers legally in the USA. The immigration of foreigners from central America has also been considerable, with a net gain in 1946–57 of probably more than 100,000. South American immigration has been comparatively slight. However the net gain to the USA from all sources of the American continent between 1945 and 1963 almost certainly exceeded a million persons.

In Latin America,[49] where each country has been essentially an immigrant area, some intra-continental movements have occurred, although their exact measurement is difficult. Generally, they appear to arise mainly from the movement of rural surpluses to urban areas, particularly to capital cities. The Haitian census of 1953 recorded 30,000 persons of Cuban origin in Haiti. The 1950 census of Honduras enumerated 20,300 persons from El Salvador, and in 1950 some 16,600 Nicaraguans were recorded in Costa Rica. There also appears to have been a migration of many thousands from Columbia into neighbouring sections of Venezuela and Ecuador. Peru had also yielded, by 1951, 30,000 or more people, mostly from rural areas, to the alpine city of La Paz in Bolivia, while the rural areas of southern Bolivia have yielded many agricultural labourers for the sugar cane plantations of northern Argentina, one estimate of these being as high as 200,000. Paraguayans have also been moving in considerable numbers into Buenos Aires, the capital of Argentina, and also into the tea-growing areas of south-western Brazil. The movements across national boundaries among these countries have probably been considerably greater than are suggested by available census and other statistical records.

In recent decades there have also been very substantial but little observed intra-continental movements within Asia and Africa, movements which might have been considered as 'internal' migration in the era of colonial rule, but which have become 'international' with the rise of new nation-states; and although some of these movements may have been relatively small in quantitative terms, their political and social significance has frequently been very great. One reason for the relatively small outflow from Asia has of course been the limited rights of entry into the major immigrant countries. A considerable part of the immigration that did occur until the 1930s was recruited and indentured labour; a system which was generally one of the basic causes of the imposition of restrictive policies in countries of European settlement. The total number of Asians living in other countries before the Second World War has been estimated at between 10 and 20 million. Most of these immigrants had come from China, India, Pakistan, Japan and Korea, and the main receiving countries had been Malaya, Burma, Ceylon, Viet-Nam, Laos and Cambodia, Thailand, Indonesia and Manchuria, where many of them were employed in mines, on plantations and in entrepreneurial enterprises in Asian cities.[50]

Many of these immigrations were concentrated in relatively small areas, often as a direct result of recruitment for specialized purposes, as in the case of Indians in Fiji, Kenya, Tanganyika, Uganda and Ceylon; and sometimes they quickly grew, partly as a result of high rates of natural increase after the initial immigration, into substantial minorities and occasionally into majority populations. For example, in Malaya before about 1945 the Chinese and Indians made up over half the population (which was 5·8 million in 1947); and in Fiji in 1963 the Indians outnumbered the Fijians in an estimated total population of 450,000. In Ceylon, immigrant Indians formed 10 per cent of the population of 607 millions in 1946.

Much of this immigration, with the important exception of Japanese immigration into Latin America, was into territories which had not received political independence before the Second World War. Since then, most of the receiving areas have achieved independence, but this has tended to be accompanied by the imposition of further restrictions among the Asian countries themselves. Nor has there been any really substantial change in the restrictive policies of non-Asian countries. Consequently, the flows of Asian migrations have tended if anything to be reduced further, and in some instances there have been expulsions of earlier immigrants back to their homelands. The most extensive international movements of Asians since the Second World War have been, as with Europeans, the compulsory transfers of populations and refugees.

One major transfer arose from the partition of Palestine in 1947.[51] By October 1948, all but 110,000 of 860,000 Arabs had left the present boundaries of Palestine for surrounding territories, particularly Jordan, the Gaza area, Lebanon, and Syria. Some of these subsequently moved back into Israel, but the majority remained to become the core of the 960,000 refugees who were in the care of the United Nations Relief and Works Agency by 1950.

By far the greatest civilian population transfer was between India and Pakistan. The refugee crisis was taking shape before the Indian Independence Act of July 1947. Hundreds of thousands of

Hindus had left their homes in the Punjab and North-west Provinces, and a flight of Moslems towards the west was also occurring. This vast two-way movement continued after Indian independence, and by 1951 there were 7·2 million refugees in Pakistan and a similar number of refugees in India. The broad distribution of these refugees in 1951 was as follows:[52]

In Pakistan		In India	
East Pakistan	699,100	Northern India	480,300
		Eastern India	2,576,000
West Pakistan	5,910,600	Southern India	16,600
		Western India	409,900
Federal District		Central India	195,900
of Karachi	616,900	N.W. India	3,617,200
Total	7,226,600	Total	7,295,900

The impact of these refugees was most severe in the Punjab in Pakistan, where they formed 68 per cent of the population; and in India in West Bengal (29 per cent of the population) and the Punjab (33 per cent). In West Bengal the numbers of incoming Hindus were three or four times greater than the numbers of emigrating Moslems. Similarly, in Pakistan there was a heavy net gain through the refugee movement in the Punjab and in the Karachi Federal District. Movements since 1951, of about 1·5 million Hindus from Pakistan into Eastern India, and of 0·5 million Moslems from West Bengal into East Bengal and a further 650,000 from India into West Pakistan, have continued to affect mainly the partitioned states of Bengal and Punjab.

The problems of resettlement were complicated by the fact that the migrating populations were dissimilar in occupational structure and skills: the Moslems were mainly rural handicraftsmen and peasants, whereas the Hindus included a much higher proportion of shopkeepers, government employees and clerical workers. The costs of resettling these transferred populations consumed substantial funds which might have been used for more profitable investment. Between 1947-8 and 1957-8 the Indian government had spent 3,011 million rupees on displaced persons, excluding a further 29 million rupees spent between 1955-6 and 1957-8 on Rehabilitation Finance Administration loans. The Second Five-Year

Plan (1956–61) also proposed the expenditure of 855 million rupees as compensation to refugees for their loss of capital. While the capital outlays for rehabilitating the refugees were very high, the achievements were also considerable: by 1957–8 1,114,000 families or over 4 million persons had been settled on the land, some 600,000 housing units for refugees had been built, and 537 million rupees had been paid in compensation.

In Pakistan, surplus land, especially in West Pakistan, and land vacated by Hindus, enabled the resettlement of Moslem refugees to be carried forward fairly quickly. The major problem remained the urban refugees, particularly in the Karachi region. The extent of the problem is apparent in the fact that although it was estimated that 1·4 million displaced persons had been housed in West Pakistan by 1957, at least a million remained to be housed. The problem remained even more serious in East Pakistan and Karachi. As in India, the government of Pakistan was also faced with the problem of compensating refugees for loss of property.

Another major population shift arising from the war and its immediate aftermath was the transfer of over 5 million Japanese by the end of 1946, with the numbers rising to 6,285,000 by 1956.[53] China (1,532,000), Manchuria (1,046,000), South-East Asia (712,000), South Korea (596,000), North Korea (323,000) and Formosa (480,000) yielded the greater part of these repatriates, who greatly exceeded the 1·2 million foreigners who departed from Japan between 1945 and 1950. Net immigration from these movements thus amounted to about 5 millions, which in turn was about half the increase in Japan's population between 1945 and 1950.

The precise impact of these repatriates upon Japan's economic recovery is almost impossible to gauge. Little is known of their age or occupational skills, but they do seem to have assisted the government-sponsored land settlement schemes which aimed at overcoming food shortages after the war. Compared with Germany, however, the Japanese population structure at the conclusion of the war was comparatively normal: Hiroshima and Nagasaki at least took a cross section of the population. In 1950, with a population of 83 million (compared with 72 million in 1941), Japan had a relatively small surplus of females (M : F = 96 : 100) and a higher proportion of its population in the working age groups (60 per cent of the population aged 15–60) than any other Asian country.

A major Asian immigration, when considered in relation to the size of the receiving country, has been from mainland China to Hong Kong. The 1961 census of Hong Kong recorded that over half the population of 3,129,600, or 1,643,000 persons, had been born outside Hong Kong. Of these, 815,800 were estimated to have arrived before September 1949 and 827,200 after that date. Most of the immigrants came from the Kwantung Province of China, from which the immigrant flow reached a peak of more than 120,000 in 1949.[54]

As already indicated, however, the post-war period, with its accompanying trend of the establishment of independent nation states, has not encouraged immigration in Asia. On the contrary, barriers have been raised against such movement, and earlier immigrants have in many cases been repatriated. Almost 100,000 Chinese were repatriated from Indonesia in 1960.[55] Indian migration has been stopped in Ceylon and Burma, and both Indian and Chinese immigrations have ceased in Malaysia. With these trends in Asia itself, and with close restrictions in almost all areas of European settlement, there seems little prospect of increased Asian emigration in the near future.

In the African continent, the movement of people beyond tribal and national limits has also largely been the product of the 'opening up' of Africa after the acquisition of territories by European governments, and again the movement has been initiated by conquest leading to treks from tribal areas and by the recruitment of labour for agricultural, mining and industrial enterprises. Since the slave trade ended, few Africans have left the continent for permanent residence abroad, and the intra-continental movement has tended to be one of male workers moving temporarily out of tribal areas for employment, with periodic return movements to tribal homes, although in recent years there is evidence of more extensive family emigration, particularly in West Africa.

Statistical data are too meagre to measure precisely the flows of international migrations within Africa, but their general directions are known. In North Africa, major movements were associated with the gaining of independence in Morocco, Tunisia, Libya and Egypt. All these new states restricted the employment and the rights of permanent residence of foreigners, and some 400,000 Europeans left North Africa. The political upheavals associated with the struggle for independence also created considerable refugee problems, with the movements of 300,000 or more people from Algeria to Tunisia and Morocco.[56]

The major intra-continental movements of Africans, however, occurred south of the Sahara. While some of this movement has been of the traditional type of nomadic pastoralists, it has been increasingly the product of three factors: the poor land resources available to African tribes, the accelerating rate of population growth, and the attraction and recruitment of wage labour into areas of relatively rapid economic growth.[57] Increasing contacts of Africans with European civilization created demands for such goods as textiles and hand tools which required a cash income in addition to the subsistence from the land. Such requirements encouraged the temporary migration of male workers to urban areas, but as wages were too low to allow these workers to transplant their families to their places of employment, they tended to return frequently to their tribal areas. African society, therefore, came to depend largely upon two types of economic activity: subsistence agriculture at the base, and industrial employment to raise cash income to the vital minimum. The complement of this situation was that employers came to rely upon an apparently inexhaustible supply of unskilled labour to supplement the European capital, entrepreneurs and skilled manpower that were associated with European immigration.

In Central and East Africa, the main movements have been towards the south. Bilateral and multilateral agreements have controlled these migrations to some extent, generally with the objects of regulating the supply to the demand or of preventing depletion of labour supplies in the areas of emigration, and of establishing minimum standards in such matters as wages and accommodation; but the great majority of African migrants continued to leave their tribal lands in the first instance on their own impulse, with little knowledge of such regulations, only to be caught in the administrative network as they approached their places of employment.

The two chief immigrant areas for labour, especially from central and eastern Africa, have been the Union (now Republic) of South Africa and Southern Rhodesia. There were estimated to be 164,000 immigrants from Mozambique in the Union in 1953, which also contained 16,500 Southern Rhodesians in 1951. In 1953 there were also 25,700 Northern Rhodesians in Southern

Rhodesia and 9,100 in the Union. At the same time, Northern Rhodesia contained about 10,000 persons from Nyasaland, Mozambique and Angola, and 160,000 Nyasalanders were estimated to be in other territories, mostly in Southern Rhodesia and the Union.[58] There were also substantial emigrations from British Protectorates of Bechuanaland and Swaziland to the Union. Tanganyika also yielded emigrants to the Union and to Uganda, but at the same time attracted workers from the surrounding territories.

These complicated patterns of movements appear to have been sustained since 1953.[59] For example, Tanganyika and Uganda took many immigrants from Ruandi-Urundi, but also continued to lose emigrants elsewhere. Heavy inflows continued into Southern Rhodesia, while there were also movements to Uganda and the highlands of Kenya. However, the Union of South Africa continued to be the principal immigrant area, with organized schemes of labour recruitment playing an important role until approximately 1959, after which many of the immigrants returned home. One estimate puts the African immigration into the Union in the late 1950s at about 112,000 persons, of whom more than 75,000 ultimately returned.

In western Africa the movement of Africans in the 1950s was to the South and West, especially into Ghana in which mining and agriculture became largely dependent upon extra-territorial labour. The 1948 census of the Gold Coast (subsequently Ghana) recorded 53,000 persons from other British territories and 122,000 of other foreign origin, and it is estimated that the number of foreigners entering Ghana temporarily or permanently rose from 108,000 in 1938 to 392,000 in 1953. The flow seems to have exceeded 300,000 a year until at least 1960. The most important source of these workers was the Upper Volta, with important supplements from Nigeria and Toga. The census of Ghana in 1960 showed that one in twelve of the population was foreign born and one in eight was of foreign ancestry.[60] In Ghana, this immigration has concentrated increasingly in urban areas; almost one-third of males aged 15–54 years in Accra in 1960 were foreign born.

Political upheavals in Africa have also added considerably to the international movements in Africa south of the Sahara. At the end of 1963, for example, there were 153,000 refugees from Rwanda in Burundi, the Congo, Tanganyika and Uganda, and also 150,000 refugees from Angola in the Congo (Leopoldville).[61] Other movements on a smaller scale have been associated with the establishment of independence in former British and French West Africa – for example, a movement of some 6,000 refugees from Ghana to Togo in 1961 and of some 12,000 from the Ivory Coast to Dahomey after 1958.

The general pattern of the international migration of Africans during this century has thus been one of very considerable movements, to be numbered in millions of persons, across boundaries which have had political purposes but which have sometimes had relatively little ethnic significance. Direct comparison between Africa and many other developing areas is, therefore, difficult because Africa is now a continent of many nations, many of them relatively small in population, whereas India, for example, is a continent with vast numbers under one government. Thus, what is measured as *international* migration in Africa may be *internal* migration in India. Despite its 'Balkanization', however, movement throughout Africa south of the Sahara has been, until recently, less restricted by social, cultural and political factors than it was in, say, the Indian sub-continent, and the migrations provided an important safety valve against the pressure of populations on scarce resources, but one that was associated with such evils as detribalization, the disruption of family life, and extremely low wages.[62] The system led to a pattern in which a majority of able-bodied men could be away from their homes for a substantial part of their adult life, leaving the communities from which they moved to suffer economic and social stagnation. The establishment of new nation-states, opposition to policies which associate migration with segregation and restrictions upon economic and social rights, and the emphasis upon economic development plans within each new nation, are tending to restrict movements across national boundaries and to accentuate internal movements from rural to urban areas, a trend particularly apparent in the Rhodesian copper belt and in the coastal towns of Ghana.

In conclusion, in reviewing the main features of the international movements of recent times, the most significant aspect has been the vast reshuffling of between 40 and 50 million people across international borders as refugees and forced migrations since the war. While this movement encouraged ethnic diversity in some of the receiving areas, as with the displaced person movement to Australia and Canada, its general tendency was to ethnic homogeneity, as with the return of Japanese to their homeland or with the transfer of Indian and Pakistani populations. Economically, these transfers were of considerable importance, for example where they replaced war losses or restored the demographic structure to more normal proportions, as in Germany; or where they reduced labour shortages, as in Australia, in the process of catching up lags caused by the war in the national stock of capital and consumer equipment.

The migratory flows of Europeans since 1945 have displayed some of the features of the traditional nineteenth-century patterns, for example in the considerable flows overseas to 'New World' countries; but, whereas emigrations from Europe throughout most of the nineteenth century were essentially movements of workers from the lower skilled and rural groups, overseas emigrations of recent times have been increasingly from among the skilled tradesmen and white collar classes. The majority of Europe's overseas emigrants have been required for industrial, not rural purposes. Again, whereas emigration from the late nineteenth century until the Second World War tended to be increasingly restricted by legislation imposed for both economic and political reasons, the flows after 1945 were increasingly free, at least in terms of temporary residence for purposes of employment. This is particularly true of north-western, central and southern Europe, which now have many of the characteristics of a free labour market. One consequence of this trend is the increasing pull of northern and western Europe upon the surplus labour of the south and east, and a further consequence is the increasing difficulties faced by the traditional overseas receiving countries in recruiting immigrants.

Whereas the demand of European immigrant areas is first and foremost for labour units, with substantial restrictions still in most cases upon family migration for permanent settlement, the overseas countries have for the most part deliberately encouraged the emigration of family units. Consequently, while most of the immigrants have been, as traditionally, under the age of about 40 years, the ratio of females to males (about 45 : 55) has been high, as has the proportion of children (generally one-fifth to one-quarter of all age groups). Migration between industrialized, high-income nations has increasingly required the operation of a whole range of state and voluntary services concerned with education, housing, transfer of pension and social service benefits, etc. Whereas the emigration of both workers and their families now involves essentially the loss to the sending country of any return upon the substantial cost of educating and rearing those family units, the process of their transfer also requires very substantial new capital outlays by the receiving country. In short, the transfer of skilled manpower and family units probably raises much more complicated problems of economic planning to absorb the immigrants than did the mass movements of the nineteenth century.[63] An important aspect of these migrations, especially within Europe, is the very large transfer of capital now involved through immigrants' remittances.[64]

But while the erstwhile emigrant countries of northern and central Europe and the immigrant countries overseas are competing for the same skilled labour, the market is imperfect and there is some evidence that the emigrants from Europe have been replaced to some extent by immigrants into Europe with lower skills, and that in the immigrant countries, where the rate of economic growth tends to be high and labour scarce, with therefore increased opportunity for mobility by the non-migrant population, the immigrants tend to be concentrated initially in occupations vacated by upwardly mobile non-migrant populations. Finally, both the high rate of labour mobility and the high immigrant absorptive capacity of European and some of the high-income overseas countries (e.g. Australia, New Zealand) have been facilitated by the demographic events of the 1930s which, with their excessively low birth rates, resulted in the 1950s in very low growth rates in the non-migrant work-forces.

Generally, the international movements of Europeans following 1945 formed complex patterns, with some countries (such as the United Kingdom) both giving and taking. While economic factors remained important determinants of these movements, the simplified long-term cyclical explanations which seemed to fit the trans-Atlantic movements of the nineteenth century cannot easily be applied to post-war European migrations, in which refugees, tensions created by international crises (e.g. Suez, Berlin, the failure of the UK to enter the Common Market), and even climatic factors, all seem to have played major explanatory roles.

Finally, many of the theories which have sought to explain the migrations among Europeans have little applicability to non-European areas. In Africa, the continent with probably the greatest migratory flows, the movements have probably been substantially motivated by economic and demographic factors, but such migrations of an essentially Malthusian character are now being resisted as the vestigial remains of imperial domination. To a greater extent the new nations of Asia and Africa are seeking the solution of their economic problems through measures to raise the rates of economic growth within their own countries, and in many instances (e.g. India, Taiwan, Korea, Turkey, Egypt) by encouraging birth control to reduce rates of population growth. In the pursuit of these objectives, the new nations of Africa and Asia are tending to raise barriers against immigration. This trend, together with a continuation among immigrant countries of European origin to sustain their barriers against Asian and African immigration, has created a situation in which work-forces (which in some cases will double within twenty years) will have to be absorbed wholly within existing national boundaries. In this event, the role of international migration to and from developing countries may tend to become increasingly, not mass movements, but temporary movements abroad for purposes of higher education and selective immigration of persons with skills essential to stimulate the rate of economic growth, with the basic solutions sought through the movements of capital and extensions of international trade.[65] These last two factors would thus play the same role as overseas investments from Europe in the nineteenth century, except that they would be investments in territories which are not underpopulated and need people, but which are overpopulated and require capital.

Chapter 6

Contemporary Patterns of the Western World

No single generalization can encompass the trend of fertility decline in all of today's 'developed' countries. As has been previously observed, a common trend became clearly apparent in many countries during the last quarter of the nineteenth century.

The United Kingdom, the Scandinavian countries and many overseas countries settled by Europeans (e.g., USA, Australia and New Zealand) fall into this category. This period also roughly coincides with the beginning of the dominance of industrial and urbanized social structures. But on the other hand the first signs of decline in fertility long preceded industrialization and urbanization in France and in Holland. Yet, while the trend towards controlled fertility occurred over different time-spans and in a great variety of economic and social circumstances, the significant fact is that by the 1930s most countries of northern and western Europe and their counterparts overseas in North America and Oceania had achieved birth rates which were frequently less than half those which had prevailed a century earlier. In western and northern Europe only the Netherlands exceeded a birth rate of 20 per 1,000 of population. England and Wales, Sweden and Switzerland were down to about 15, and even the United States, Australia and New Zealand were between 17 and 19.[1]

Comparatively little accurate demographic information was available at this time about the non-European peoples; but the situation described above was frequently compared with the past experience of the low-birth-rate countries themselves, or with the contemporary situation in south and eastern Europe where birth rates were in most cases still well above 30, and in the case of the USSR above 40 per 1,000 of population. The advantage held by the low-birth-rate countries was that they had all established lower levels of mortality than had ever before existed, with expectations of life at birth around or above 60 years. Birth rates around 18 per

1,000 of population, accompanied as they were by death rates of about 11 or 12 per 1,000 still left them with natural increases of 0·5 per cent or above, which were about half the growth rates that had applied in the middle of the nineteenth century, but were nevertheless much above the rates that had applied throughout most of their earlier history. France alone, because of relatively high mortality, was experiencing a natural decrease. By contrast, however, the USSR and many of the southern and eastern European countries were experiencing growth rates of 1 per cent or higher by demographic patterns that fairly closely resembled those which the north and west had experienced about seventy years earlier. These patterns have already been illustrated in Table 4.6.

One point needs emphasizing here, although full discussion of the matter will be left until Chapter 10. The people who produced the low levels of fertility of the 1930s among northern and western European countries and their counterparts overseas had no magic contraceptive pill or sophisticated intrauterine device to assist them; yet they managed to exercise control to an extent seldom before achieved, and never before achieved over so many classes of the people or over such wide geographical regions. The methods of control used were rudimentary and traditional – the sponge, douching, the condom, the use of the safe period and especially onanism or *coitus interruptus*. Nevertheless, the controls so exercised were remarkably effective. As emphasized in Chapter 4, an additional factor among these European peoples was the relatively late age of marriage and the relatively high proportions who remained unmarried. These European peoples were both Malthusian and Neo-Malthusian.

The motivations that led to this situation must have been very compelling and from the present point of time might be broadly classified as the product of the revolutionary change that had occurred in the societies of the countries concerned during the previous half century or so – the establishment of industrial, urbanized society, the escape from subsistence, the spread of universal education, the emancipation of women, and so on – but another compelling factor was undoubtedly the strengthening of the life-force of the new societies, or the expectation of parents that they themselves had a fair chance of living until the end of their working careers and that most of the children they bore would also live to replace them in adult life. For the first time in human history the life cycle had assumed permanent characteristics that required a new approach to fertility.[2]

Yet fertility control had become almost too effective. The natural increase of the north-western European populations was frequently a function of favourable age distributions rather than inherent reproductive capacity. When this was pointed out and popularized by neat indexes which standardized current fertility performance by age and related it to current mortality to provide a synthetic measure of the extent to which a population might be expected to replace itself over a generation, widespread concern about the low level of the birth rate tended to degenerate into panic about the impending decline of the Western peoples.

The indexes of measurement that caused so much concern, were the female gross and net reproduction rates, which have been briefly described in Chapter 2. The *gross* rate, which is the sum of the age-specific female fertilities of the women in a population in a given year, provides an estimate of the number of female children who would be born should the specific rates of a given moment continue indefinitely. The *net* rate, by applying a mortality schedule of the same moment, provides the further refinement of estimating the numbers of these female children who would survive to replace their mothers over a generation, assuming the continuation indefinitely of fixed fertility and mortality schedules.

The basic concept in these rates is that of the stable population, that is a population in which age and sex structures have become fixed with constant birth and death rates and therefore constant rates of increase or decrease. A. J. Lotka had stated the basic principles of the stable population in an article. 'Relation between Birth Rates and Death Rates', published in *Science* in 1907, but the most widely used interpretation of Lotka's stable theory as applied to human populations was his article with L. I. Dublin in the *Journal of the American Statistical Association* of September 1925, 'On the true Rate of Natural Increase as exemplified by the Population of the United States, 1920'. Stable theory applied to human populations appeared to bring demography close to acceptance as a respectable science. It was left to R. R. Kuczynski to popularize the concept in terms of gross and net reproductive rates and to give in effect a generation perspective over many countries of what would happen if current fertility and mortality levels continued to prevail.[3] For example, a net reproduction rate above or below unity provided an index of the extent by which each generation of child-bearing women would increase or decrease: a rate of 1·25 would mean that each thousand women would be replaced in the next generation by 1250; a rate of 0·75 would mean a decrease per generation of 250.

The index, which corrected for variations in age composition and mortality, was widely felt to cover the main variables that had inhibited comparisons among different countries at a given time or within a given country (or other area) over time. Marriage was not felt to be an important variable, and in any case the principles used in the calculation of the Life Table could also be applied to produce a nuptiality table by which estimates of nuptial fertility could be calculated.

The widespread use of the gross and net reproduction rates caused great concern in the 1930s, among governments as well as demographers, because they revealed that few western European countries were near replacement rate; only in southern and eastern Europe, and notably in the USSR, did continued growth appear to be the future prospect. The decline in the birth rate which had been causing considerable public concern for some years past amongst European peoples became the subject of a most painstaking inquiry by a Royal Commission of the Legislative Assembly of New South Wales in Australia in 1903-4.[4] This was the first inquiry of its kind in the English-speaking world. In England, a National (but unofficial) Birth Rate Commission also conducted an extensive investigation into the situation there and published its findings in two substantial volumes in 1916 and 1920.[5] At this stage the concern was rather with the relative slowness of growth compared with other parts of the world, than with decline. By the 1930s the fear had become centred on decline. This prospect seemed a reasonable deduction from the available evidence, particularly when examined in terms of reproduction rates. Among western European countries, only the Netherlands had a net reproduction rate above unity. The Belgian rate was as low as 0·67 (1941) and the Austrian (1935) had fallen to 0·64. England and Wales stood at only 0·81 in 1938, France at 0·98 (1940), Sweden 0·79 (1940) and Switzerland 0·90 (1941). Indeed only improvements in mortality had prevented natural increase being converted to decrease, as was in fact the case in France.

Table 6.1: Crude Birth and Death Rates and Reproduction Rates, Selected Countries (Annual average per 1,000 of Population)[6]

Region and Country	Birth Rate			Death Rate			Natural Increase			Reproduction Rates		
	1898 to 1902	1908 to 1912	1935 to 1939	1898 to 1902	1908 to 1912	1935 to 1939	1898 to 1902	1908 to 1912	1935 to 1939	Gross	Net	Year
N.W. & Central Europe												
England and Wales	28·8	25·2	15·0	17·4	14·2	12·0	11·4	11·0	3·0	0·90	0·81	1938
Scotland	29·7	26·6	17·7	18·0	15·6	13·2	11·7	11·0	4·5	1·07	0·91	1936
France	21·7	19·4	14·9	20·7	18·5	15·6	1·0	0·9	−0·7	—	0·90	1939
Germany	35·7	30·0	19·3	20·8	16·9	11·9	14·9	13·1	7·5	—	0·98	1940
Austria	31·4	26·5	14·8	22·7	19·8	13·9	8·7	6·7	0·9	—	0·64	1935
Netherlands	31·9	28·7	20·3	17·1	13·8	8·7	14·8	14·9	11·6	1·26	1·16	1941
Switzerland	28·7	25·1	15·4	18·1	15·4	11·6	10·6	9·7	3·8	1·00	0·90	1941
Sweden	27·9	26·8	14·5	16·2	14·1	11·7	10·6	10·6	2·8	0·89	0·79	1940
Denmark	29·7	27·5	17·9	16·0	13·4	10·6	13·7	14·1	7·2	1·09	0·96	1941
Belgium	28·8	23·6	15·3	18·0	15·8	13·0	10·8	7·8	2·3	0·80	0·67	1941
S. & E. Europe												
Italy	33·3	32·7	23·2	22·6	20·8	13·8	10·7	11·9	9·3	1·43	1·13	1935–7
Poland	43·7	38·2	25·4*	25·0	21·2	14·0*	18·7	17·0	11·4*	1·50	1·11	1934
Romania	39·2	41·5	30·2	26·4	25·6	19·6	19·6	15·9	10·6	2·16	1·40	1930–1
Yugoslavia	38·5	38·2	28·3	22·8	23·7	16·1	15·7	14·5	12·2	2·10	1·45	1930–2

											Year
USSR	48·8	45·6*	44·2*	31·8	28·9*	20·8*	17·0	16·7*	23·4*	—	1·70	1925–8 (RSFSR)
Beyond Europe												
USA (White)	—	—	17·1	—	—	11·0	—	—	6·1	1·09	1·00	1940 (white)
Canada	20·2	26·1*	20·2	12·1	12·5*	9·7	8·1	13·6*	10·4	1·42	1·27	1940–2
Australia	27·1	27·2	17·3	12·7	10·7	9·6	14·4	16·5	7·7	1·16	1·06	1942
New Zealand	25·7	26·7	18·8	10·0	9·4	9·0	15·7	17·3	9·8	1·30	1·21	1942
Union of S. Africa (White)	—	31·8	24·8	—	10·3	9·8	—	21·5	15·0	—	1·30	1938
Chile	38·4	39·5	34·2	32·2	31·7	24·7	6·2	7·8	9·5	2·26	1·30	1930–2
Argentina	36·3*	37·3*	24·3	18·4*	17·2*	12·1	17·9	20·1*	12·2	—	—	—
Asiatic and Pacific												
China	—	—	38·4*	—	—	—	—	—	—	—	—	—
India	37·4	38·3	34·7*	31·3	32·8	23·2*	6·1	5·5	11·5*	2·96	1·40	1930–1
Japan	32·1	33·8	29·7*	20·6	20·8	17·2*	11·5	13·0	12·5*	2·15	1·44	1937
Java and Madura	—	—	41·4*	—	—	—	—	—	—	—	—	—
Philippines	—	—	32·5*	—	—	—	—	—	—	—	—	—

* Poland 1935–38; Russia 1906–9, 1935–38; Canada 1911–13; Argentina 1899–1902, 1909–23; India 1935–38; Japan 1935–38; China 1931–35; Java and Madura 1931–35; Philippines 1936–40.

The causes of the decline in fertility have been quite copiously written about but still remain obscure.[7] Indeed a scientific evaluation is now impossible because dead persons cannot give their accounts of how they viewed and acted upon what Godwin termed 'the passion between the sexes' and no adequate contemporary records exist on the subject. The Commissioners of the official inquiry in New South Wales, Australia, in 1904 attributed the decline of the birth rate to:

1 an unwillingness of women to submit to the strain and worry of children;

2 a dislike of the interference with pleasure and comfort as a result of having children;

3 a desire to avoid the physical discomfort of gestation, parturition and lactation;

4 a love of luxury and of social pleasures which the Commission found to be increasing.

They found one element in common in all these, namely selfishness!

From a study of nineteenth-century society, there is fairly clear evidence that fertility decline was associated with increasing mobility of the middle and upper classes, increasing urbanization, lengthening of the period of dependency, increasing concern of parents for the maintenance and improvement of material living standards, and an increasingly rational approach to family limitation with the spread of contraception and universal literacy.[8] A. Dumont summarized most of these factors in his theory of social capillarity, which is still probably the most satisfactory general theory to explain the social and cultural reasons leading to controlled fertility.[9]

The spread of contraceptives is much too simple an explanation as a *cause* of the decline in fertility, although it must of course have encouraged the efficiency of rational attempts to control family size. The evidence of the Royal College of Obstetricians and Gynaecologists presented in 1948 to the UK Royal Commission on Population, which revealed the extent to which age-old methods of control were still practised in the twentieth century, or the control of fertility in France or Ireland long before modern improvements in contraceptives, emphasizes the point that the significance of moral restraint in the Malthusian sense and of such practices as *coitus interruptus* should not be underrated.[10]

Nevertheless the significance of the publicity emanating from early campaigners in the field of population control cannot be ignored. More detailed consideration of the birth-control movement will be given in Chapter 10. The movement may be said to have originated in England, with Francis Place's book, *Some Illustrations of the Principles of Population*, published in 1822, and with his subsequent handbills recommending the sponge as a contraceptive.

The trend of fertility suggests no immediate reaction to this early propaganda, but the same can probably *not* be said of the activities of the remarkable Annie Besant and Charles Bradlaugh when in 1877 they challenged a court decision by reprinting and selling some 200,000 copies of Dr Charles Knowlton's *Fruits of Philosophy*, an American book first published in England as long ago as 1834. N. E. Himes[11] estimated that there were also more than a million tracts on sale between 1876 and 1891 giving advice on contraception. The subject of pamphlets and itinerant pedlars was also a major subject of concern to the New South Wales Commissioners.

Yet while the publicity of the Besant-Bradlaugh trial no doubt gave impetus to the movement towards rational fertility control, other more fundamental forces were at work, and effective birth control had an application far too general to be to any substantial extent the result of the proceedings of an English court. The fundamental forces leading to birth control were summarized in the 1949 *Report* of the UK Royal Commission as follows:

The explanation lies we think in the profound changes that were taking place in the outlook and ways of living of the people during the nineteenth century. The main features of these changes are well known. They include the decay of small-scale family handicrafts and the rise of large-scale industry and factory organization; the loss of security and growth of competitive individualism; the relative decline in agriculture and rise in importance of industry and commerce, and the associated shift of population from rural to urban areas; the growing prestige of science, which disturbed traditional religious beliefs; the development of popular education; higher standards of living; the growth of humanitarianism, and the emancipation of women. All these and other changes are closely interrelated; they present a complex web rather than a chain of cause and effect; and it would be exceedingly difficult to trace how they acted and reacted on each other or to assess their relative importance[12]

The decline in fertility is generally represented in statistical series on *national* bases. The nature of available statistics frequently offers little alternative to this approach, but more meaningful time-series would be by social and economic class rather than by national units. Where evidence permits studies of differentials, the trend seems clearly to have begun in the upper and middle social classes, the higher educated sectors and the urban as against the rural areas (France and Ireland again substantially excepted). The pattern may be illustrated from two countries on opposite sides of the world. In Australia the pattern which had emerged by 1911 and 1921 is illustrated in Table 6.2.

Table 6.2: Occupational Category and Average Number of Children of Husbands, Australia – 1911, 1921[13]

Occupational Category	1911			1921		
	Age 40–44	Age 50–54	All Ages	Age 40–44	Age 50–54	All Ages
Agricultural	4·10	5·99	4·57	3·81	4·98	4·02
Pastoral	4·17	5·83	4·49	3·72	4·80	3·94
Mining & Quarrying	4·15	5·66	3·94	4·01	4·94	3·89
Industrial	3·94	5·40	3·81	3·39	4·37	3·27
Transport & Communication	3·88	4·48	3·61	3·55	4·39	3·19
Commercial	3·33	4·33	3·39	2·98	3·67	2·86
Public Administration & Professional	3·13	4·18	3·37	2·73	3·54	2·80

In Great Britain the pattern appears to have been similar. The UK Royal Commission *Report*, 1949, shows from 1911 census data that, among women who married between 1851 and 1861, the completed families were smallest among professional and higher administrative classes, and largest amongst miners and agricultural workers, and that between those women marrying in 1851–61 and those marrying in 1881–6, the decline in family size was 33 per cent amongst social class I compared with only 10 per cent in class VI and 15 per cent in class VII. From the Family Census conducted in Great Britain in 1946, the distinction between the completed families of manual and non-manual workers was still very marked amongst women marrying in the twentieth century.

Table 6.3 : Great Britain – Estimated Average Size of Completed Families[14]

	(1) Non-manual workers	(2) Manual workers	(3) (2)(1) %
Married 1900–9	2·79	3·94	141
„ 1915–19	2·05	2·91	142
„ 1925–9	1·73	2·49	144

Studies in the USA[15] and Canada[16] produced similar results, and in particular showed clearly the negative correlation between educational attainment and family size. This last pattern encouraged fears about the outbreeding of national intelligence, as well as slow extinction of the total population – a theory which might have considerable validity given perfect educational and social mobility according to intellectual capacity, but one which could have had only very limited application in the educational and class structure of Britain (or of most other countries) at that time.[17]

For the major European participants, the First World War was undoubtedly responsible for some of the decline in birth rates in the 1920s and for some of the failure to recover in the 1930s. In that war some 15 per cent of all men mobilized in Europe died in service; a loss of some 8 per cent of all male gainful workers. These losses, which were mostly of persons in the armed services, were heavily concentrated between ages 20 and 34, with consequent effects upon marriage rates and the reproductivity of marriages: post-war Europe carried substantial female surpluses as a result of war. Notestein has estimated that the First World War with approximately 10 million dead, cost Europe the equivalent of its natural increase from 1914 to 1919.[18] The births to the cohorts reduced by war losses were reaching marriageable age near the outbreak of the Second World War. Consequently birth rates in these countries would have remained low even though fertility of new marriages may have increased.

But clearly factors other than war effects were applying in the 1930s, as the evidence of non-belligerents (e.g. Scandinavia) and overseas countries indicates. The response to the economic recession of the 1930s was to some extent the classical postponement of marriage, but this was now accompanied by a postponement of births which attained much more effective proportions than ever before. As has been emphasized, the nature of these fertility trends

137

could not be fully understood from the measurements of gross and net reproduction rates made in the 1930s. It was not until fresh inquiries applying new methods of cohort analysis were begun after the war that it was realized that the very low birth rates of the 1930s were due in considerable measure to the postponement rather than the cancellation of births. Had the Second World War not occurred, a moderate rise in birth rates would almost certainly have appeared in the early 1940s, as births 'postponed' during the worst years of the depression were 'made up' and as 'postponed' marriages became effective.

In terms of total loss of life, the Second World War was even more severe than that of 1914–18, but whereas the losses in the first war were mainly confined to the armed forces, this was far from being the case in the second war. For Europe excluding the Soviet Union, the 10 million dead in the first war included only 500,000 civilians. By contrast, the Second World War cost Europe over 15 million dead of whom only 5,824,000 were estimated to be military, compared with 4,922,000 non-Jewish civilians and 4,372,000 Jews. To these must be added the heavy losses from all causes to the Soviet Union, variously estimated for the second war at between 13 and 17 million. Next to the Soviet Union, the heaviest losses were in Poland (4,300,000), Germany (4,200,000) and Yugoslavia (1,700,000).[19] Outside these areas of heavy losses, the second war had a much less severe effect on demographic structure than the first; and, the Soviet Union excepted, the demographic structures of the heavy losers were restored to some degree by the massive post-war population transfers, as discussed in the previous chapter. This was particularly the case in Germany. A comparison of age structures about 1950 for some of the countries which suffered the heaviest losses during the war is of considerable interest. The age selectivity of war casualties is apparent amongst the younger adult age groups, particularly in those aged 30–34; among the population aged 15–49 there is also a considerable deficit of males per 100 females; but, nevertheless, considering the devastation in these areas during the war, structures had revived to a remarkable degree by the early fifties. In the case of Poland and Yugoslavia their high pre-war fertility has provided a good underpinning to their population profile, and this also applies to a considerable degree in West Germany, especially for ages 10–14 years. (See Figure 6.1.)

Figure 6.1 : Profiles of Some Major Belligerents of the Second World War, about 1951–53

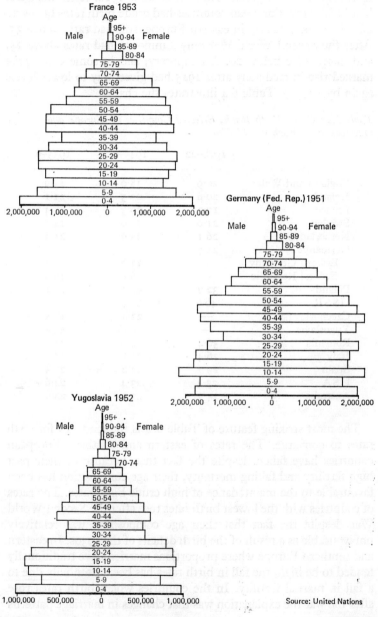

France 1953

Germany (Fed. Rep.) 1951

Yugoslavia 1952

Source: United Nations

At the end of the Second World War the demographic patterns in Europe differed greatly from those after 1918. After the First World War few European countries had crude birth rates below 20 and some, particularly in eastern Europe, still had rates above 35. After the Second World War only a minority had rates above 25, and many were below 20. A temporary, and in some cases *quite* marked rise immediately after 1945 had given way to lower levels again by 1955–9. Table 6.4 illustrates the change.

Table 6.4: Crude Birth Rates, Selected Countries of Europe and Europe Overseas, after Each World War

	1918–22	1945–9	1955–9
England and Wales	20·9	18·0	15·9
Ireland	20·6	22·5	21·1
France	17·3	20·3	18·4
Sweden	21·0	19·0	14·5
Netherlands	26·1	25·9	21·3
Germany:	21·7		
Eastern Germany	—	13·0	16·3
Federal Republic	—	16·9	16·9
Poland	32·7	28·4	27·1
USSR	40·9	25·8	25·3
Czechoslovakia	—	22·4	18·5
Yugoslavia	—	28·2	24·8
Romania	36·4	24·9	22·9
Italy	26·4	21·1	18·0
Spain	29·7	22·2	21·3
USA	23·4	23·4	24·6
Australia	24·7	23·1	22·6

The most striking feature of Table 6.4 is the tendency for birth rates to converge. The rates of eastern and southern European countries have fallen despite the fact that, because of their past high fertility and falling mortality, their age composition has been favourable to the maintenance of high crude birth rates. The rates of countries with the lowest birth rates rose after the Second World War despite the fact that their age composition was relatively unfavourable as a result of the birth deficits of the 1930s. In eastern and southern Europe where proportions married have traditionally tended to be high, the fall in birth rates has been essentially due to a fall in marital fertility. In the countries where birth rates rose after the war the explanation was that changes in marriage patterns and higher marital fertility had, temporarily at least, more than offset unfavourable changes in age composition. Compared with pre-war years, women in low-fertility countries of western and northern Europe after 1945 were marrying younger, fewer were remaining single, fewer couples remained childless and more couples had at least three children.

The very significant change since the Second World War in marriage patterns in western and northern Europe may be illustrated by considering the proportions ever-married in selected age groups, as recorded in censuses around 1920 and 1960. This revolutionary change in marriage patterns within Europe has been accompanied by similar and even more striking trends in 'Europe overseas'.

Table 6.5 : Proportions Ever-Married per 1,000 Males and Females in Age Group[20]

Males	Age 20–24 c. 1920	Age 20-24 c. 1960	Age 25–29 c. 1920	Age 25-29 c. 1960	Age 40–44 c. 1920	Age 40-44 c. 1960
England and Wales (1921,1961)	178	309	554	706	863	893
Denmark (1921, 1960)	122	228	507	676	885	897
Netherlands (1920, 1960)	115	166	446	631	843	923
Finland (1920, 1960)	106	250	383	631	744	889
Norway (1920, 1960)	115	211	446	593	843	855
Sweden (1935, 1960)	62	176	336	587	805	850
Females (Same censuses as listed above for Males)						
England and Wales	274	579	590	844	821	903
Denmark	277	541	609	854	722	919
Netherlands	235	406	529	816	769	899
Finland	232	460	490	759	754	864
Norway	235	503	529	821	769	888
Sweden	217	425	514	793	760	905

In the USA in 1962, for example, almost 71 per cent of women and 48 per cent of males aged 20–24 were or had been married. In Australia the corresponding figures in 1961 were 61 per cent and 27 per cent, compared with only 34 per cent and 15 per cent in 1921. A similar change took place in New Zealand.

No satisfactory sociological explanation of these changes has yet been attempted.[21] They are undoubtedly associated with high levels of employment and real incomes of the younger age groups, the increasing opportunities for the employment of young women, and increasing efficiency and sophistication in the use of contraceptives – all factors that would tend to encourage early marriage and the planning of families within desired economic goals. A further interesting aspect is that this post-war crop of young married persons have not used family planning to avoid, or even to defer pregnancies to any extent, but primarily to prevent higher-order births after an average of about three children.

In other words, the marriage revolution which has recently occurred in a great part of the western world is part of the institution of a highly rational, efficient reproductive system in which child-bearing is an episode within the first six to eight years of married life – a pattern which is already having a major sociological and economic impact upon the status and role of women in industrial societies.

By about 1955–60 the levels of fertility of married women in these 'European' societies had approached or exceeded those of their mothers of the 1920s. This is illustrated in the examples in Table 6.6 which gives the cumulative fertility after five and ten years per 100 women married between 1920–1 and 1924–5 on the one hand and 1949–50 on the other.

Table 6.6 : Births to Married Women after Specified Durations of Marriage in selected Countries

| | At Five Years' Duration Marriages of | | At Ten Years' Duration Marriages of | |
	1920–1 to 1924–5	1949–50	1920–1 to 1924–5	1949–50
Norway	151	141	206	202
Sweden	133	120	171	162
France	127	149	168	169
Australia	158	165	213	212
New Zealand	158	175	210	220

Two interesting features emerge from these figures: first, after five years, marriages of 1949–50 exceed the fertility of marriages of 1924–35; and second, during the second quinquennium of marriage, marriages of 1949–50 which showed a high fertility after five years (France, Australia, New Zealand) tended to add fewer births in the second five-year period than did the marriages of the

1920s. The whole pattern suggests rather a strengthening of rational planning than a trend towards much larger ultimate family size. Cohort analysis cannot lead to any firm conclusion about the ultimate fertility of recent marriages which still have most of their reproductive years ahead of them; but falling trends in crude birth rates and in age-specific fertility rates in many countries since about 1960 support the view that families of two and three children are the family sizes 'desired' by most of the modern generation of parents in affluent societies. The convergence since 1945 of birth rates in much of eastern and southern Europe towards western and northern patterns suggests further that the parents of these countries are also moving rapidly towards similar family goals. What at least seems clear in 1967 is that fertility is sufficiently above the levels of the 1930s to sustain reproduction above replacement level, although trends generally since the war, and the rapidity of the decline in age-specific fertility rates between 1961 and 1966 in such countries as the USA, Australia and New Zealand, show once again how quickly parents in a society of planned families can trim their reproductive patterns to the winds of social and economic change. In an affluent world of planned families survival cannot be *guaranteed*, even although a life expectation of 70 years (in which only about 8 per cent of women do not live from birth to menopause) is demographically speaking, almost as effective as immortality.

The whole trend of fertility among Europeans, whether within Europe or overseas, since the Second World War may again be examined in terms of differentials by income, occupation, social class and the degree of urbanization. Is the downward trend in relatively low income and more rural areas of eastern and southern Europe merely a continuation of the spread of family limitation from the 'upper' to the 'lower' social and economic classes? Further, is not the fact that fertility in the USSR is now similar to that of the USA the typical response to increasing urbanization, industrialization and universal literacy?

Recent studies have also shown that within separate Western countries the increase in fertility of marriage in post-war years may have been more the result of the pre-war low fertility groups (e.g., higher occupational classes and city dwellers, and non-Catholics compared with Catholics) having more children than a marked rise in the fertility of those with the highest pre-war birth rates. In

143

other words, post-war trends to higher birth rates may have been marked by some narrowing of the traditional patterns of differentials. In some cases the negative correlation between fertility and economic/social class seems to have been reversed. For example Judith Hubback,[22] formed the following pattern from the 1 per cent sample census of Great Britain in 1951.

	Duration of Marriage		
	5–6 years	10–14 years	15–24 years
Age at Marriage 24			
Graduates	1·9	2·6	2·8
All British Women	1·5	2·1	2·6
Age at Marriage 25–29			
Graduates	1·7	2·3	2·6
All British Women	1·3	1·7	1·7

In Sweden, too, in 1945 the average number of children per couple married during 1931–5 was smallest for the lowest income class and increased up to the middle and then dropped again.

While the *reversal* of the traditional differentials still appears to have been the exception rather than the rule, some *narrowing* of those differentials has been more generally apparent. A study of the recent trends and patterns in European countries concluded:[23]

1 That fertility differences between various population strata of the now industrialized countries have existed for at least a century and a half.

2 That the historical decline of the birth rate was characterized by a gradual development of an inverse association of fertility with socio-economic status and by a broadening of fertility differentials.

3 That during the long-term decline in the birth rate, the increased differentiation of groups by residence and occupational status *resulted largely from differences between them in the rate of fertility decline.*

4 That the contraction of group differentials during the recovery of the birth rate after the Second World War primarily reflected the higher rate of increase in fertility among groups of previously low fertility.

5 That where inverse relationship between fertility and status or class has traditionally applied, it generally still prevails, but has

been modified, and the smallest families are now found among the middle classes rather than those of highest status.

6 That, while little is known of the relation between family size and the level of educational attainment, such evidence as does exist suggests that the fertility of those with the highest education exceeds that of the general population. This pattern has existed for some time in England and Wales and in Sweden, and has recently become evident in the Netherlands.

The most extensive literature on differentials in fertility comes from the USA, and much of it has been admirably summarized by C. V. Kiser[24] who points out that the decade of the 1940s was a time of sharp contraction in differentials. Among the non-Negro population nativity differentials have almost completely disappeared; urban-rural differentials have contracted; differentials by occupation and income remain; and the most distinct differential remaining is between Catholic and non-Catholic.

Even so, the important fact remains that, although the average fertility of the whole of the Western World, in Europe and overseas, may now be considerably higher in the post-war world than it was in the 1930s, the general pattern is increasingly towards an average family of controlled size. Judged from USA and some European experiences, infertility is lower than it was before the war; but the fall in the number of large families of five and more children has persisted. Within Europe, this trend has been particularly marked since the 1940s in the predominantly Catholic areas of southern Europe.

In short, there is little in the patterns and trends in post-war Western fertility which implies any weakening of the rational control of fertility: quite the contrary. In the USA where intensive studies have been made of *desired* family size, the near universality of the desired family of from two to four children is the most striking conclusion: the rejection of the one-child family is matched by a rejection of the large family. The consensus of opinion throughout America on desired family size appeared to have converged by the decade of the 1950s towards a family of three children. To achieve such a goal the majority of the population irrespective of creed or class, must be practising some fairly effective form of birth control. For the majority the goal of desired family size has been approached by the use of contraceptive devices, although often in conjunction with 'natural' methods such as *coitus interruptus* and the use of the safe period. On the other hand, the relatively high proportion of women (13 per cent by age 30–39) who declared themselves in one survey to have been sterilized to prevent further conceptions suggests how far short even one of the most sophisticated populations was still (in the 1950s) from complete certainty in the matter of birth control.[25]

For purposes of international comparison at given points of time and of comparison in each country over time, the gross reproduction rate is a convenient index standardized for age to control the marked variations in age composition among the areas discussed in this chapter, variations caused by declines in fertility and by the ravages of wars. Table 6. 7 presents the female gross reproduction

Table 6.7 : Female Gross Reproduction Rates, Selected Countries of Europe and Europe Overseas[26]

	1935–9	1955–9	c. 1966
England and Wales	0·90	1·18	1·33 (1966)
Ireland	1·43	1·74	1·86 (1966)
France	1·02	1·32	1·35 (1966)
Sweden	0·87	1·10	1·15 (1966)
Netherlands	1·27	1·51	1·48 (1965)
Germany:			
East Germany	1·34	1·09	1·22 (1965)
Federal Republic	—	1·12	1·22 (1965)
Poland	2·16 (1925–9)	1·71 (1955–7)	1·22 (1965)
USSR	2·15	1·37 (1958–9)	1·37 (1960–1)
Czechoslovakia	0·97 (1936)	1·30	1·22 (1964)
Romania	1·81	1·34	0·94 (1964)
Italy	1·46	1·14	1·30 (1964)
Spain	1·35	1·27	1·35 (1960)
USA	1·00	1·77	1·33 (1966)
Australia	1·06	1·65	1·40 (1966)

rates of the countries listed in Table 6. 4, in the pre-war years, in 1955–9 and at the latest available year. For western and northern Europe and 'Europe overseas' these three points of time mark approximately the period of lowest fertility, the peak of post-war fertility and the pattern which appears to have emerged after the disturbances (e.g., in marriage trends and in age composition) following the Second World War.

In terms of the gross reproduction rate there seems little danger of population decline among European peoples, although the low

146

birth rates of some countries (e.g., England and Wales, and Sweden) are again bringing reproduction very close to replacement level. The crucial factor determining the margin above replacement level is likely to be marriage trends. As was previously emphasized, the revolutionary change that has occurred during the last twenty years in the proportions of women married has been a major element in sustaining birth rates, especially at a time when those attaining reproductive age were the cohorts depleted by economic depression and war. One factor in the recent declining trend in fertility in many western European and European overseas countries is the tendency for the proportions married to stabilize (as they were bound to do, sooner or later) instead of constantly rising. Indeed in some of the 'most married' countries there seems to be a downward trend in the proportions married. In USA, for example, the proportion of young women who were married between ages 20 and 24 years fell from 69·6 per cent in 1960 to 66·7 per cent in 1964. Similar trends in other countries could have a significant effect on birth and reproduction rates of the future in countries where the average 'desired family size' appears to cluster closely around the two to three children mark and where the knowledge and means of attaining this goal are widely available.

Another factor which has become increasingly important as a determinant of short-term fluctuations in the birth rates of the areas discussed in this chapter is the increasing dependence upon the numbers and fertility performance of women within a relatively small part of the reproductive span. In the countries with relatively low fertility, almost two-thirds of the births each year occur to women between ages 20 and 30. Relatively minor changes in their sociological behaviour and demographic composition (e.g., as a proportion of the rest of the population) will quickly affect the levels of births and birth rates. The significance of these young women in the reproductive schedule is apparent in the figures in Table 6.8. By comparing the reproductive schedules of Australia in 1966, 1961, and 1921, Figure 6.1 reveals the extent of the change that has occurred in forty-five years. Note that the 1921 fertility curve produced the higher birth rate (24·9 compared with 22·9 in 1961) but that the 1961 curve produced the highest gross reproduction rate (1·724 compared with 1·511 in 1921). The Australian illustration is typical of most of the countries of western and northern Europe and particularly of the USA and New Zealand.

Table 6.8 : Births per 1,000 Women by Age – USA, New Zealand (non-Maori), Australia

Age Group	USA			New Zealand			Australia		
	1954	*1961*	*1963*	*1954*	*1961*	*1964*	*1954*	*1961*	*1966*
15–19	91	88	77	33	47	51	39	47	49
20–24	236	254	231	221	258	232	198	225	173
25–29	188	198	185	234	271	227	194	220	184
30–34	117	113	106	150	157	132	122	131	105
35–39	58	56	51	77	77	66	64	63	51
40–44	16	16	14	23	23	20	20	19	14

Turning now to total growth rates, a review of the contemporary situation in Europe and the Soviet Union and in 'Europe overseas' reveals considerable differences. Around 1960 the lowest rates, averaging 0·6 per cent, were found in the countries of the European

Figure 6.2 : Australian Age-specific Fertility Rates, 1921, 1961, 1966

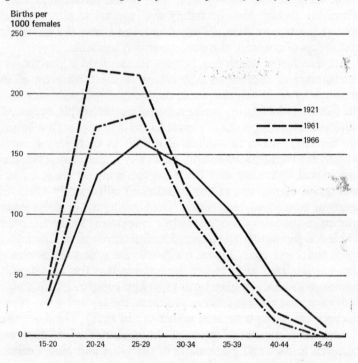

Free Trade Association (Denmark, Norway, Sweden, Austria, Switzerland, Portugal and the United Kingdom). Among these only Switzerland added substantially to natural increase through immigration. The Common Market Group (Western Germany, Italy, France, Netherlands, Belgium, Luxembourg) averaged a growth rate of 0·9 per cent, the higher rate compared with the EFTA countries being due to the substantial immigration into Germany and France and the relatively high fertility of the Netherlands. The Soviet Union and its satellite countries of Europe still displayed a high growth rate of 1·5 per cent, but fertility appeared to be declining in most of this region. Among people of European origin overseas the highest percentage rates came from the USA (1·8), Canada (2·7), New Zealand (2·1) and Australia (2·2). Their natural increase was higher than that of most countries in the first three groups and in addition they were still important immigrant countries (See Chapter 5).

The differences remaining in the *natural* increase of these areas are, however, less significant than their basic similarities. By 1960, the countries within them had all established a demographic system unique in human history. Reproductive waste had given way to reproductive efficiency. Historically speaking, death had lost its sting and further improvements in mortality can have only a marginal effect on growth rates, since only a small proportion of female infants now fail to live to the end of the reproductive period. A life expectation of 70 years, which was approximately the average of all these countries around 1960 (with the virtual certainty that those still below this level will soon attain it) implies a loss of only about 5 per cent of female births by age 40. Hence, the growth potential of such populations, should women approach their maximum fecundity, is enormous. Rates exceeding 4 per cent a year would be possible; but with few very minor exceptions, such as the Hutterites, this potential has never been realized, because fertility control has been quite firmly exercised in western and northern Europe and Europe overseas by both Malthusian constraints (deferred marriage and, for 10 to 15 per cent of women, non-marriage) and by neo-Malthusian practices (contraception); and in eastern and southern Europe and the Soviet Union by birth control rather than by marriage control.

The process of control is nowhere yet perfect – many unwanted pregnancies occur; but the basic fact remains that by one method

149

or another, mean family size has been reduced to cluster around the two and three children mark – a size which in terms of *living* children is not so very much less than formerly, but which is achieved without massive reproductive loss through infant and child deaths. 'Baby booms' in many countries after 1945 did not break this system of controlled fertility, and the declines after 1945 in fertility in southern and eastern Europe, and since 1960 in many western, northern and overseas countries, both emphasize the extent to which the marginal child is rationally determined by parents' interpretation of their immediate environment and not by physiological capacity.

This emphasis upon similarity should not be taken to mean that there is a single causal explanation of the demographic processes that have led to it, such as density of population, degree of industrialization, urbanization and so on; but it is probably fairly safe to conclude that mortality decline was an underlying cause in all areas, particularly as it tended to occur when the costs of rearing children were rising through the institution of such laws as compulsory education and a minimum age of employment. Yet even this broad generalization is difficult to sustain. As emphasized in earlier chapters the decline in fertility occurred first in France and Ireland in the 1830s and 1840s, where mortality remained fairly high and industrialization relatively backward. These exceptions pose difficult problems of explanation, although short-age of land for the indigenous population in Ireland and the Napoleonic Code which encouraged the fragmentation of land in France, together with the lack of alternative employment opportun-ities because of tardy industrial development, may have been significant factors. The exceptions apart, however, the move to-wards lower fertility over many countries during the last quarter of the nineteenth and into the early twentieth century did coincide with major industrial and social changes. Between about 1880 and 1910 there was a marked reduction in fertility in most of western and northern Europe, in the USA and Canada in North America, and in Australia and New Zealand in Oceania. The trend appeared in the 1920s in Italy, Spain and Portugal, in the 1930s in Poland, Bulgaria and Romania, in the 1940s in the Soviet Union and in the 1950s in Japan and Yugoslavia. There is no common bundle of socio-economic factors associated with the onset of fertility decline in all these countries, but in most of them some part was played by declining mortality, increasing costs of rearing children with the establishment of universal primary education, emancipation of women, weakening of religious constraints, the strengthening of secular and rational attitudes in social behaviour, and a reduction of the proportion of the population in rural employment. As has been emphasized, the last factor did not always apply, as evidenced by the cases of France and Ireland; in many southern European countries fertility decline also began when mortality was still very high, as in Spain and Bulgaria. It is significant, as Coale has observed, that every nation in the world today in which no more than 45 per cent of the labour force is engaged in extractive industry, in which at least 90 per cent of the children of primary school age attend school, and in which at least 50 per cent of the population lives in urban areas, has experienced a major decline in fertility.[27] Fertility decline has at times preceded the onset of these conditions but apparently has never failed to be present once they have occurred.

Figure 6.3: Birth Rate Trends, Selected Catholic and Non-Catholic Countries of Europe

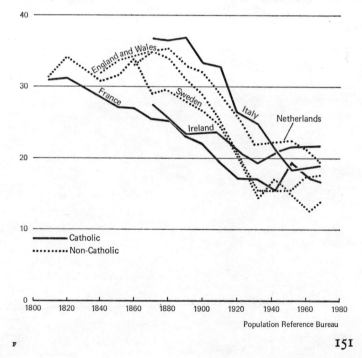

Population Reference Bureau

In absolute terms the number of people in the regions covered in this chapter who have achieved this unique demographic balance of very low mortality and controlled fertility is impressive – about 680 million in Europe, including the USSR; 220 million in north America; and 14 million in Oceania; some 914 million in all, or 28 per cent of the world's people. If these people decided to maximize their fertility they could, at present levels of mortality, create a population explosion which would considerably exceed the highest rates found in the developing world. Growth rates of 4 per cent would be possible, but there seems no likelihood of this occurring, and even if it did the pace could not be held for long. Europe already contains the world's most densely populated countries, and Americans already look with some trepidation towards a likely US population of over 350 million by the end of the century. The evidence is fairly plain that for several decades at least the growth rates of the 'developing' areas will outstrip those of the regions discussed in this chapter; but even if the latter fall to a quarter of the world's population, their affluence is likely to remain sufficient to ensure that they will use some three-quarters of the world's available resources.

Chapter 7

Population Growth in the Developing World: The Asian Giants

Generalizations made today about the problem of population growth in relation to available food resources and production, or about the fear of world overpopulation usually, and for the most part rightly, pick as the danger spots the high growth rates of Asian countries, and particularly of the land masses of India–Pakistan and Communist China; but, as emphasized in Chapter 3, these great areas of the world, which now contain some 40 per cent of mankind, have not suddenly exploded into rapid growth after centuries of stagnation. The European world began to outstrip their rates of growth in the eighteenth and nineteenth centuries, but for long periods in earlier times the Indian and Chinese sub-continents were probably holding their own, and indeed, in the case of China in the seventeenth and eighteenth centuries, may have been growing at a faster pace than the European peoples (Chapter 3).

In other words, relatively speaking, throughout much of history Asia has not been underfed and undernourished compared with the rest of the world, and at times parts of Asia probably held the advantage. Nor has the food position of the Asian countries suddenly become worse in the twentieth century compared with earlier times. In some cases there have been real improvements. The important point is that by the standards of all previous eras, European societies have created *mass* levels of nutrition that are unique, so that in relative terms the situation in the developing world appears to have deteriorated, and when famine strikes, as it did in the northern provinces of India in 1966–7 primarily as the result of the failure of monsoon rains, the conclusion is easily drawn that the cause is simply overpopulation.

Famines caused by natural tragedies such as drought, floods and wars are not new to Asia; but their occurrence in the demographic situation of the twentieth century has rightly been increasingly

153

feared because population growth rates are now two and even three times the levels of the nineteenth and earlier centuries. In almost all the developing countries there have been marked improvements in agricultural productivity as well as extensions of the area of land under production (otherwise mass starvation would have gripped many of these areas long ago), but the rate of population growth has continued to rise commensurately and sooner or later this nexus must be broken. The problems of economic and social organization which are unique in the developing countries today, compared with the past, are not created by any deterioration in agricultural, industrial, social or political efficiency, but by their expanding rates of population growth; and the unique element in their demographic situation is not the levels of their birth rates but the decline in their death rates.

The use of the word 'developing' in the title of this chapter may seem imprecise. In one sense the most 'developing' societies today are those of the high-income countries generally classed as 'developed' which have achieved expectations of life from birth around or above 70 years and whose population growth rates are controlled by efficient family planning. These countries are 'developing' in the sense that their *per capita* incomes are still leaping ahead of their rates of population growth; but if 'developing' is restricted to countries with annual *per capita* incomes below $200, compared with about $480 for the world as a whole, or $1800 for North America, the territories covered will be those in which fertility control has scarcely begun or not even started. In terms of continents these major areas and their estimated populations around 1960 are:

The ECAFE region	1,659 million
Latin America	212 million
Africa	273 million
Total	2,144 million

This covers about two-thirds of the world's population, and clearly the dominating area is Asia, and within Asia, the great political units of mainland China, India, Pakistan and Indonesia.

While emphasizing the uncertain nature of the Chinese population counts – which were not censuses in the real sense but enumerations usually made for fiscal or military purposes – the historical picture up to the seventeenth century which seems to find general acceptance, particularly from the scholarly reappraisals made by Durand[1] and Ping-ti Ho,[2] are summarized with relation to China proper (i.e. excluding Manchuria, Mongolia and other outlying areas) in Table 7.1.

Table 7.1 : Estimates of China's Population to 1620

Dynasty	Approximate Period	Approximate Population (in millions)
West Han	AD 2	71
East Han	156	62
Sung	1014	60
Sung Ch'in	1193–95	123
Ming	1381	60–80
Ch'ing	1620	130–150

One must remember (see Chapter 3), that these figures are highly conjectural and are as much deductions based upon evidence of the political state of China as evidence from statistics: during long periods of peace and prosperity associated with stable dynasties population was assumed to increase; during revolutionary turmoil often associated with the end of a dynasty or invasion from outside population was assumed to decrease. Thus the downfall of the Han dynasty in AD 156 is felt to have been associated with a period of decline; the peace and prosperity of the Sung dynasty (1006–1223) may have led to population increase; the invasion of China by Kublai Khan and the Monguls in 1280 was accompanied by slaughter and turmoil which probably reduced population, perhaps from about 120 to 80 million; the great period of the Ming dynasty, 1381–1626, was probably accompanied by steady population increase again.

It is probably safer to argue that growth rates were accelerated during long periods of peace, which were accompanied by expansion of settlement and improvements in food supplies, as Ping-ti Ho does in relation to the Sung and Ming dynasties, than it is to conclude that population declined drastically during revolutionary and turbulent times. Simulation of assumed trend effects on population models shows how difficult it is to achieve sudden and drastic population decline in response to major catastrophes, especially where these occur within a large political area or land mass, such as China. The invasion of China was almost certainly accompanied by heavy slaughter, but this probably affected the northern provinces most severely and may not have seriously affected the trends in the rest of China. An increase of China's population from about 120 million at the end of the twelfth century to 150 million around the middle of the seventeenth century may be more likely than a decline to 60 or even 80 million during the Mongul occupation around the end of the thirteenth century.

As indicated in Chapter 3, the organizational framework of *Chia*, *Li* and *Hsien* during the Ming dynasty for the collection of statistics seemed admirable, but in practice the system never seemed to operate efficiently, and most scholars have concluded that the relatively stable number of households enumerated between 1381 and 1620, ranging between 9,128 million (estimated 50,565 million persons) and 10,621 million (estimated 60,693 million persons), was rather a mark of increasing inefficiency of the system than comparative stability of population.

The initial Ming count of 1381 was made shortly after the time of the Black Death, and bubonic plague swept China as well as Europe. Yet there were many other reasons for the apparent lack of population increase and the small initial counts of the Ming dynasty compared with the late twelfth century. These have been summarized by Ping-ti Ho[3] as:

1 The emphasis of the population counts was fiscal and as such was probably careless in its enumeration of women and children.

2 Registration for fiscal purposes was evaded by people under the protection of powerful rural interests, particularly in the lower Yangtze and south-eastern coastal provinces.

3 Official corruption was rife: evidence suggests that sometimes only a tenth of the taxes due were entered in the tax registers.

4 Several clans often merged into one to lighten the fiscal burden.

5 People often illegally forsook or changed their allocated status to reduce the dues and services for which they were liable, and frequently they avoided registration completely. Further, by rendering services to military garrisons commoners could escape tax as well as the *li-chia* population registration.

Durand also adduces evidence of corruption, clerical incompetence and arithmetical inability amongst those whose job it was to enter the population figures in the registers. According to an edict of 1370, penalties for evasion or corruption associated with the censuses were terrifyingly severe. Soldiers were to go to every household to check the returns. If in their search the military came across minor officials who had suppressed the facts, those officials were to be decapitated, while common people suppressing the facts were to be punished 'according to law' and to be 'drafted into the army'. But despite all this, corruption and evasion appeared to have continued. Ping-ti Ho[4] quotes the report of an early Chi'ing official that in some of the 1642 Yellow Registers the population returns had been compiled in advance for the year 1651!

From such evidence both Durand and Ping-ti Ho conclude that Ming population data are relatively useless, and increasingly so as the dynasty moved to a close. Ping-ti Ho elaborates upon other evidence – the writings of contemporary and local historians, the long centuries of peace, and relative prosperity – and concludes that population *should* have increased linearly over the fifteenth and sixteenth centuries. He also shows that the aggregate of the five northern provinces increased from 15·5 million in 1393 to about 26·7 million in 1542 – a gain of 72 per cent in 150 years, or an average growth rate of 0·34 per cent, a rate which would have doubled China's population between 1381 and 1600. He acknowledged that the northern provinces were not necessarily representative of all China, but emphasized that the south had ample land resources and that most of the writers testifying to continued increase were southerners.

On the basis of such evidence, Ping-ti Ho 'guesses that China's population had increased from some 65 million in the late fourteenth century to the neighbourhood of 150 million by 1600'. Even if the south had been increasing 'at the same moderate rate revealed in official figures for the northern population, it may be hazarded that China's population had exceeded 130 million by the turn of the sixteenth century'.

By the second quarter of the seventeenth century, events were again moving against population increase, with peasant wars and rebellions as destructive as Europe's Thirty Years War which were not brought under control until 1683; but from this point, under the Ching (Manchu) dynasty a new phase of population growth seems to have started. Evidence for this comes from analysis of recorded statistics of *ting*, and after 1740 of the *pao-chia* system of annual population enumeration.

Precisely what is represented by the statistics of *ting* is open to conjecture. Some demographers and historians have assumed them to represent taxpayers defined as males aged 16–60 and have estimated total population by making estimates of females and 'dependent' age groups. Others have assumed that the statistics again refer to households and have used a multiplier. Assuming the registration of *ting* to be consistent over time, the increases suggest substantial population growth. Durand gives the following *ting*:

1651	10·6 million
1680	17·1 million
1710	23·3 million
1734	27·4 million

Assuming the *ting* bore a constant ratio to population, Durand concludes that the above figures imply a rate of growth of population rising from 0·37 per cent in 1657–71 to 0·90 per cent in 1708–34. That the high rate of increase of the latter period did obtain is at least partially confirmed by the *pao-chia* system introduced in 1741. This scheme was based on the following system:

10 households	=	1 *pai*
10 *pai*	=	1 *chia*
10 *chia*	=	1 *pao*

Originally each household was required to keep a tablet hanging by the door with a list of members. These were later replaced by lists kept in *pai* and *chia* offices. Like the earlier system of the Ming dynasty the *pao-chia* appeared on the face of it to be an admirable scheme of registration; but again its weakness lay in the inefficiency and inexperience of the minor officials administering it. I. Taeuber and Wang Nai-chi[5] have argued that once a provincial population was established it was carried forward by constant arbitrary increments, until a request from higher-up for a report or revision would often lead to a substantial rise in the base. There was also further evidence of undercounting in some areas. Yet these figures present probably the most reliable series in China's long history and that their record of growth is summarized in Table 7. 2.

Table 7.2 : Estimated Population of China 1741–1851

	Population (in millions)	Implied Percentage Rate of Natural Increase
1741	143	1741–61: 1·6%
1761	198	1761–81: 1·7%
1781	280	1781–1801: 0·3%
1801	298	1801–21: 0·9%
1821	356	1821–41: 0·7%
1841	413	1841–51: 0·2%
1851	431	

The *pao-chia* reflect a rapid increase in recorded population in 1775 after the Emperor complained about alleged inaccuracies in statistics. Durand is inclined to accept the view that the recorded figures following 1741 were too low, rather than that those after 1775 were over-inflated. Assuming that the ratio of 1774 to 1775 may be the ratio of underestimation he produces a figure of 212 million in 1749, or 35 million above registered numbers. This would then give an average natural increase of 0·9 per cent in 1749–75, which may not be unreasonable in the light of other factors encouraging growth at this time.

As evidence of rapid growth over the period 1725–1851, Ping-ti Ho refers to: the steady rise in the price of rice to 1750 despite bumper harvests; the filling up of the important rice-producing lowlands and low hills in the early eighteenth century; the exhortation by central and provincial officials to experiment with new crops, especially the sweet potato; the systematic migration in the eighteenth century to dry hills and mountains and the introduction of maize and sweet potato crops to these parts; the invasion of the inland Yangtze highlands and Han River drainage by millions of farmers; the exploitation of mountain regions by the end of the eighteenth century to the extent of diminishing returns in agriculture and soil erosion; increases in prices of a wide range of commodities (silk and cotton fabrics, vegetables, fruits and meats); growth and luxurious living in great cities.

The whole of this story has a rather familiar 'Western' ring, except that city growth and rising standards of living in China were not associated with great scientific and industrial revolutions. Nevertheless, the parallel is also close in other respects, because the upsurge of population produced theories of the relation between growth and resources very similar to those of Malthus. Generally the attitude to population growth in China had been thoroughly expansionist or mercantilist: more people meant more taxpayers, more soldiers, more labour and the opportunity to increase the areas under cultivation. But by the mid-eighteenth century some were questioning this theory, and one such who, like Malthus, had his predecessors, was *Hung Liang-Chi* (1744–1809).[6]

In two essays, 'Reign of Peace' and 'Livelihood' written in 1793 while serving as Educational Commissioner of Kweichow, Hung expounded the following theories relating to population:

1 The increase in the means of subsistence and the increase of population are not in direct proportion. The population within a hundred years or so can increase from five-fold to twenty-fold, while the means of subsistence, due to the limitation of the land-area, can increase only from three to five times.

2 Natural checks like flood, famine and epidemic, cannot diminish the surplus population.

3 There are more people depending on others for their living than are engaged in productive occupations.

4 The larger the population, the smaller will be the income *pro rata*; but expenditure and the power of consumption will be greater. This is because there will be more people than goods.

5 The larger the population, the cheaper labour will be, but the higher will be the prices of goods. This is because of the over-supply of labour and over-demand for goods.

6 The larger the population, the harder it will be for the people to secure a livelihood. As expenditure and power of consumption become greater than the total wealth of the community, the number of unemployed will be increased.

7 There is unequal distribution of wealth among the people.

8 Those who are without wealth and employment will be the first to suffer and die from hunger and cold, and from natural calamities like famine, flood and epidemics.

As to the possible remedies for overpopulation and their effectiveness, Hung says:

Some may ask: 'Do Heaven and Earth have remedies?' The answer is that their remedies are in the form of flood, drought, sicknesses and epidemics. But those unfortunate people who die from natural calamities do not amount to more than 10 or 20 per cent of the population. Some may ask: 'Does the government have remedies?' The answer is that its methods are to exhort the people to develop new land, to practise more intensive farming, to transfer people from congested areas to virgin soils, to reduce the fiscal burden, to prohibit extravagant living and the consumption of luxuries, to check the growth of landlordism, and to open all public granaries for relief when natural calamities strike. . . . In short, during a long reign of peace Heaven and Earth could not but propagate the human race, yet their resources that can be used to the support of mankind are limited. During a long reign of peace the government could not prevent the people from multiplying themselves, yet its remedies are few.

Hung failed to elucidate, as Malthus did, a law of diminishing returns, or to study population data for empirical support of his theories; but clearly he did grasp some of the basic economic consequences of population growth. His ideas were carried further by Wang Shi-to (1802–89) whose diary, written in 1855–6 while he was a Taiping captive, foresees the overpopulation of China forcing people to plant cereals on mountain tops and to reclaim sandbanks and islets, and to destroy the forests. 'Yet there is still not enough for everybody. This proves that the resources of Heaven and Earth are exhausted.'[7] To Wang, the ills of the mid-nineteenth century were not due to misgovernment, or to the people's lack of ingenuity and diligence, but to the increasing disproportion between population and economic resources. To remedy the situation he wanted to relax the prohibition against female infanticide and to encourage the practice *en masse*, to establish more nunneries and to forbid widow remarriage, to propagate the use of sterilizing drugs, to raise marriage age, to graduate tax *against* the family with more than two children, and to drown all but the fittest infants!

Ping-ti Ho goes a long way towards accepting the view that the breakdown of the Manchu dynasty was in fact caused basically by increasing overpopulation, against which the Manchus had no answer. He considers the Taiping wars that rent China after 1851 may have cost China 20 to 30 million lives. The catastrophe almost certainly checked the population growth in the lower Yangtze area, but the growth of the low plain provinces of north China continued, and population by the end of the nineteenth century may well have been equal to or in excess of the 1851 estimate of 431 million. However the continued absence of any major technological evolution offered no long-term relief to the population-land ratio. The Opium War and contact with the west did nothing in China, as it did in Japan, to change the whole basis of economic organization.

A new census planned in 1909 was interrupted by the abdication of the Emperor in 1911. The Republican government then attempted a new census in 1912 and further enumerations were made in 1928-9. These were based substantially on the *pao-chia* system, but Durand considers them to have been inaccurate, particularly in regard to the counts of females.

Further enumerations were carried out in the provinces in the 1930s and 1940s, but in no case were they complete censuses. Estimates based on the enumerations of 1911-12 and of 1928-9 put the Chinese population at 411 million (Willcox) in the former period and between 445 million and 475 million in the latter period. These may be compared with the official results of the last census in 1953, which was 583 million. Taking this and the 1851 figure of 417 million as accurate, the implied rate of increase over the century is only 0·2 per cent.

Taeuber and others have doubted the accuracy of the 1953 census on the grounds of incomplete coverage, inadequate time for processing the data, the method of enumeration (with householders calling at census offices to record data), and the long spread of about a year over which the data were collected. If the 1953 census is an undercount, the growth rate may have been rising again in the preceding years. Other data now available imply a growth rate after 1953 that may have been as high as 2 per cent a year, made up of a birth rate of 37 and a death rate of 17 per 1,000. Chandrasekar[8] quotes birth rates in Shanghai and Peking around 40 and death rates under 10, or growth rates over 3 per cent. Just how accurate these statistics are, or how typical they are of wider areas, is still a matter of conjecture; but even allowing for wide margins of error they do suggest that China's population was moving forward around 1953 to another major growth phase. One estimate[9] suggests the population in 1953 was probably nearer 608 million than 583 million, and considers that with growth rates rising slowly from 2·3 to 2·5, the population may have reached over 700 million in 1959. This is the figure postulated by the Foreign Manpower Research Office of the US Census Bureau.[10]

In the absence of precise data, these figures must be treated cautiously, but given an economic situation where the supplies of food and other essentials of life are sustained above famine levels, the growth potential of the population is clearly very high. This potential is again clear from the estimated age distribution in 1953 which placed over 35 per cent of the population under the age of 15 and 90·9 million aged 0–4, compared with 63·8 million aged 5–9 and 54·5 million aged 10–14, compared with only 44·4 million aged 25–9 and 29·1 million aged 45–9.

Barring a major catastrophe, far more severe than that associated with the failure of 'the great leap forward' following 1957, or than that which appears to be occurring at the political level in 1967, the Chinese population seems set for a long period of growth. If the estimates of Aird, Chandrasekar and others are to be accepted, China's growth rate in the 1950s was probably over 2 per cent a year, a rate which if maintained from an estimated base of 700 million in 1960 would produce a population exceeding 1,400 million by the end of the century. If the growth rate around 1960 is assumed to have been around 2·5 per cent, which Aird considers possible, and if this rate is reduced by half during the 1960s, which is perhaps the maximum reduction that could be expected, the population of China would still reach 1,000 million by 1985 and 1,200 million by the end of the century, or about the same number of people as have been estimated for the whole world around 1850.

Admittedly the 'evidence' concerning present trends of China's population is substantially conjectural, but the patterns indicated above are in no way unusual for areas in which *per capita* incomes are very low, the majority of the population live as peasants, illiteracy levels are comparatively high and food production has just been keeping pace with population growth. The growth pattern which has been suggested for China around 1960 is in fact similar for that of India for which recent demographic data, although far from perfect, are much more adequate.

In British India a uniform system for registering births and deaths was begun as early as 1864, and about 1875 the system was supposed to cover the whole area under British control. However it is now clear that the system was far from complete. Fortunately, however, the initiation of a vital registration system was accompanied by systematic censuses. The first attempt to count the whole population of India was made almost a hundred years ago, between 1867 and 1872. A second census followed in 1881, since when regular decennial censuses occurred. The history of the Indian sub-continent as revealed by these vital data and censuses has been adequately described by Davis and need only be briefly summarized here.

Davis[11] gives the figure of 255 millions in 1871 as 'the 1871–2 census figure corrected for territory omitted and for defective methods', and thereafter the figures as shown in Table 7. 3.

Table 7.3 : Estimated Population of Pre-Partition India 1871–1941

Year	Census Population (in thousands)	Estimated Population (in thousands)	Estimated Increase per cent during decade previous
1871	203,415	255,166	—
1881	250,160	257,380	0·9
1891	279,593	282,134	9·4
1901	283,870	285,288	1·0
1911	303,041	302,985	6·1
1921	305,730	305,679	0·9
1931	338,171	338,171	10·6
1941	388,998	388,998	15·0

The striking feature of this Indian growth is its clearly cyclical character up to 1931 – periods of relatively rapid growth followed by near stability. The fluctuations almost certainly had little to do with changes in fertility, which appears to have remained high throughout the period. Davis estimates birth rates between about 45 and 49 over the whole period. These are estimated from censuses and are much above the rates calculated from registration data, and if correct they imply periodic periods of devastating mortality. Two great famines occurred in 1876–8 and 1898–1900, which may provide much of the explanation of the limited population growth in the decades 1871–81 and 1891–1901. The third such decade, 1911–21, included the disastrous influenza epidemic of 1918 which is estimated to have killed some 15 million people.

Throughout the whole period, however, mortality was appallingly high. Official life tables for the period 1871–1911 show expectations of life at birth varying between 22·9 and 25·0 years, and

Davis estimates an expectation between 1911 and 1920 of only 20·1 years. By comparison, therefore, the expectation of 1931–41 of 31·8 years, which is often quoted today as evidence of the plight of India at approximately the time of partition, is a pronounced advance on earlier times. The influenza epidemic appears to have been the last great check on the expansion of population growth in the Indian sub-continent. The Bengal famines of the Second World War, the upheavals associated with partition, and the famines of the northern provinces of India in 1966–7 have all been minor episodes compared with the great checks of 1876–8, 1898–1900 and 1918–19. At the time of partition, India and Pakistan appear to have been launched firmly on the road of expanding growth rates. Before passing to this post-partition era, the figures of India for 1881–1941 as estimated by Davis[12] and presented in Table 7. 4 should be carefully studied.

Table 7.4: Birth, Death and Natural Increase Rates per 1,000 of Population, British India 1881–1941

| | Registered | | | Estimated | | |
	Birth Rates	Death Rates	Natural Increase	Birth Rates	Death Rates	Natural Increase
1881–91	—	—	—	49	41	8
1891–1901	34	—	—	46	44	2
1901–11	37	—	—	48	43	5
1911–21	37	34	3	49	48	1
1921–31	33	25	8	46	36	10
1931–41	34	23	11	45	31	14

These figures show the oscillating movements in India's population with advance and check alternating in Malthusian fashion. The pattern was probably similar to that of many European populations before the eighteenth century. After 1921, however, something new is suggested, with natural growth rates in 1931–41 as high as almost anything achieved by the European countries. Since then the trend to expanding growth rates as a result of further improvements in mortality has continued after the manner of the European populations of the nineteenth century.

The analogy with European countries must not however be too closely drawn. As emphasized earlier, late marriage and considerable proportions remaining unmarried were features of Western society which helped to check population growth rates. The relatively low birth rates of most European countries during their periods of maximum growth, compared with those of Table 7. 4, were due to marriage control rather than to birth control. The fertility of married women was in most cases very high. In pre-partition India, and indeed in India and Pakistan separately today, marriage is almost universal and is consummated at an early age – estimated by one demographer to be around an average age of 17 for Indian women.[13] At the 1961 census of India, only 6 per cent of women aged 20–24 had never married, and only 1·9 per cent were unmarried at age 25–9. The mean age of women at marriage was 15·8 years.

Death rates of post-partition India have declined steadily to bring about a consistent expansion of growth rates and a rise in the expectation of life at birth from about 32 years in 1931–41 to about 46 years in 1961. Fertility has, however, remained high, although its exact level is difficult to assess. Registration of vital events is still very deficient so that estimates have to be made from census data and sample surveys, which have provided the crude birth rates indicated in Table 7. 5.

Table 7.5 : Estimated Birth, Death and Growth Rates per 1,000 of Population, India 1941–64

A   Intercensal estimates, annual averages

	Birth Rate	Death Rate	Growth Rate
1941–50	40	27	13
1951–60	42	23	19
B Rates derived from National Sample Survey			
1958–59	38	19	19
1963–64	38	13	25

Note : The later figures from the national sample survey should be read in the light of the comment in the UN *Demographic Yearbook* for 1967, i.e.: 'At the request of the Government of India, data for 1963–64 from the eighteenth round of the National Sample Survey and data for the Registration Area were suppressed in this issue because the intercensal rates compiled from 1951 and 1961 census data were considered to be more reliable.'

The high birth rate in India in recent decades is the product of high fertilities in the early reproductive years as a result of the very early age at marriage. High mortality has greatly reduced the numbers of mothers in the later reproductive years, and among those still living through these years restraints upon remarriage have created a considerable pool of widows not at risk of pregnancy. It is of some interest to compare the age-specific fertility pattern of India around 1961 with that of the Hutterites of North America – one of the highest fertility groups known in this century. The comparison in terms of births per 1,000 women at each age group shows that the Indian rates imply a completed family size by age 45 of about 6·4 children, compared with a Hutterite figure of 7·8. The Indians marry much younger and so lead the Hutterites markedly to age 24, but thereafter the latter take the lead and at higher ages far outstrip the Indian performance.

Table 7.6 : Births per 1,000 Women in each Age Group, Ethnic Hutterites 1946–50 and India 1961[14]

Age Group	Hutterites	India
15–19	11·96	154·3
20–24	230·95	305·0
25–29	382·73	314·2
30–34	391·11	252·2
35–39	344·61	168·1
40–44	208·34	76·3
Total Fertility Rate*	7·8	6·3

* Sum of columns × 5.

It might seem, therefore, that a rise in the marriage age in India would greatly reduce India's birth rate. An initial rise say from 16 to 18, might in fact have the opposite effect by decreasing the heavy mortality of young women associated with childbearing and thus leaving larger cohorts to bear children in later years; but almost certainly a rise in mean marriage age to say 20 years would have a considerable effect, although here again any such change is likely to be associated with other economic and social changes associated with still further decreases in mortality and fewer restrictions on the remarriage of widows, therefore again raising the average number of years during which each woman is exposed to the risk of pregnancy.

Estimates of the reduction in birth rates that could be made by raising the average age at marriage by about five years vary considerably. One estimate puts the savings in births by raising average marriage age from 15·6 in 1961 to 19–20 in 1961 at 21 per cent.

167

another which takes fuller account of some of the variable factors referred to above considers that the saving between 1961 and 1966, with marriage age raised to 20 years would be only about 10 per cent.[15] The latter seems the more reasonable estimate, and even if too conservative does not invalidate the argument that changing marriage patterns will not by themselves be sufficient to bring about a marked redirection in growth rates in India, particularly if mortality continues to decline. Such a decline is likely to remain a cardinal aspect of Indian policy for even at 46 years, the expectation of life at birth is amongst the lowest of the modern world, and an infant death rate, still estimated to be as high as 139 per 1,000 live births between 1951 and 1961, is still far above the tolerance level for any modern society.

The main feature of the Indian situation since independence has therefore been a steady growth rate over the whole period, with a marked increase over the last decade. If sustained, the estimated rate of 2·5 per cent in 1963–4 would double the population of India in just about twenty-eight years. The policy of successive Indian governments has been to prevent this, so far obviously without success, and the momentum of growth is now so great with such large increases amongst those who will soon be approaching the reproductive ages that at least a doubling of India's population must be expected before controls can become really effective. For the moment, we will merely note the effect in terms of population growth which has already flowed from the consistently high fertility and declining mortality which have been briefly illustrated in this chapter. The estimated population inside the present boundaries of India (excluding the Indian-held part of Kashmir-Jammu) has more than doubled this century, and the greatest part of this increase has occurred since 1921. While indices such as *per capita* incomes may show little real improvement since the 1920s, thus suggesting decades of stagnation, demographic indices can give an entirely different picture. During the doubling of the Indian population since the 1920s, the expectation of life at birth moved from around 26 years to 46 years in 1961 and may pass the mark of 50 years before this decade closes. This index suggests that a vast social change has been taking place which has brought India to the threshold of modernity. Traditional economic indices are no longer sufficient to measure the rate of change in developing societies. The question now is whether economic development can be stepped up to the level where it can cope with the present unprecedented level of population growth. The Indian government has decided that it cannot do so and is now bringing in population control as a fundamental aspect of economic as well as social welfare.

Table 7.7 : Estimated Population of India, Post-Partition Boundaries

	Population (in millions)	Increase or Decrease in each Period (in millions)	Per cent Change in the Period
1891	235·9	—	—
1901	235·5	−0·4	−0·17
1911	249·0	13·5	5·73
1921	248·1	−0·9	−0·36
1931	275·5	27·4	11·04
1341	312·8	37·3	13·54
1951	356·9	44·1	14·10
1961	439·0	82·1	23·00
1966	498·7	59·7	13·60

In Pakistan, which was born as an independent nation from the partition of the Indian sub-continent in August 1947, the demographic picture of recent times has been broadly similar to that of India. The demographic basis of Pakistan is the Moslem population of pre-partition India. Partition involved massive transfers of non-Moslems from the new territories of Pakistan and of Moslems from the territories of the Indian Union, with close upon 10 million moving in each direction. By 1949 over 83 per cent of the population of Pakistan were Moslems, compared with 11 per cent in the Indian Union.

At the first post-partition census of 1951, Pakistan's population was recorded at 75,800,000. Over the next decade this had increased to 94,547,000, a population over twice the size of that estimated for the same boundaries in 1901. Table 7. 8 provides an estimate of the population this century within the boundaries of present-day Pakistan, excluding the Pakistan-held part of Kashmir-Jammu.[16]

To the extent that these estimates can be trusted, it would appear that, compared with Indians, the Pakistanis experienced a considerably higher growth rate in the first two decades of the century, that they suffered less of a set-back at the end of the First World War and that their recent growth rate has con-

7.8 : *Estimated Population and Population Increase of Pakistan 1901–66*

	Population (in millions)	Increase (in millions)	Per cent Change in Period
1901	45·5	—	—
1911	50·9	5·4	11·9
1921	54·4	3·5	6·7
1931	59·1	4·7	8·8
1941	70·3	11·2	18·9
1951	75·8	5·5	7·9
1961	94·5	18·7	24·7
1966 (est.)	105·0	10·5	11·1

tinued to be somewhat higher over recent years. The implied higher fertility of Moslems is consistent with historical evidence. In 1881 the Indian census reported that Moslems were 19·97 per cent of the total population: by 1941 their proportion had increased to 24·28 per cent. The ratios of children aged 0–4 to women aged 15–39 was also consistently higher for Moslems than for Hindus. W. S. Thompson,[17] also points out that most of the great irrigation schemes in the Indus River valley between approximately 1901 and 1940 were located within the present boundaries of Pakistan, thus encouraging an immigrant flow from India. The higher growth rate of Pakistan before 1941 appears however to have been due primarily to the fact that its territories suffered less than those of India from famines and epidemics of cholera or other disease. On the other hand the relatively low rate of growth in Pakistan between 1941 and 1951 may be attributed in part to the severity of the Bengal famine in 1943, which caused 1·5 million deaths or sufficient to halt population growth in East Pakistan. By contrast West Pakistan continued to grow from 1941–51 at about 2 per cent a year.

The higher growth rate of Pakistan in recent years, compared with India, is probably due to higher fertility, although an exact figure cannot be provided for Pakistan because of inadequate registration data and known deficiencies in the age data from the census from which fertility estimates can be made. Very high fertility is common among predominantly Moslem countries, although again few of them have vital statistics or other data which permit exact measurement. Kirk[18] estimates that annual birth rates of Moslem countries range from the low forties to as high as sixty per 1,000 of population. United Nations estimates put the birth rate of Pakistan in 1963 at 43·4 per 1,000, with a death rate of 15·4 and therefore a growth rate of 2·8 per cent. This may be compared with the corresponding estimated rates of 38, 13 and 2·5 per cent for India in 1963–4 (Table 7. 5). Using stable population analysis, birth rates around 1961 of 55 – and in one case of 60 – per 1,000 have been suggested. Other estimates, based upon carefully prepared sample populations by the Pakistan Population Growth Estimation project, a joint venture of the Central Statistical Office and of the Pakistan Institute of Development Economics, have placed birth rates around 1963–4 at figures ranging between 52 and 55 and crude death rates around 20 per 1,000.[19] These imply a rate of natural increase of between 3·3 and 3·6, a total fertility rate (births expected per woman living through the child-bearing years) of about 7·9 children, a gross reproduction rate of almost 3·9, a net reproduction rate of 2·6 and, at these levels of fertility and mortality, a doubling of the population in about twenty years.

As with India, a factor in the extremely high fertility rates of Pakistan is the low age of marriage and the universality of marriage. The mean age at marriage for women is around 17 years and marriage is almost universal by age 20.

Table 7.9: Proportion per cent of Women Single and Married, Widowed, etc., in each Age Group, Pakistan, 1961

Age	Proportion per cent	
	Single	Married, Widowed, etc.
10–14	77·4	22·6
15–19	25·5	74·5
20–24	5·8	94·2
25–29	2·5	97·5
30–34	1·5	98·5

As Moslems have none of the restrictions on remarriage of the Hindus, the great majority of those classified as not single would be married. In other words, from age 20 few women in Pakistan are not exposed to the risk of child-bearing, even more so than in India, and a raising of the marriage age could have an important effect upon growth rates. One estimate[20] is that birth rates could be reduced by some 30 per cent if the mean age of marriage could be raised by five years, but even if this goal could be quickly achieved (which is unlikely) growth rates would still be high and other measures of fertility control would seem necessary. High as Pakistan's growth rate is, it could go even higher, for there is still ample room for a considerable decline in mortality. For example, infant mortality (deaths of infants under 1 year of age per 1,000 live births) was estimated to be still as high as 145 in 1963, compared with an estimate of 139 for India, and the expectation of life at birth is still probably below that of India.

The situation of Pakistan is all the more acute because the highest growth rates are found in the most densely settled area. East Pakistan has higher proportions married and higher birth and fertility rates than West Pakistan, but while the former has the richer agricultural areas, the density is already very high. East Pakistan carried 56 per cent of the population in only about one-seventh of the total area, and the density per square mile already exceeds 1,000 persons, compared with only about 76 persons in West Pakistan. Ease of flow from overpopulated to underpopulated areas or from rural to urban areas in search of non-agricultural employment is hampered by the great distance separating East and West Pakistan. Thus both higher growth rates and geographical factors hampering internal mobility combine to give Pakistan an even more formidable population problem than that of India.

Indonesia, the other predominantly Moslem country among the Asian 'giants', with a population enumerated at the 1961 census of 96,319,000 people, and an estimated population in 1966 of 107 million, has even more demographic uncertainties than Pakistan. In total population, Indonesia is probably very similar to Pakistan, but its total land area of 576,000 square miles is greater (364,700 in Pakistan). As with Pakistan much of the population is concentrated in a relatively small part of the archipelago: Java and Madura with one-eleventh of the land area carry about two-thirds of the population, compared with East Pakistan's 56 per cent of all Pakistan.

In 1816 Java's population was estimated to be only about 4·5 million, or half the population of England and Wales: in 1955 it had an estimated 53 or 54 million people, or more than England and Wales.[21] Growth rates during much of the nineteenth century may have exceeded 2 per cent a year, and as death rates must have been fairly high, such rates could only have been sustained by a combination of high fertility and immigration from the outer islands. Growth rates appear to have declined by about one half in the early years of the twentieth century suggesting that the population may have been pressing towards the subsistence capacity of the areas then settled, but they increased again after about 1920 in response to better health services, the extension of irrigation, and the opening of new areas for settlement. Nevertheless the Dutch were conscious of the pressing problem of increasing numbers and attempted to encourage emigration from Java to the outlying areas, without significant success. In 1955 Java already had a density between 1,025 and 1,050 persons a square mile, or higher than East Pakistan today, and when allowance is made for the extensive mountain areas, the settled parts of Java are amongst the most dense in the world.

At the beginning of the nineteenth century about a seventh of the land was estimated to be cultivated; by the Second World War cultivation covered about three-quarters of the land area. The expansion of export crops, especially sugar from cane planted on land leased from the peasants, the embargo placed by the colonial government on the sale of land to non-Indonesians, the interest of the export industries which encouraged the Dutch authorities to install major irrigation works so as to expand the areas available for sugar, and relatively efficient health services, all combined to encourage population growth. The peasant had some cash income from the lease of his land, and security of yet other land for subsistence rice cultivation; hence food supplies were reasonably secure and labour surplus to subsistence-farming had some opportunity for employment on the sugar plantations. Keyfitz[22] has emphasized the difference between the situations of Java and France in the nineteenth century. The French peasant's livelihood was wholly confined to the piece of land he had inherited and his children had little chance of finding employment off the farm: two or three children were quite sufficient to ensure that a son could take over the farm, provide security in old age and avoid subdivision in the next generation into sub-economic small plots. In Java, the staple diet of rice, the fertility of the soil, and the opportunities for supplementing subsistence farming with cash income from rents and employment off the farm provided few disincentives to fertility. The demographic response to this economic and ecological situation in Java is apparent in Table 7.10.

Table 7.10 : Estimated Population of Indonesia (in thousands)[23]

	Java & Madura	Other Areas	Total
1845	9,374	—	—
1870	16,233	—	—
1900	28,386	—	—
1930	40,891	18,147	59,138
1961	63,060	34,025	97,085
1966	—	—	107,500

Table 7.11 : Distribution of Population by Region, 1930 and 1961

	Per cent of Total Population 1930	1961	Per cent of Total Area
Java and Madura	68·0	64·9	6·9
Sumatra	13·6	16·2	24·9
Kalimantan	3·6	4·3	28·3
Sulawesi	7·0	7·3	9·9
Other Islands	7·8	7·3	30·0
Indonesia	100·0	100·0	100·0

There is no similar historical series for the outer islands of Indonesia, but from 1930 the situation over the whole archipelago is reasonably clear at census dates, and annual estimates of the United Nations since 1947 imply a steady expansion of population in all areas, with the population of Java still holding about two-thirds of the people, despite its density. There has been some movement from Java to other islands, for example of labour attracted by the higher wages of the rubber plantations in North Sumatra and by the coconut producers of the Celebes. Between 1932 and 1961 about half a million people were transferred with government support from Java to Sumatra and Celebes, but the basic concentration of population within Java continued, for natural increase was on much too vast a scale to be offset by the emigration schemes initiated by governments.

. The capacity of Java to carry such a large population has been, and will continue to be conditioned by the capacity of the other islands to sustain their exports (for example of minerals, oil, rubber) on the world's markets. The collapse of those markets or the secession of the outer islands in which most of these raw materials exist would leave Java in an impossible situation unless population growth could be quite suddenly brought to a halt. If present growth rates continue it is difficult to see how the extension of peasant settlement to the outer areas on a massive scale can long be avoided. Assuming the logistics of massive population transfers could be handled, the Indonesian territories can provide subsistence livelihood for a population far in excess of present numbers. Conservative estimates put the upper limit at 250 millions,[24] but whether political realities will allow free and massive movement is quite another matter. Yet only a political system which accords with economic realities seems likely to save much of Indonesia, and particularly Java, from Malthusian overpopulation.

The role that population control measures might play as one measure to alleviate the pressing problems of Indonesia will be discussed in a later chapter. Here it is intended only to set out the basic aspects of the demographic situation, to the extent that these are known or can be reasonably estimated.

The total population of Indonesia, excluding West Irian, was estimated to be 40,400,000 in 1905. The census of 1930 recorded 59,138,000. Thirty-one years later (1961) this had grown to 97,085,000 and thirty-six years later (1966) it had reached 107,500,000 (Table 7.10). Since 1930 therefore the growth rate has averaged about 1·8 per cent and in recent years has been estimated to be between 2·0 and about 2·4 per cent.

Precisely what have been the fertility and mortality schedules behind these growth rates is somewhat conjectural as there is no efficient registration system; but estimates derived from census data have suggested birth rates per 1,000 of population between 42 and 45 and death rates of 21 or 22. Lower figures have however been postulated for Djakarta, where a survey of 1957 yielded a birth rate of 36·4.[25] The lower urban fertility implied in these figures would however have only a marginal effect upon the total Indonesian situation as only 7·5 per cent of Indonesians lived in areas designated as urban in 1961. While some form of fertility control might have been practised traditionally amongst some groups, birth rates are still high and yield an average of about five births per married woman by the end of her fecund years. Few women do not marry, but the age at marriage appears to be considerably higher than in either India or Pakistan. Kartono[26] gives a mean age at marriage for Djakarta of 19·2 years for women and 24·3 years for men.

Generally the Indonesian situation seems broadly similar to that of Pakistan, with mortality still high enough for growth rates to expand still further if public health systems and applied medical science are more efficiently supplied. Mortality schedules are still high by the standards of developed countries, but they are much better than those that applied in the Indian sub-continent until twenty or thirty years ago. Life Tables prepared by the Institute of Demography in the Faculty of Economics of the University of Indonesia on the basis of 1951 and 1961 census data have expectations of life at birth of 44·3 years for males and 48·5 for females, and tables for Djakarta prepared by the Department of Health and based on survey data for 1957 and 1958 give a combined male and female expectation as high as 51·3 years.[27] These rates, although giving Indonesia a possible edge on India or Pakistan are still considerably below the levels now applying in some of her smaller neighbours. Malaysia, for example, had rates for males and females respectively of 55·8 and 58·2 in 1956–8, almost identical with the rates in Thailand in 1960.

A final feature to be illustrated from the Indonesian situation and applicable to the other Asian giants discussed in this chapter is the age composition now existing as a result of constantly high fertility and considerable improvements in mortality which have tended to have their initial effect upon the saving of lives of infants and young children. In 1961, 42 per cent of the population were between the ages 0 and 15 years; and only 2·5 per cent were aged 65 and over. These figures may be compared with Australia as an example of a developed country with a very high expectation of life and controlled fertility: there in 1961 only 30·2 per cent were aged 0–14 and 8·5 per cent were aged 65 and over. In developing countries like Indonesia – or India, or Pakistan – the size of the young cohorts aged 0–14 in relation to the older groups means, of course, that reductions in fertility will tend to be offset for the next fifteen to twenty years by the increase in the proportion of young persons attaining marriageable age. In countries aiming at the attainment of complete literacy such an age distribution also requires extremely heavy investment in education. In Indonesia in 1961 less than two-thirds of the children aged 9–12 were attending schools.

This chapter has discussed some of the major features of only four political units; mainland China, India, Pakistan and Indonesia:

Figure 7.1 : World Population Growth and Distribution by Major Areas, 1920 and 1961

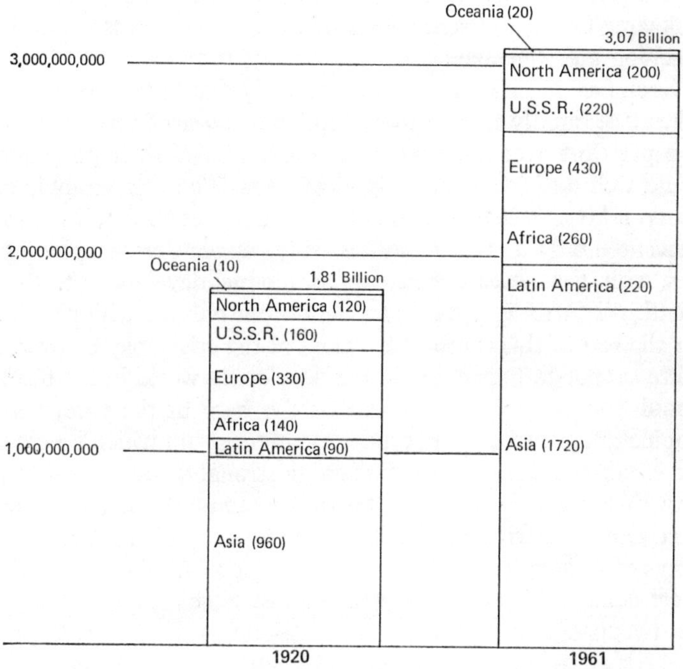

Source: OECD Observer, August 1963

but they contain over 40 per cent of the world's population. Among these vast groupings there is yet little sign of fertility control. So far they have experienced only one aspect of demographic transition in the form of some improvement in mortality. But while improvements in this regard may seem comparatively slight from the standpoint of people in countries with life expectations now exceeding seventy years, the improvements are already sufficient to bring these huge agglomerations of people to a point not far from the situation attained by the Western world some seventy years ago. If demographic events in these countries follow the sequence of most Western countries since that time, with further reductions in mortality before fertility can be effectively brought under control, their present growth rates – which probably all exceed 2 per cent a year, with the possible exception of China –

177

will rise even further. Furthermore even if the number of births per married woman can be reduced, their age composition is now such that the effect of such a reduction would tend to be offset for the following fifteen to twenty years by the greatly increased numbers reaching marriageable ages.

Such factors make it extremely unlikely that fertility control can take place rapidly enough to prevent an increase of between 75 and 100 per cent over the next forty years. Indeed their populations could well double within thirty-five years. The demographic patterns and trends suggest this to be a distinct possibility, likely to be prevented only if these countries fail to match demographic realities with the necessary rate of economic development. But if Malthus's tortoise of food production can only be whipped along for the rest of this century the worst of the crisis may be over, for there is enough happening in the developing world in the form of population control to suggest that the hare in the race, that is population growth, has not quite the momentum which he used to have. Nevertheless, he is still running strongly, and the pattern of growth suggested in this chapter is likely to be paralleled and even exceeded, in Africa and South America, thus giving the world's population a great thrust towards the 7,000 million mark which most demographers now accept as an inevitable event by early in the twenty-first century.

Chapter 8

Population Growth in the Developing World: Latin America

Latin America – that is the American continent south of the borders of the United States – is one of the fastest growing regions of the world and it has been so for some fifty years. The precise trends before that are substantially a matter of conjecture, although it is known that international immigration was a major factor promoting growth. Gross immigration into Argentina, Uruguay and Chile is estimated to have approached 3 million between 1900 and 1930, and over the same period some 2·5 million immigrants entered Brazil and 857,000 entered Cuba. By 1920 the Latin American population was estimated to be about 87 million. The native population of Latin America around 1492, when Columbus first visited the region, has been variously estimated to have been between approximately 8 and 15 millions, so that over the whole intervening period to the twentieth century, the average growth rate must have been very slight. Since early in this century, however, despite poor statistics which prevent precise measurement, a great acceleration of growth is certain, and since the 1930s when international immigration ceased to play a significant role, the increasing growth rates have mostly come from natural factors. An estimate of the background to the present situation, by major regions is given in Table 8. 1.

The main factor in this expansion was the rapid improvement in mortality, which was widespread throughout most of the region and reached remarkable rates of decline in some countries. In Mexico, for example, estimated crude death rates fell from 25·6 per 1,000 of population in 1930–4 to 11·5 in 1960 – a decline of 55 per cent in approximately twenty-eight years. Similar falls occurred in El Salvador and Costa Rica. In Chile the death rate fell over the same period by 49 per cent; and in Brazil, in a matter of about ten years between 1945–50 and 1955–60, the rate came down by almost a third from 20 to 13·5. These trends, when

Table 8.1 : Estimated Populations and Growth Rates by Major Regions of Latin America, 1920–60[1]

Region	Populations in Millions					Annual Growth Rates, per cent			
	1920	1930	1940	1950	1960	1920–30	1930–40	1940–50	1950–60
Middle America	19·4	22·4	26·8	34·6	46·7	1·4	1·8	2·5	3·0
Caribbean	7·5	9·2	11·0	13·3	16·3	2·0	1·8	1·9	2·0
Tropical South America	45·2	54·0	66·2	83·3	111·6	1·8	2·0	2·3	2·9
Temperate South America	14·8	18·9	22·3	26·8	32·8	2·4	1·7	1·8	2·0
All Latin America	86·9	104·5	126·3	158·1	207·4	1·8	1·9	2·2	2·7

matched against high and largely constant fertility throughout most of the region set the pattern of the extremely high current growth rates of Latin America.

'Middle America', made up of Costa Rica, El Salvador, Guatemala, Honduras, Mexico, Nicaragua and Panama, has been estimated to contain no country with current growth rates below 3·0 per cent a year and to contain five countries with rates equal to or exceeding 3·5 per cent. Birth rates are estimated to be between 41 and 50 and death rates between approximately 8 and 16 per 1,000 of population. The gap between births and deaths is therefore enormous and the expectations of life at birth range between 50 and 60 years in Guatemala to 58–64 years in Mexico and 62–65 years in Costa Rica.[2] Furthermore the future growth potential is even greater than it has been in the recent past because of the changes in age composition brought about by rapid declines in infant mortality. Every country of Middle America has between 42 and 51 per cent of its population in the juvenile age group, 0–14 years. In the global sense, however, these rapidly increasing populations will have a marginal effect on the world's future, for their total numbers in 1968 were estimated to be only about 63 millions, of whom 47 millions were in Mexico; but within each country the population issue has now reached a critical level in terms of the political, social and economic capacities to handle such high growth rates.

To the south of these countries lies the Caribbean where the situation is now much more variable. In some of the Caribbean region birth control and emigration have greatly reduced growth rates. Barbados has a birth rate below 30 per 1,000 of population and a growth rate below 2 per cent a year. Cuba, with a birth rate now estimated at about 35, has a death rate of around 8 per 1,000, and therefore an increase of about 2·7 per cent, with little relief through emigration. Jamaica, on the other hand, has a somewhat higher natural growth pattern (approximately a birth rate of 38 and a death rate of 8), but the natural growth rate of about 3 per cent has been greatly reduced by emigration to 1·7 per cent a year or lower. Emigration has also been a significant factor in reducing growth rates in Puerto Rico, where, however, birth rates are now comparatively low (estimated at 28·3 in 1968). The fastest growing country of this region is the Dominican Republic with birth rates of 45–48 per 1,000, death rates of 14–16, and a growth rate around 3·6 per cent. The populations of all the countries of the Caribbean region (Barbados, Cuba, Dominican Republic, Haiti, Jamaica, Puerto Rico, Trinidad and Tobago) amounted to about 23 million people in 1966, and while their average growth rate of about 2·5 per cent is considerably below that of their northern neighbours in Middle America, it is still well above world average and is capable of doubling populations in about twenty-eight years, or about each demographic generation. In general the major factor encouraging growth has been the very rapid and extensive fall in mortality. Only the Dominican Republic, with a life expectation at birth between 35 and 45 years, or lower than that of India, has any longer a substantial check through the factor of death. Its infant mortality rate (deaths of infants aged 0 years per 1,000 live births) probably exceeds 110, whereas the rate of each of the other countries is less than 50, with life expectation rising to 65 or over in Barbados, Jamaica and Trinidad. Thus in terms of both birth and death rates some of the Caribbean countries seem to be approaching the patterns of the 'developed' Western countries.

The greater part of the population of Latin America is however to be found in Tropical South America (Bolivia, Brazil, Colombia, Ecuador, Guyana, Peru and Venezuela) with approximately 141 million people, and Temperate South America (Argentina, Chile, Paraguay and Uruguay) with about 38 million.

In Tropical South America the birth rates of every country are estimated to be between approximately 40 and 45 per 1,000 of population with Ecuador possibly rising to almost 50 and Venezuela to 48. Death rates are now relatively low, with infant mortality rates around 45 per 1,000 live births and crude death rates per 1,000 of population mostly around 10 to 14. The clearest exception to this pattern is Bolivia with a rate of 20 or more. Consequently growth rates are high, and are estimated to exceed 3 per cent in most countries, to be close on 3 per cent in Guyana and 2·4 per cent in Bolivia. Brazil, with 88 of the 141 million people of the region, has a growth rate of about 3·2 per cent a year, or sufficient to double the population every twenty-two years. Indeed this is approximately the average for the region as a whole.

In Temperate South America, the situation is much the same in Paraguay, with birth rates per 1,000 between 42 and 45 and a growth rate of 3·2 per cent; but the other countries of this region are beginning to approach the 'Western' patterns. Argentina has a birth rate of only 21 and Uruguay about 24, with Chile in an intermediate position for the moment with a rate around 32. Relatively high death rates, with an infant mortality rate exceeding 100 infant deaths per 1,000 live births, provide some check to Chile's growth rate which, however, still exceeds 2 per cent, compared with only 1·5 per cent in Argentina and 1·2 per cent in Uruguay. The average growth rate of the whole of this region of 38 million people – with 23 million in Argentina – is approximately 1·9 per cent a year, which is a little above the world average but is still low enough to separate it clearly from Tropical South America and Middle America.

The impetus to growth emanating from Tropical Latin America, and to a smaller extent from Middle America, gives the whole Latin American continent probably the highest growth rate of any major continental region of the world. From an estimated 91 million people in 1920 the population has grown today to some 263 million and unless fertility is controlled this could increase almost threefold by the end of the century. The maintenance of such a growth rate would demand increasing efficiency in the use and distribution of resources both in terms of food and export crops, but the social structure and political systems of many of the countries of the region provide no guarantee of the achievement of this goal – which, of course, emphasizes the necessity for alternative measures to reduce the threat of overpopulation, namely fertility control; and here the religious compositions of the majority of the populations together with the high degrees of illiteracy have probably complicated the achievement of such an alternative route to salvation.

Table 8.2 : Estimated Populations and Vital Indices of Latin America, 1968[3]

	Population mid-1968 (millions)	Birth Rates*	Death Rates*	Infant Mortality Rates†	Annual Growth Rates ‡ per cent	Years required to double population
Middle America						
Costa Rica	1·6	44–46	7·7	75·1	3·5	20
El Salvador	3·3	47–49	9·9	61·4	3·7	19
Guatemala	4·9	46–48	16·6	91·5	3·1	23
Honduras	2·5	47–50	15–17	70–90	3·5	20
Mexico	47·3	44·1	9·6	60·7	3·5	20
Nicaragua	1·8	47–50	14–16	60–80	3·5	20
Panama	1·4	41–42	10–11	40–60	3·2	22
	62·8					
Caribbean						
Barbados	0·3	25·2	8·2	49·3	1·7	41
Cuba	8·2	34–36	8·9	35–45	2·6	27
Dominican Republic	4·0	45–48	14–16	81	3·6	20
Haiti	4·7	45–50	17–21	110–130	2·5	28
Jamaica	1·9	38·8	7·7	35·4	1·8	39
Puerto Rico	2·7	28·3	5·9	42·0	1·5	47
Trinidad & Tobago	1·0	37–39	6·9	35·3	2·8	25
	22·8					
Tropical South America						
Bolivia	3·9	43–45	20–24	—	2·4	29
Brazil	88·3	41–43	10–12	—	3·2	22
Columbia	19·7	40–45	11–13	82	3·2	22
Ecuador	5·7	45–50	12–14	93	3·4	21
Guyana	0·7	39·9	8·1	39·8	2·9	24
Peru	12·8	44–45	11–13	—	3·1	23
Venezuela	9·7	46–48	9–10	—	3·6	20
	140·8					
Temperate South America						
Argentina	23·4	21·5	8·2	60–65	1·5	47
Chile	9·1	32·0	10·7	107·1	2·2	32
Paraguay	2·2	42–45	12–14	—	3·2	22
Uruguay	2·8	23–25	8·9	40–45	1·2	58
	37·5					

* Per 1,000 of population.
† Deaths of infants aged 0 per 1,000 live births.
‡ Growth rates include effect of international migratory movements.

As systems of vital statistics in many Latin American countries are fairly rudimentary, many of the rates given in Table 8·2 can only be accepted as approximations. Nevertheless the fact of high growth rate in the region as a whole is incontrovertible, and if fertility control is the response to social change, advancing literacy and economic development, the prospects for reducing growth rates are not bright. On the other hand it is to be noted that the countries with the lowest birth rates (e.g. Argentina and Uruguay) have also the highest literacy rates, with over 90 per cent of the population over the age of 15 years so described. In an area in which estimates of national incomes *per capita* range between US $80 in Haiti to $959 in Puerto Rico, Argentina ($740) and Uruguay ($537) stand reasonably high. Although low by the standard of most Western European countries, these average *per capita* figures are comparable with those of many countries of eastern and southern Europe (where incidentally most birth rates are already quite low) but a feature of the Latin American scene is the tendency for there to be an extremely wide variation around the average. Wealth, as well as political and economic power, tends to be concentrated in a small minority of each population. The masses of the populations are poor peasantry or unskilled urban dwellers, among whom adult illiteracy rates range to as high as 50 per cent. They have neither the skills nor the capital to break from the bonds of poverty and in more than half the countries serious programmes of agrarian reform which might relieve the situation have not yet been attempted; and where such attempts have been made they have tended to founder through political instability at the centre and the failure to break down regressive tax systems.

The inability of many of the governments to acquire the capital for investment in education, agrarian reform and industrial development exacerbates the situation already created by the remarkable decline in death rates throughout much of the region which, in combination with the very high-fertility rates, has resulted in population structures in which most countries of Middle America, the Caribbean and Tropical South have between 40 and 45 per cent of their people as young 'dependants', that is under the age of 15 years.

The precise course of vital events which have resulted in relatively low fertility rates in a few countries (Argentina, Barbados, Uruguay) and considerable falls in mortality rates in most, cannot be plotted with accuracy. Argentina, Chile, Guatemala, Mexico and Uruguay, with about a third of the Latin American population, have now relatively good vital statistics, but in the remainder of the area death registration is incomplete, with at best only two population censuses against which vital events can be checked with reasonable accuracy. In general, however, the decline in mortality appears to have set in around 1915, when the campaigns to eliminate hookworm and yellow fever were initiated.[4] These were followed by improvements in water supplies and sanitation, and later by the control of malaria by DDT. At their lowest levels, death rates correspond to those of the United States ten to fifteen years ago; but in some areas, as already emphasized, the rates remain very high in absolute terms, and again there are wide variations between the highest and the lowest economic and social classes.

The relatively low death rates which now apply in many Latin American countries reflect to some extent the extremely high fertility rates of the past, which have created population profiles with very high proportions of the total populations between ages of early childhood (say 5 years) and early adult life (say 25 years), that is within the ages where exposure to the risk of death is relatively low. Nevertheless, the reductions shown in Table 8. 3 and the low rates of recent years shown in Tables 8. 2 and 8. 3, reflect very real improvements in death rates over all ages. However, in some countries infectious diseases are still taking heavy tolls of life, and are estimated to account for about one-third of all deaths. Prominent causes of such deaths are tuberculosis, diphtheria, whooping cough and infantile diarrhoea. Progress in preventing these is still hampered by both inadequate investment in public health and the scarcity of qualified doctors and nurses. It was estimated in 1965 that there were only 100,000 doctors practising in the entire region – a ratio of 5·8 doctors for every 10,000 persons compared with 15·1 per 10,000 in the United States.* The situation regarding hospital accommodation is similar. While there has been a considerable increase in hospital beds, with an estimated increase from 670,000 in 1960 to 760,000 in 1967, this increase has not kept pace with the requirements of population growth.[5] Again a

* The Latin American situation in this regard, while poor compared with USA, is on the other hand infinitely better than those of the Asian and African regions.

Table 8.3: Estimated Death Rates and Percentage Decreases in Selected Countries[5]

	First Period Date	Rate per thousand	Second Period Date	Rate per thousand	Percentage Decrease	Number of years
Middle America						
Mexico	1930–34	25·6	1960	11·5	55	28
Guatemala	,,	26·1	,,	17·5	33	28
El Salvador	,,	23·0	,,	11·0	52	28
Panama	1945–50	15·5	1955–60	11·0	29	10
Caribbean						
Cuba	1930–34	11·3	1960–62	7·0	38	30
Dominican Republic	1945–50	22·5	1955–60	18·0	20	10
Puerto Rico	1930–34	19·7	1962	6·7	66	29
Tropical South America						
Brazil	1945–50	20·0	1955–60	13·5	33	10
Columbia	,,	19·0	,,	15·5	18	10
Peru	,,	21·0	,,	15·5	26	10
Venezuela	1926–30	18·9	,,	12·5	34	29
Ecuador	1945–50	22·5	,,	17·5	22	10
Bolivia	,,	25·0	,,	22·5	10	10
Temperate South America						
Argentina	1930–34	11·6	1960–62	8·1	30	29
Chile	,,	23·9	,,	12·0	50	29
Uruguay	,,	11·6	1963	8·6	26	31
Paraguay	1945–50	17·5	1955–60	14·0	20	10

basic problem remains inefficient distribution both between countries and between urban and rural areas within each country. Most of the medical facilities are available in the large urban centres, which have up to five times as many doctors per 1,000 inhabitants as rural areas.

Until about a decade ago, international immigration played an important role in the population growth of Latin America (see Chapter 5). Much of the planning of this immigration was aimed at rural settlement and improved agricultural efficiency, but in fact the majority of the immigrants tended to drift into urban employment. Now international immigration is surplus to the requirements of most Latin American countries except in so far as it can supply technical skills not provided by under-educated populations. But in quantitative terms, with the exception of very few countries, such as Argentina, Chile and possibly Venezuela, the

Figure 8.1 : Natural Increase Trends; Examples of the 'Old' [European] and the 'New' [Latin America]

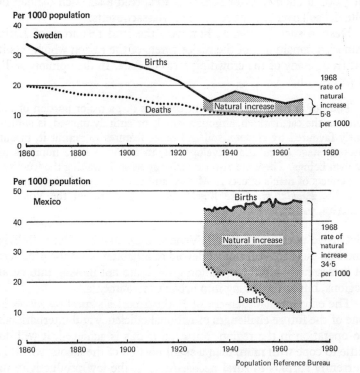

Population Reference Bureau

problem is no longer supplementation of populations by international immigration, but the employment of the swelling masses of young workers derived from the high fertility and falling mortality patterns already noted.

For the region as a whole, density of population is still relatively low. In 1960 South America had only 20·4 persons to the square mile, compared with 50·5 in the USA and 340·1 on the US Middle Atlantic Seaboard. This does not mean, however, that South America has limitless land resources for an expanding rural peasantry. So far the cost of bringing new areas into production has tended to exceed the economic returns to be expected. Furthermore, in Tropical Latin America, jungle soil has failed to produce many crops before exhaustion and much of the land is sloping and susceptible to erosion once cleared of its shield of natural overgrowth. It has been estimated, for example, that the silt load carried away each year by the Amazon into the Atlantic is of the order of 5,000 million tons, or sufficient to spread a six-inch blanket of alluvial soil over the entire State of Massachusetts.

Despite such problems, however, the land resources of Latin America remain one of the major assets of the region which sets it off from many of the crowding areas of Asia. In the opinion of T. Lynn Smith,[7]

The South American continent contains . . . a major portion of the land on the earth which, although largely or entirely unused, is sufficiently favoured by climate, soil and other features to permit it, in our present stage of cultural development, to maintain large numbers of human beings. There are also extensive areas still awaiting the fructifying effects of man's efforts in Mexico and Central American countries. (In *The Population of the World,* Forum Lectures of the Voice of America, p. 107.)

Extensive portions of Brazil, Venezuela, Colombia, Peru, Bolivia and Paraguay are still almost devoid of inhabitants yet the products of increasingly rapid population growth are not moving into rural regions, but are crowding into urban environments.

The efficient management of Latin America's rural resources is one of the future challenges of national efficiency and international co-operation in the region, but even if this is achieved, it will do little to cope with more than a small portion of the labour which is currently surplus to rural needs. As it is, the low productivity in agriculture increases the pressure of rural population upon resources and sustains a 'push' off rural areas towards towns, and particularly towards a few major metropolises.

On the basis of censuses taken around 1950 and 1960, the Economic Commission for Latin America estimated that the mean intercensal annual growth rate of all Latin America was about 2·8 per cent, with a growth rate of rural population of only 1·5 per cent, compared with a growth rate of urban areas (population, 2,000 and over) of 4·5 per cent. Differential fertility favoured rural rather than

188

urban growth rates, although mortality may have tended to favour the urban sector; but the major factor in these differential growth rates was the migration of surplus rural labour to the cities. This urban drift is illustrated in Table 8. 4.

Table 8.4: Percentage of Population in Rural Areas, and Estimated Annual Rates of Growth per cent, around 1950 and 1960[8]

Country	Percentage Rural		Intercensal Annual Rate of Growth, per cent		
	1950	1960	Total	Rural	Urban Capital City
Costa Rica	67	66	3·8	3·7	4·0	—
El Salvador	64	62	2·8	2·4	3·3	—
Mexico	57	49	3·0	1·5	4·7	4·9
Nicaragua	65	57	3·3	2·2	4·9	—
Panama	64	59	2·9	2·0	4·1	5·2
Dominican Republic	76	70	3·4	2·5	5·7	7·3
Brazil	64	55	3·1	1·6	5·2	3·2
Chile	40	34	2·5	0·5	3·7	—
Ecuador	72	65	3·1	2·3	4·6	4·7
Paraguay	65	65	2·6	2·5	2·8	3·3
Peru	64	53	2·4	1·5	3·5	—
Venezuela	52	38	3·9	0·7	6·3	6·6

As this table indicates, the decline in the *proportion* of the population in rural areas has been very marked in some countries, particularly in Mexico, Chile, Peru and Venezuela, but this has not been sufficient to prevent substantial increases in absolute numbers of rural dwellers, and the investments in urban development that have tended to draw people to the cities have not been matched by commensurate investments to improve rural productivity. The drift to the cities is still the result of the push of rural poverty, and this push has been draining off about half the natural increase of the rural population.

Throughout most of the Latin American region investment is still inadequate to meet the pressure of population growth. This is indicated by the estimated relationship between the trend in gross national product and the trend in population. In almost every country growth in *per capita* income is below the population growth rates. Recent estimates for some of the major countries, based on the population growth rates given in Table 8· 2, are indicated in Table 8. 5.

Table 8.5: Population and Per Capita *Income Growth*[9]

	Annual Increases Per Cent	
	Population Growth	*Per Capita* GNP
Mexico	3·5	2·5
Guatemala	3·3	2·4
Venezuela	3·4	1·7
Colombia	3·0	1·8
Ecuador	3·4	1·3
Peru	3·1	3·3
Brazil	3·0	2·1
Chile	2·4	1·4
Bolivia	2·4	1·9
Argentina	1·6	1·1

While these figures must be accepted with some caution, the gap between the two series is very wide, with only Peru showing a GNP rate matching population increase. There seems little chance of reversing the trend until the very large estates are broken up and utilized more efficiently, until the tiny subsistence farms which are so widespread in Latin America are combined into larger units, and until the millions of landless peasants are given security of employment. Yet, so far, very little change has taken place in the distribution of the land and even where distribution has occurred the basis has often been political. As one commentator has written: 'To raise farm yields substantially, Latin America will nevertheless have to restructure its rural life by one means or another, dragging millions of acres out of the Middle Ages.' Only in this way can Latin America feed the 750,00 new mouths which are added to the population each month.

Some progress has been made by the development of farmers' co-operatives, extension of credit facilities, increased use of fertilizers, the extension of thousands of miles of feeder roads to serve new agricultural areas, crop diversification to relieve national economies from dependence on single commodities, and the introduction of courses in agronomy and animal husbandry in schools and universities. But such investments still fall far below needs and, when matched by educational and housing budgets which are also still inadequate in the face of the high growth rates and young age structures of the populations, they do little to engender a sense of optimism – the more so when to all these can usually be added the unstable political systems within which social and economic reforms must be created.

Investment in rural development can however be only a partial solution to Latin America's problem for, as previously pointed out, the region is already much more highly urbanized than other major 'developing' regions of the world, such as Africa, India or Pakistan. It is also more urbanized than southern Europe, and in most countries the urbanization is highly 'megalo-cephalic', that is with a high proportion of the urban population concentrated in major cities. Around 1960 twenty of the twenty-two Latin American countries for which data were available had more than 60 per cent of their urban population in cities of 100,000 or more people. During 1950–60 Brazil's urban population grew by almost 80 per cent, compared with a national growth of some 37 per cent, and half of Brazil's urban growth of about 13 millions came from rural-urban migration. Similar trends occurred in Mexico over the same decade: the urban population rose by 61 per cent in a national increase of 35 per cent, and in an urban growth of 6·7 millions probably some 2·8 millions came from rural Mexico.

If this 'push' to the cities was the product of high-population growth and inadequate investment in rural productivity, it was not matched by compensating investment in urban areas, for the maldistribution of land and wealth in rural Latin America had its counterpart in urban areas. The *Wall Street Journal* of November 12, 1964, said of the economic boom then evident in Mexican cities:

... underneath these glittering hallmarks of prosperity lies the festering poverty of what many Mexicans call their country's 'second economy', comprising two-thirds of the nation's 39 million people. Like many other developing countries Mexico has built industrial enclaves which are bringing rising incomes to many businessmen and skilled workers, but offer little, if anything, to untrained workers and peasants.

The pace of urbanization has not been matched by a corresponding degree of economic industrialization, so that unemployment and underemployment are as rife amongst the unskilled workers in urban as in rural areas, thus exacerbating a situation in which the ratio of workers to dependants is already low as a result of demographic factors alone. In 1960 only 55 per cent of the population was of 'working age', that is 15–64 years; 42 per cent was under the age of 15 years and 3 per cent over the age of 65 years. This pattern was common throughout most of the region with the exception of the relatively low fertility countries of temperate South America (e.g. Chile and Argentina). The above figures can also be compared with those of the 'developed' region of North America in 1960.

	Percentage of Population	
	North America	Latin America
Under 15 years	31·3	41·7
15–64 years	59·7	55·0
65 years and over	9·0	3·3

In a 'developing' situation, the high 'dependency' ratio is offset to some extent by the use of juvenile employment and sometimes by the high proportion of females employed in agriculture. In Latin America, on the contrary, the economic activity of women is particularly low. Around 1950 only 14 out of 100 females of all ages were economically active, as against 21 in North America and 28 in both Asia and Europe, and this helped to increase the ratio of *inactive* to *active* persons, which was then 1·84 in Latin America compared with 1·35 in Asia and 1·22 in Europe. While these ratios have probably improved in Latin America since then, there is certainly still inefficient use of manpower resources and the problems ahead in the field of manpower employment are only too apparent in the very high ratio of 41·7 juvenile dependants in the 1960 population.

The high proportion of juvenile dependants which, as already indicated, ranged in 1960 between about 42 and 44 per cent of the populations of the countries of Middle America and Tropical South America – compared with only 30 per cent and 26 per cent in the 'low' fertility areas of Argentina and Uruguay – are of course the products of high fertility and declining mortality and especially the saving of infant lives. One factor in the high birth rates illustrated in Table 8. 2 is the high proportion of the fecund female populations, particularly of rural areas, 'exposed to risk' of childbearing. Studies have shown that in at least seven countries of the region consensual unions occur amongst more than 20 per cent of the population aged 15 years and over. The practice is particularly common in rural areas. A high proportion of such unions are thought to be stable, although some studies in the West Indies suggest that they are less so than legal marriages. However, there is no clear evidence that the former are less fertile than the latter, and the combination of consensual unions and legal marriages tends to produce a situation, at least in rural areas, in which high proportions of young women at relatively young ages are potential bearers of children. In addition the fertility of *married* women appears to be high in rural regions. In urban areas, on the other hand, there is considerable evidence of some control over both marriage and fertility.

In Middle and Tropical Latin America census data of 1950 showed that child-women ratios (children aged 0–4 years per 1,000 women aged 15–44 years) were extremely high, ranging from a minimum of 553 in Cuba to a maximum of 798 in the Dominican Republic. In seven out of the ten countries (Costa Rica, Cuba, Chile, El Salvador, Guatemala, Mexico, Nicaragua, Panama, Paraguay, Dominican Republic) examined the ratio exceeded 700. In all the countries, whatever the child-women ratios, there was also a marked difference between rural and urban ratios, with the former ranging between 1·3 and 1·9 times the latter. To some extent the difference might have been attributable to differences in age and sex ratios in rural and urban areas, but where tested by another index (the number of children ever born alive to women by age) the rural-urban differential remained. Examples of such differentials are given in Table 8. 6. This indicates that urban women begin child-bearing later than rural women and that the gap apparent by age 20–24 years has probably been a phenomenon over a considerable period, for the differential is revealed in the older as well as the young age groups.

A factor accounting for the differential may be the tendency for later marriage and lower proportions marrying in cities compared with rural areas. It has already been emphasized that, over all, the proportion of women 'exposed to risk' of child-bearing appears to be high; but surveys carried out in three Latin American cities in 1963–4 (Panama City, Rio de Janeiro and San Jose) indicate that the proportions of young women who were ever married or who were in common-law marriage were comparatively low, thus reducing to comparatively low figures the numbers of live-born children as measured against *all* women (Table 8. 7).

Table 8.6 : *Average Number of Live-born Children to Women in Selected Age Groups*[10]

Age Group	Cuba 1953			Brazil 1950		
	Rural	Urban	Ratio R/U	Rural	Urban	Ratio R/U
20–24	1·26	0·69	1·83	1·28	0·83	1·54
30–34	3·54	1·85	1·91	4·59	2·94	1·56
40–44	4·99	2·68	1·86	6·81	4·43	1·54
45–49	5·41	3·01	1·80	7·27	4·92	1·48

Age Group	Panama 1950			Mexico		
	Rural	Urban	Ratio R/U	Rural	Urban	Ratio R/U
20–24	1·82	1·16	1·57	1·55	1·06	1·46
30–34	4·46	2·56	1·74	4·29	3·47	1·24
40–44	5·40	3·02	1·79	5·69*	4·44*	1·28*
45–49	5·48	3·28	1·67			

* Age group 40–49.

The proportion married legally and otherwise at age 20–24 years may be compared with the proportion of the same age group 'ever married' in the United States of America in 1960 (about 70 per cent) and Australia in 1961 (almost 61 per cent). On the basis of this survey material, early marriage does not seem to be a factor inducing high growth rates in these major cities, but they are probably far from typical of the countries in which they are situated, and they will continue to be fed with population springing from the much higher natural growth rates of rural areas – rates which are the product of both higher proportions married and higher marital fertility. Yet one important finding of the 1963–4 survey of the three cities referred to above was that in each case

Table 8.7 : *Conjugal Status by Age, and Live-Born Children, Three Cities*[11]

	Percentage of Age Group ever Married, including Common-Law Marriage			Average number of Live Births to all Women in each age Group		
	20–24	30–34	40–44	20–24	30–34	40–44
Panama City	59·3	90·9	94·8	1·18	3·48	3·72
Rio de Janeiro	47·2	87·4	96·6	0·69	2·57	3·52
San Jose	51·8	82·5	86·2	1·18	3·22	4·22

over half the women in legal or common law marriage declared that they were or had been using some method to control conception, although to the time of the survey the controls had not proved very efficient. Nevertheless the extent of the practice of control, which was positively correlated with literacy and degree of education, seemed to cut across the religious factor, suggesting that the predominance of Roman Catholicism in the region may no longer be the greatest barrier to the spread of efficient family planning practices.

However, the trend towards more widespread and efficient family planning in major cities cannot be taken as evidence of imminent and major reductions in growth rates: the predominant numbers and high fertility of the rural masses will prevent any rapid decline in national growth rates and, as in so many 'developing' areas, the swollen numbers of young people arising from past falls in mortality and now pressing towards the age of marriage will more than offset the modest declines in marital fertility which may be achieved over the next decade or so. The graph of growth may thus rise above even today's high levels before it can be brought down.

Yet population growth in Latin America is less to be feared than it is in the Asian continent. Densities are still low and the resources to be brought under control are still ample. The problem is not so much resources as the need for stable political systems that can both redistribute their allocation and turn to good account the capital inflows that have been and are likely to continue to be available from North America.[12] There seems no reason why the American continent as a whole cannot carry several times the present population; but it is important that the growth of the Latin American segment be checked to bring population growth into line with its capacity to increase gross national product – a capacity which seems likely to remain restricted because of the relative inefficiency of its political systems. Finally, in the light of the demographic and economic situation now facing Latin America, there seems no reason to believe that international immigration will again assume a significant role in quantitative terms, although it may still be important as a means of supplementing the skills required for economic and social development.

The old theme song of Brazilian history, *falta de bracos*, or lack of hands, now seems strangely inappropriate in a continent made up of countries with annual growth rates climbing to, and even above, 3 per cent and with close on half their populations as young dependants. The earlier concern for lack of hands now seems to be giving way to a concern about too many mouths. The Inter-American Conference in Rio de Janeiro in 1965 emphasized the political and economic problems arising from too rapid population growth. In 1967 the Secretary-General of the Organization of American States saw population as 'the most dynamic – and in all probability the most significant – factor of all those currently affecting the overall development picture in Latin America'. This concern is now being expressed in increasing official attention at national levels to the question of population control. The controlled fertility in major cities, already referred to, and the low-fertility rates already achieved in Argentina and Uruguay, without any official assistance, indicate that effective birth control can occur. Five Latin American countries (Chile, Colombia, Peru, Venezuela, Honduras) now extend official sanction to population control programmes, and there is evidence that the movement is spreading. Despite its late start and the prevalence of Catholicism, Latin America may yet prove to have the greatest potential for the spread of birth control of any of the 'developing' continents, and much of the incentive and know-how for such programmes is likely to come again, as in the case of the public health measures that led to falling mortality, from the United States. The winds of demographic change are beginning to blow strongly over Latin America, but their economies will still have to prepare for a doubling of populations before the end of this century and almost certainly a doubling again before three decades of the twenty-first century have passed. But this is the lucky continent – the resources are there; it is all a matter of organization.

But that is too facile and overlooks the fact that no continent has ever, in all human history, faced demographic forces as explosive as those in Latin America. Whereas the developed regions of the world grew by 40 per cent between 1940 and 1960, Latin America grew by 138 per cent. Over the same period the decline in death rates in some Latin American countries (and notably in Mexico) probably created world records, and almost as remarkable was the pace of urbanization. After citing these facts, J. Mayone Stycos and Jorge Arias[13] perceptively concluded in 1966, that 'the demographer's dream can be the social planner's nightmare', and these authors imply that some of the bad dreams facing the social planners in Latin America are the need to supply over the next fifteen years 28,000 additional hospital beds and 4,800 additional doctors just to keep pace with demographic forces. Haiti, they continue, will require twelve times the number of school places available in 1960 even to enrol 30 per cent of its 15–19-year-old children in 1980. 'Over the past decade in Central America, for every death or retirement from the labour-force there were three or four new job applicants in rural areas and two or three in urban areas. In the next decade additions to the labour-force will be even greater.'

These are the dimensions of social and economic operations that have now to be faced by most of the countries of Latin America. Their scale is unique in terms of their investment requirements and they arise directly from the demographic forces discussed in this chapter. However steeply the fertility graph can be curved downwards in the future, there is no escaping over the next thirty years the consequences of the demographic history of the past thirty years.

Chapter 9

Population Growth in the Developing World: Africa

Difficult though the reconstruction of the population history of most of the 'developing' regions may be, most of them have some data that can form the basis of analyses. In the Indian sub-continent decennial censuses go back a hundred years; in China population counts of one kind and another go back 2,000 years; but over most of Africa darkness prevailed until the twentieth century, and even today there must be as much informed guesswork as fact. Much of the knowledge of tropical Africa in particular is derived from the ingenious manipulation, using sophisticated statistical techniques, of scarce data, particularly those derived from surveys, rather than from reliable censuses or any kind of registration system.

Africa was carved into fragments by the major European powers in the nineteenth and early twentieth-century game of imperial expansion. Whereas in some cases (e.g. British India) imperial intervention led to the introduction of reasonably reliable and regular censuses, this was not generally the case in Africa until well into the present century. As Africa was divided into spheres of influence, economic development by the metropolitan powers gave rise to the necessity for head-counts for purposes of recruiting labour supplies, and as administrative controls were expanded so did the reports on the size and characteristics of the indigenous populations. In some cases periodical estimates of populations were based on tax registers and in others upon essentially impressionistic surveys by officials of commercial corporations or of the colonial authorities.[1] Lorimer emphasizes that 'the so-called censuses of the native population of South Africa, prior to 1936, as well as the official statistics on the population of most countries in tropical Africa prior to the Second World War were of this type'.[2] However the accuracy of most of these data was open to doubt. Carr Saunders,[3] for example, points out that there were 'so-called

198

censuses' in some parts of Africa in the later years of last century (Gambia and Lagos in 1881, and Basutoland and Bechuanaland in 1891) but neither these nor others subsequently taken up to the time he was writing (e.g. Nyasaland in 1911 and Kenya 1921) could be claimed as more than very rough approximations. A report from the Government of Kenya in 1930 stated that little reliance could be placed on the official figures of population which were arrived at largely as a result of the enumeration of huts as a necessary part of the collection of a hut tax. The only firm conclusion from such figures seemed to be that the populations enumerated were increasing.

R. R. Kuczynski, who made the first systematic analysis of the materials relating to British spheres of influence in Africa,[4] commented that thousands of reports submitted as facts that were no more than reasoned guesses, so that many of them had to be dismissed or submitted to further reinterpretation and guesswork – albeit by a most skilful demographer – to yield what seemed reasonable estimates of fertility, mortality, migration and growth rates.

This lack of data makes virtually impossible any reinterpretation of the estimates of the population of Africa before the nineteenth century. In Chapter 3 (Table 3. 1) of this book it was pointed out that J. Beloch attributed a population of 11·5 million to the African colonies of the Roman Empire. The next figure generally accepted in the literature is an African population in the mid-seventeenth century of 100 million, or over 18 per cent of the estimated population of the world (see above, Table 1. 1) compared with only about an estimated 9 per cent by 1960. The figure for 1650 seems extraordinarily high, and it is curious that while the world's total was estimated to have doubled over the next 200 years, most estimates leave Africa's population stationary, or even with a slight decline to 95 million. There seems little reason to assume that the peoples of Africa would have remained stationary for two hundred years while the populations to the east and west were doubling. The factors controlling death would not have been all that different between the major regions of the world over these centuries and there is nothing in our more precise knowledge of current fertility patterns of present-day Africa to warrant an assumption that their fertility was below that of, say, China, India, or the European peoples.

Whatever the early history of the African population, and an advance from around 60 million in 1650 to 120 million in 1920 would seem more reasonable in the light of our current demographic knowledge than a base of 100 million in the earlier year, there is little doubt that the growth rate in Africa is now very high and is likely to go higher to bringing it into line with the other major 'developing' land masses, such as Pakistan, India or Latin America. The figures estimated by the United Nations for the present century give the following progression: 1900 (120 million), 1920 (140 million), 1940 (191 million), 1960 (278 million).

While there is not conclusive evidence in many regions of Africa of the precise levels of fertility, sufficient is known to support the generalization that throughout most of the continent growth rates now exceed 2 per cent a year. For the period 1850–1900 Carr Saunders and Willcox suggested average annual growth rates for the whole continent between 0·5 and 0·7 per cent. Other estimates suggest that the growth rates did not vary greatly over the next thirty to forty years, but that then a steady expansion began, as elsewhere, in response to falling death rates. Rates of 1·3 per cent a year between 1930 and 1950 were estimated by the United Nations, but it was emphasized that 'little reliance . . . can be placed on this estimate and there is some evidence that it is an inflated rate'.[5] There was support for the view that some African communities were still suffering from the factors that were considered to have imposed severe checks upon growth in the nineteenth century, such as intertribal wars, epidemics, exposure to communicable diseases introduced from European penetration of the country, and famines following periodic crop failures. There was also evidence of continuing population decline in some areas, such as French Guinea and Sierra Leone, but by contrast, expanding growth rates were almost certainly occurring elsewhere. In response to improvements in irrigation and immigration, the Egyptian population had begun a steady expansion by the middle of the nineteenth century and between the censuses of 1882 and 1937 is estimated to have increased from 7·6 to 15·9 million – an implied average annual growth rate over the whole period of 1·2 per cent. In Algeria official statistics also showed a population increase from 2·5 million in 1856 to 7·2 million in 1916 – an average annual rate of 1·3 per cent, with an estimated rate from 1931 to 1936 of 2 per cent. It was also estimated that the population of

Tanganyika, after a period of relative stagnation between 1913 and 1921, then leapt ahead with an average annual rate of increase of 2·0 per cent between 1921 and 1948.

In the decade or two preceding the Second World War the broad pattern was that there was fairly substantial evidence of high growth rates in the northern and southern regions of the continent, but with some evidence from the more tropical central regions of sporadic growth at best, and even of stationary and declining situations.[6] The evidence, however, seems fairly clear that over the continent as a whole, the era of expansion had begun. The estimated growth rate for the whole continent in 1960–2 was 2·4 per cent, subdivided into 2·3 per cent for North Africa and 2·5 per cent for sub-Sahara Africa.[7] An examination of age structures of the populations around 1960 also supports the view that in most areas growth rates had been accelerating from quite early in this century.

As far as tropical Africa, south of the Sahara, is concerned, considerable light has been shed on the demographic situation during the last two decades or so by both more complete censuses and extensive use of samples and field surveys. Complete house-to-house censuses had been carried out by 1948 in British East Africa (i.e. Kenya, Tanganyika, Uganda and Zanzibar) and in the Gold Coast (Ghana). The Union of South Africa had also carried out extensive village-to-village enumerations in 1936 and 1946, and by 1950 similar studies had been completed in Angola and Mozambique. Sample surveys were commenced in Southern Rhodesia in 1948 and such methods were to be extensively used during the next decade. Nation-wide demographic sample surveys were carried out in Guinea in 1955–6, in the Congo in 1955–7 and in the Sudan in 1955–6. Subsequently sample surveys were carried out in most French-speaking areas; and in Ghana, East Africa and Gabon sampling inquiries were used to supplement complete enumerations. The only large country today with virtually no information concerning the size and structure of the population is Ethiopia; but the existence of figures in other regions is not in itself sufficient – they must be accurate – and the problem of accuracy was illustrated in the censuses of 1962 and 1963 in Nigeria, which became a demographic *cause célèbre*. The Nigerian census taken in 1962 was officially repudiated as being in part fraudulent. A new census of 1963 suggested a Nigerian population of 55·7 million, compared with only 30 million in 1952–3. The increase is clearly too large and indicates that either the earlier census is an under-count or the later census is inflated – or both, as indeed now seems to be accepted. Such doubts about some of the census materials are all the more serious because of the absence of reliable vital registration systems. Consequently great reliance has still to be placed upon the results of special sample surveys, but again the problem is that while these may be taken as accurate for the populations sampled they cannot strictly be held valid for wider areas. In other words inference at best and speculation at worst is still necessary to try and secure a total picture of tropical Africa.

A review of the situation presented to the First African Popula-tion Conference, held in Ibadan in 1966, indicated that information collected by systematic surveys relating to fertility and mortality was available for about half the population of tropical Africa,[8] and it is from these data rather than the regular censuses (in which age data were usually insufficiently accurate or detailed) that approxi-mate growth rates have been derived.

The most extensive and thorough reconstruction of fertility and mortality rates in tropical Africa has been the work of the Office of Population Research, Princeton University.[9] Working on data produced from some twenty-four censuses or surveys carried out since 1950, Professor Ansley J. Coale and his colleagues have produced estimated birth rates, total fertility rates (i.e. the number of children that would be born during the lifetime of each woman given the age-specific rates at the time of investigation), rates of infant and child mortality, and general death rates, for approxi-mately 110 provinces or other sub-national geographical units. Some illustrative figures are given in Table 9. 1 and the patterns relating to fertility based on the complete results are shown in Figures 9. 1 and 9. 2.

As many of the data for demographic analysis are based on sur-veys which lend themselves more readily to fertility than to mortality estimation, there is more confidence in the estimated birth rates and total fertility than in the levels of infant mortality. Moreover the detailed analysis of sub-national regions which lies behind the illustrative figures of Table 9. 1 indicates a wide variety of fertility and mortality levels within national boundaries. Total fertility rates were estimated to range between 3·5 and over 8; estimates of crude death rates were as low as 15 and as high as 40 per 1,000 of population; infant mortality rates range between less

Table 9.1 : Estimated Fertility and Mortality in Selected Populations of Tropical Africa[10]

Area	Year of Census or Survey	Births per 1,000 of Population	Deaths per 1,000 of Population	Total Fertility per Woman	Infant Deaths per 1,000 live births
West Africa					
Dahomey	1961	49	33	6·4	221
Ghana	1960	50	—	6·5	—
Guinea	1954–55	46	38	5·8	246
Niger	1960	58	29	7·7	211
Portuguese Guinea	1950	37	31	4·8	211
Upper Volta	1960–61	49	36	6·5	270
Central Africa					
Congo	1955–57	45	26	5·9	163
North Cameroon	1960	38	31	4·9	232
Southern Rhodesia	1962	49	—	7·1	—
Zambia	1963	49	—	6·9	—
East Africa					
Burundi	1952–57	46	22	6·4	156
Kenya	1962	48	18	6·8	132
Sudan	1955–56	49	21	7·3	—
Uganda	1959	48	25	6·7	172

than 100 to over 300 per 1,000 live births; and expectations of life at birth fall as low as 30 years and occasionally rise to over 45 years. Coale[11] concludes that even allowing for the margins of error arising from imperfections of the data, '. . . a fair generalization is that mortality in tropical Africa is amongst the highest in the world, although some provinces have already secured the advantages available in modern health techniques'.

The wide variations in fertility are difficult to interpret until much more accurate and extensive data are available. Carr Saunders[12] writing in 1936 commented upon the relatively low birth rates estimated for some regions of tropical Africa and considered that this was 'due to the maintenance of an ancient custom which keeps the family small – the custom of abstaining from intercourse until the child has been weaned'. (Carr Saunders 1936, pp. 302–3.) The soundness of the observation has since been confirmed, though it must be emphasized that while the practice of

Figure 9.1 : Natural Increase Rates

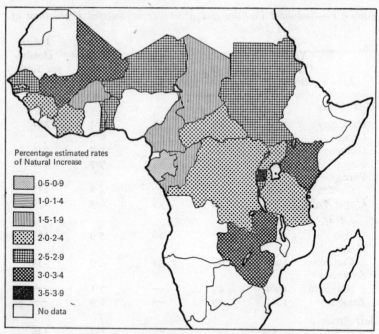

Source : J.C. Caldwell, C. Okonjo (eds.) *The Population of Tropical Africa* Longmans, London, 1968.

prolonged lactation may prevent very high fertility it is not in itself sufficient to bring about low fertility. Carr Saunders also considered that the areas of high birth rates tended to be found in areas where tribal organization, and therefore tribal practices inhibiting large families, had been disrupted. In support of this view he referred to high birth rates, over 50 per 1,000, in Capetown and Port Elizabeth; but he also considered that such an upsurge of very high fertility was not likely to be a permanent phenomenon, adding that 'some observers are of the opinion that the native women, who have no religious motives for desiring a large family and are of a realistic turn of mind, will rapidly adopt the practice of family limitation'. 'Indeed,' he continues, 'an observer in Nigeria says that some native women are now limiting their families by means of abortion, and are doing so not because they are following an ancient custom but for the same sort of reason that leads to family limitation in Europe.'

The existing state of data, better though it is than when he was writing, does not enable Carr Saunders's arguments to be thoroughly tested. Certainly there are few areas in which birth control

Figure 9.2 : Total Fertility* Rates

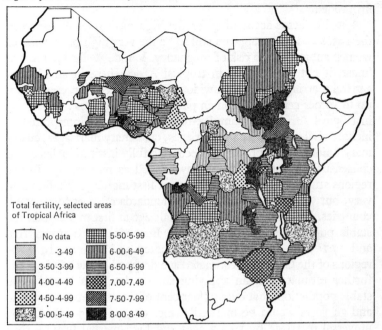

Total fertility, selected areas of Tropical Africa

No data	5·50-5·99
-3·49	6·00-6·49
3·50-3·99	6·50-6·99
4·00-4·49	7.00-7.49
4·50-4·99	7·50-7·99
5·00-5·49	8·00-8·49

Source : J.C. Caldwell, C. Okonjo (eds.) *The Population of Tropical Africa* Longmans, London, 1968.

* 'Total fertility' is the number of children that would be born during the lifetime of each woman experiencing the current fertility rates.

in the 'Western' sense of the small family unit is yet accepted. Caldwell found some tendency in Ghana for urban families to be some 10 per cent smaller than rural families, but among the urban élite, who might be expected to be the first to accept birth control, the most commonly desired family size was still between four and six children.[13] The forces likely to encourage lower birth rates were still relatively weak: marriage tended still to be accepted as the 'natural' state; the cost of rearing children in an urban and literate environment was the subject of comment but was not felt to be a significant factor encouraging birth control; the impact of mortality decline upon the survival rate of children was also noted but again was not felt to be a strong reason for limiting births. In short, if contacts with European influences had created an upsurge of fertility, as Carr Saunders suggested in 1936, there was still not much evidence from research in Ghana a

205

generation later that motivations for birth control had yet found firm roots.

A major factor accounting for the high birth rates of Africa in the 1950s and 1960s appears still to be the very high proportion of women subject to the risk of pregnancy. Van de Walle[14] notes that 'most, if not all, cultures in tropical Africa share in an ideal of general marriage – although widows and divorcees represent often up to 50 per cent of all women past childbearing ages'. 'Marriage' in tropical Africa is a complex term and must be interpreted to include civil and Christian marriages, customary marriages, customary unions in the process of becoming fully institutionalized and consensual unions, and polygamy as well as monogamy. In the regions studied by van de Walle age at first marriage was found to vary, but was still very low by the standards of most 'developed' countries. He estimated that the female age at first marriage in the stable population was 19·4 years in Burundi, but between 16·0 and 17·1 years in the Congo, Dahomey and Guinea. In some regions of the Congo the estimated age dropped below 16 years. He further estimated, again applying survey data to a hypothetical stable population, that over 95 per cent of women between ages 20 and 34 years would be married[15] (loc. cit., pp. 205–28). Almost universal marriage by young ages and high marital fertility thus appear to be the main factors in the high growth rates of tropical Africa. Polygamy was not a factor, for on the whole the age-specific fertility rates of monogamous unions was higher than among those in which husbands had two or more wives.

While the studies presented by the Princeton group show considerable variations region by region, the general pattern of tropical Africa is one of very high average fertility rates, high growth rates generally exceeding 2 per cent a year, and a potential for a considerable expansion of growth rates because of still relatively high death-rates. Coale concludes:[16]

The variations in fertility . . . should not be allowed to convey a false impression that the average fertility of tropical Africa is anything other than very high. The birth rate of all of the population analysed is about 49 per 1,000 and total fertility for tropical Africa is probably about 6·1–6·2 children (per woman). Only Latin America from Mexico to Peru and Brazil has fertility approximately this high. These extremely high-fertility rates are combined with mortality that also is amongst the highest in the world. The recent experience of other developing areas

206

suggests that tropical Africa is in the early phase of rapidly accelerating population growth. In some areas . . . the rate of natural increase has apparently already reached about 3 per cent per annum. . . . tropical Africa is now beginning to encounter the whole range of new problems that other developing countries know very well – the barriers to social and economic progress that come with extremely rapid population increase.

The areas discussed so far in this chapter, designated as 'tropical' Africa were estimated by the United Nations to have a population of 189·3 million in 1960 or almost double the estimate of 96·8 million in 1920[17] (UN *World Population Prospects . . . 1963*, p. 201). But both to the north and to the south of these regions equally rapid growth rates are to be found. Between 1920 and 1960, northern Africa (United Arab Republic, Sudan, Morocco, Algeria, Tunisia, Libya. Spanish North Africa, Spanish Sahara and Ifni) was estimated to have grown from 35·1 to 66·0 millions in a steadily expanding decennial progression of growth rising from 11·5 in 1920–30 to 25·4 in 1950–60.[18] Details of these growth rates are not very accurately known, for neither censuses nor vital registration systems are yet considered wholly reliable and there have been few surveys of the type alluded to in the regions of tropical Africa. However there is little doubt that like tropical Africa, northern Africa also ranks high on the world's growth chart. Table 9. 2 provides the most recent estimates published by the United Nations.

Table 9.2 : Estimated Populations and Birth, Death and Natural Increase Rates per 1,000, Northern Africa[19]

Country	Estimated Population in 1965	Year of Estimate	Rates per 1,000 of Population		
			Births	Deaths	Natural Increase
United Arab Republic	29,600,000	1966	41·2	15·8	25·4
Sudan	13,540,000	1955	51·7	18·5	33·2
Morocco	13,323,000	1962	46·1	18·7	27·4
Algeria	11,923,000	1963	48·2	10·0	38·2
Tunisia	4,360,000	1966	45·2	10·7	34·5
Libya	1,617,000	1964	25·1	4·1	21·0
Spanish North Africa	158,000	1966	17·3	6·7	10·6
Spanish Sahara	48,000	1965	14·0	4·0	10·0
Ifni	52,000	1960	35·4	12·1	23·3
	74,621,000				

The low birth and death rates of the small countries are almost certainly in error, but they have little effect on the average of the whole region, which was estimated to have in 1966 a total birth rate of 45, a death rate of 19 and a natural increase rate of 26 per 1,000 of population. Throughout most of the region mortality rates still appear to be relatively high, although in most countries specific measurement is extremely difficult because of faulty data. UN estimates suggest an average expectation of life from birth for the whole region in 1950–60 of 42·5 years, but there have been sufficient signs of improvement in mortality to suggest that by the 1960s the expectation exceeded 45 years.

Thus in northern Africa the demographic picture is dominated by the high growth rates of the most populous countries of the region, the majority of which probably have annual rates exceeding 3 per cent. With scope for extensive improvements in mortality, the potential of growth is still considerably higher than current rates, unless effective fertility control can be rapidly introduced. North Africa must therefore be added to tropical Africa both as currently one of the world's most rapidly growing regions and as one of the regions with potential for raising growth rates even higher in the near future.

Turning to southern Africa, comprising (and with an estimated population in 1960 of): South Africa (15,822,000), Basutoland (685,000), South West Africa (522,000), Bechuanaland (330,000) and Swaziland (260,000) (total 17,619,000), the picture is one of very high fertility rates amongst the non-European peoples of the region, but a 'Westernized' demographic pattern amongst the European populations of the Republic of South Africa. The lowest *growth* rates of the region since the 1920s were found in Basutoland and Bechuanaland, but to a considerable extent this was probably the result rather of out-migration than of low fertility. Over the region as a whole growth rates have considerably exceeded 2 per cent and the growth pattern has been dominated by the Republic of South Africa which in 1965 was estimated to contain 17,867,000 of the total population of 20,104,000 in the whole region.

The demographic history of the economically and politically dominant group of the Republic of South Africa, that is those of European stock, can be traced with some certainty over the past century. A census of 1865 enumerated more than 350,000 Europeans in South Africa. A high rate of natural increase and a steady

Table 9.3 : *Estimated Populations and Birth, Death and Natural Increase Rates, Southern Africa* [20]

| | Estimated Population in 1965 | Rates per 1,000 of Population | | |
		Year of Estimate	Births	Deaths	Natural Increase
South Africa	17,867,000				
Bantu Population	12,185,000	1950–55	46·0	8·1	37·9
Asian Population	533,000	1966	33·9	7·7	26·2
White Population	3,398,000	1966	22·8	8·6	14·2
Coloured Population	1,751,000	1966	45·6	14·2	31·4
South West Africa	574,000	1964			
Coloured Population		1964	57·3	15·2	42·1
White Population		1964	23·0	6·9	16·1
Basutoland	740,000				
Bechuanaland	559,000				
Swaziland	364,000				
	20,104,000				

inflow of immigrants raised the figure to 1,276,000 in 1911 when the first census was taken in the new Union of South Africa. Since then the annual growth rate has averaged about 1·8 per cent, with a range between about 2·24 in 1921 and 1·60 in 1946. With expectations of life at birth of 64·6 for men and 70·1 for women reached as early as 1950–2, the European population has been in the forefront of the 'healthy' populations of the world. Their fertility has also conformed broadly with those populations, with a birth rate below 30 per 1,000 since 1911–15. The birth rate did not fall in the 1930s as it did in so many other 'Western' countries, but remained around 25. This level was sustained until 1961, after which the European birth rate declined slightly to 23 in 1965. Thus the Europeans of South Africa come well within the small family pattern of developed, industrialized countries, but among these they have been in the higher fertility group. With a total fertility rate around 3·5 children born per woman by the end of her childbearing years, and with the low levels of mortality prevailing, Europeans in South Africa still show a substantial natural increase and a female net reproduction rate exceeding 1·5. Few European populations equal this, but their growth rate is far outweighed today by the other elements of the population of South Africa. The growth rate for South Africa as a whole is estimated to be around 2·4 per cent and this derives primarily from the high-fertility patterns of all the non-European groups, among some of whom mortality patterns still seem to be comparatively high, thus leaving a potential for even more rapid rates of increase in the future. For example, the infant mortality rate was estimated in 1958 to be 132 per 1,000 live births for the coloured population and 68 per 1,000 for the Asiatic population of South Africa, compared with only 29·4 for the Europeans.[21]

In his study of the major components of the population of South Africa to 1946, L. T. Badenhorst[22] emphasizes that, despite their high fertility, the growth rates of non-European peoples were still held back by the end of the period by high mortality. This was particularly true for the coloured population and, despite the paucity of data, almost certainly for the Bantus. Until then only the Asiatics had benefited clearly from mortality decline. In 1950–2 their expectation of life at birth was approximately 55 years for both men and women, compared with only 45 for coloured men and 40 for coloured women. In projecting into the future, Baden-horst allowed for substantial mortality declines, but even so his figures fall a considerable way short of the UN estimated populations for the components of South Africa in 1965. The full discrepancies appear to arise from Badenhorst's underestimate of fertility and immigration in the case of Europeans, and from even higher fertility and more sharply declining mortality than he estimated for the non-European components, for the period 1946–65 (Table 9. 4).

The rates of increase shown in Table 9. 4 up to 1947 now appear to have been substantially exceeded in the cases of the Bantu and Coloured populations. Amongst the latter, birth rates averaging between 44 and 48 per 1,000 have been consistently recorded, whereas crude death rates fell from an average of 21·3 per 1,000 in 1945–9 to 15·8 per 1,000 in 1960. For the indigenous Bantu peoples no vital statistics are available, but estimates of fertility and mortality derived from census data using reverse-survival methods, yield a gross reproduction rate 1950–5 of 3·0, compared with 3·2 for the Coloureds and only 1·8 for the Europeans. The Bantu growth rate was still being substantially reduced by high mortality, with the expectation of life estimated to be still only

Table 9.4: Growth of Component Populations of South Africa 1904–65[23]

	Europeans	Coloured	Asiatics	Native
Estimated Population 1904	1,116,806	445,228	122,734	3,491,056
Estimated Annual Growth Rates				
1904–11	1·91	2·41	3·12	2·03
1911–21	1·76	0·37*	0·86*	1·57*
1921–36	1·86	2·32	1·90	2·29
1936–46	1·71	1·89	2·65	1·69
Population in 1946	2,372,690	928,484	285,260	7,805,515
Badenhorst's projected population for 1965	3,166,500	1,452,400	515,700	10,977,600
UN estimated population 1965	3,398,000	1,751,000	533,000	12,185,000

* The low rates here were probably partly due to the inroads of the influenza epidemic following the First World War.

about 40 years around 1951, and about 46 years by 1960. Thus while the birth and death rates attributed to the Bantus in Table 9.3 can be accepted as only very rough approximations, and while the derived rate of natural increase may be an overestimate because of deficiencies in registration, particularly of deaths, such evidence as does exist all points to a very high rate of growth indeed, and with the age distribution to be expected from continuing high fertility and falling mortality a natural growth rate exceeding 3 per cent would not be an unreasonable expectation. In addition the native populations have been augmented in the last two decades or so by immigration from neighbouring African states. The higher economic growth rate in South Africa has apparently proved a 'pull' factor sufficient to outweigh the 'push' of apartheid.

The only non-European group of South Africa which may move towards controlled fertility patterns in the near future appear to be the Asiatics. Their birth rates fell from 38·5 in 1945–9 to 31·5 in 1955–9, but then rose again to 35·4 per 1,000 in 1960, with a subsequent decline again to an estimated 33·9 in 1966 (Table 9.3). Their main advantage from the point of view of growth is their already low and still improving death rates. A growth rate well in excess of 2 per cent a year seems assured for some way ahead, but their future numbers are likely to depend wholly on natural increase, without the supplement of immigration, and their growth will almost certainly be exceeded by that of the Coloured population with their still very high birth rates and apparently quite rapidly improving death rates (Table 9.3). Again, apartheid, whatever its long-term objective, does not appear to be hampering the acceleration of growth rates amongst the Coloured population. Moreover the policy gives the Coloureds an identity which helps to determine their increasing role in the demographic scene of South Africa, whereas previously miscegenation was tending to blur that image and to leave a considerable part of that increase to fade into the European population.

In 1950, Badenhorst[24] wrote that a reasonable expectation based on contemporary trends was that during the following thirty years to 1980 the Bantu population would increase by three-quarters, the Coloured population would double, and the Asiatic population would increase by 150 per cent, whereas the European population would increase by less than half. His projections for the non-European population are likely to be exceeded as far as the Bantu and Coloured populations are concerned, but the Asiatic growth rate may be coming down faster than Badenhorst anticipated. Nevertheless his general proposition that the European population will be a declining proportion of the total population of South Africa seems inevitable. His anticipated changes in proportions between 1946 and 1980 were:

	1946	1980
European	20·8	17·8
Bantu	68·5	68·8
Coloured	8·2	9·5
Asiatics	2·5	3·9

Immigration based upon apartheid, and therefore limited to settlers of European stock, is certainly not likely to give the European population a total growth rate for the rest of this century equal to the natural increase alone of the non-European population.

Thus Africa remains a continent in which no nation has a low rate of growth, in which most nations are already increasing at rates which will double their populations within thirty years, and in which the potential for future growth is likely to continue to increase as a result of very high fertility and very considerable room for further and quite rapid declines in mortality. Few African countries, with Egypt as a major exception, are yet pressing against subsistence limits in terms of food resources or land. Densities are still low. The danger is less a scarcity of land and food than political fragmentation within frameworks of nationalistic fervour that will prevent the substantial flows of labour that have been a feature of Africa since the Second World War. The current tragic struggle between the Nigerians and Biafrans illustrates this point.

Finally it must be again emphasized that the figures presented and discussed in this chapter cannot be accepted as better than approximations, for almost nowhere in Africa can censuses be accepted as accurate and in few areas are there satisfactory vital registration systems. Nevertheless information that can now be pieced together from intercensal analyses and surveys all convey pictures of growth that establish Africa as one of the most – and possibly *the* most – rapidly growing major regions of the world. There is no reason to believe that the rates assessed by the United Nations for five major sub-regions of Africa since 1960, and sum-

Table 9.5 : *Estimated Mid-Year Population and Annual Rates of Growth, Major Regions of Africa*[25]

Region	Density per Sq. Kilometre	Estimated Population in Millions			Annual Rates per 1,000 of Population		
	1967	1940	1960	1967	Births	Deaths	Natural Increase
Western Africa	17	58	88	104	51	27	24
Eastern Africa	14	54	77	90	44	20	24
Northern Africa	9	44	66	79	45	19	26
Middle Africa	5	23	29	34	42	23	19
Southern Africa	8	12	18	21	40	16	24
All Africa	11	191	278	328	46	22	24

marized in Table 9.5, are in any way excessive. Nor is it improbable that some of these rates may approach an annual average of 3 per cent before they turn down, for the African does not feel the pressures on resources that are so severe in the Indian sub-continent. On the other hand, as in the Indian sub-continent, what are still felt to be the necessary preconditions of demographic transition (e.g. literacy and rising expectations of living associated with the spread of a cash economy) are not yet much in evidence throughout most of central and northern Africa. Yet the speed with which changes can come should not be underestimated. Despite apartheid, the exposure of the Bantu to industrial economic developments in South Africa is equipping him with new sets of values concerning the role of the family in society. Mauritius (with a birth rate in 1967 of only about 30 per 1,000 compared with over 40 in 1963) may also be one straw in the wind to indicate once again how a society can draw back from the brink of demographic disaster when the Malthusian pressures are really applied. Another sign of potential change may be the falling birth rate of the Asiatics in South Africa. However, most of Africa is still far removed from the pressures that have applied to Mauritius in recent years, and the traditions of tribalism are still probably more powerful influences inhibiting change than are the innovations associated with urbanization and industrialization as agents of change. Straws in the wind though there may be, as was suggested above by the illustration of Mauritius and the Asians in South Africa, the full cycle anticipated by Carr Saunders in the 1930s (of a release of rapid growth among African tribes as contact with European influences broke down traditional practices of inhibiting fertility, followed again by new forms of control) has not yet generally appeared. Indeed it is not yet clear that the first phase, of expanding growth rates, has yet been completed among most African societies.

Chapter 10

Population Policies and the State: From Expansion to Control

Throughout most of man's recorded history conscious efforts have been made to attain some balance between the quantity and quality of population and the environment in which he has lived. He has endeavoured to attain that balance in two ways: first, by increasing the supply of foodstuffs and other materials necessary for the maintenance of life, and second, by rites and customs designed to check human fecundity. At most times his command of the resources of nature has been so tenuous that he has not been able to free himself from the devastation of famine and disease, and seldom has he been confident enough of his powers to control his social environment to relax his conscious control of the reproductive power of the human species, through customs relating to marriage (e.g. endogamy, monogamy), and the birth and survival of children (e.g. infanticide).

The nature of these controls has varied according to prevailing conditions, but seldom, if ever, have the controls been the result of a scientific investigation to determine the end which they should serve. Generally they have been applied in the belief that they would maximize the material well-being of a given community, that they would maintain the *status quo*, or that they would help to provide security, at least for the dominant class. Utopian plans have at times been made to provide a complete integration between demographic and environmental factors. Plato, for example, planned what he considered to be an ideal social environment and then proceeded to outline demographic controls to fit his scheme. He visualized a community with a constant population of 5,040 citizens; at most forty or fifty thousand people in all, including slaves and children; in which the government should control the age of marriage for men and women, the persons who should mate, and the number of children who should be born.[1] Much later, Sir Thomas More's *Utopia* postulated the same notion of a community with a constant population, in which no city should contain more than 6,000 persons and in which no family should have fewer than ten or more than sixteen children. More suggested that there could be no determined number of children at my age, but the balance of the size of families would be kept by removing some of the children of fruitful couples to those who did not abound in them. In like manner, the size of cities would be controlled, some of the people from those which bred rapidly being removed to those which bred slowly. If the whole Commonwealth bred too rapidly, emigration was to be resorted to.

Plato's abstract theories dealing with the functions of the state in regard to population were essentially a reflection of measures that had already been adopted. In actual practice the Greek City-State, even idealized Sparta, had none of the precision of Plato's plan, but the approach to the population question was similar. The City-State was considered to be the most satisfactory socio-political unit and population was to be regulated to fit that unit. When wars took their toll of young men, early marriage was to be urged by the State and bachelors were to be subject to legal and political disabilities; in times of peace late marriages and emigration were to be encouraged. Infanticide was seen, and frequently resorted to, as a eugenic device to preserve quality. The City-State was a work of art, in which the balance between demographic and environmental factors was to be maintained by law.

The Greeks came nearer to a scientific plan to control population than any other civilized people, either before or after them. After them, the emphasis was upon expansion rather than upon stability of numbers, and frequently the aim was security. The Emperor Augustus of Rome, who was probably more concerned with the maintenance of the Senatorial families than with the increase of the people of the Empire as a whole, decreed that men and women must be married and have children before the men attained the age of 25 and the women 20. The partners of sterile marriages were liable to penalty, and those of prolific marriages were to be the recipients of state honours and privileges. But these measures did little to change the social environment of Rome, which (as the writings of Polybius indicate) had been unfavourable to procreation for more than a century before Augustus took action. For this reason the Augustan legislation proved of little avail. The ruling classes of Rome, bent upon the pursuit of luxury, were in no mood to be bound by the bills of pains and penalties devised by their Emperor.

With the Romans there was not the same attempt as with the Greeks to identify population policy with environmental factors. The same is true of the later history of Europe in Christian times. Expansionist policies were encouraged when it was considered that more manpower would increase the security of the state or nation, or after some catastrophe had severely reduced numbers. Thus, after the Thirty Years War, which is believed to have reduced the population of the German Empire by a third, German literature contains many works which emphasize the need for greater populations. The rise of nation-states, which were struggling for political and economic supremacy in Europe in the sixteenth and seventeenth centuries, also encouraged the adoption of measures to increase population. Population growth was but part of the general theory of expansion in both the commercial and industrial fields which was a fundamental tenet of the mercantile system. But again there was no scientific basis for these views regarding population, and in general the Roman view was accepted that the number of people could be increased by a system of bribes to the fecund and penalties to the sterile.

A good example of the bribes and penalties theory was the edict of Colbert in 1666 in France, by which persons liable to taxation would be exempted from all taxes until their twenty-sixth birthday if they married by age 20. Those marrying at 21 years of age were to receive tax exemption until their twenty-fifth birthday, and so on. Fathers who had ten living legitimate children, provided none of them were priests or nuns, were to be exempt from all taxes and public charges for life. Further, to ensure the maintenance of the nobility who were considered essential to the support of the crown and the power of the State, nobles with ten living legitimate children were to receive an annual pension of 1,000 livres a year, while those with twelve children were to receive twice this amount. Half of these amounts were to be paid to bourgeois inhabitants of free cities who had the requisite number of living legitimate children. So few of the nobility applied for pensions that the funds were offered in 1667 to all subjects without distinction of class, and in 1683 the measure was withdrawn altogether, partly because it was feared that it would encourage marriages between Protestant and Catholic.

Later, in 1767, Maria Theresa was also concerned to expand the influence of her empire. She attempted to encourage offspring amongst her soldiers by permitting them to marry and by granting an endowment for each legitimate child. Measures similar to those of Colbert were also applied in Savoy and Lorraine.

Nevertheless, this expansionist view did not imply unlimited growth. The states which encouraged population expansion also accepted as fundamental certain tenets of the Christian religion, which discouraged bastardy and polygamous marriages, and which were in other ways probably as restrictive in their effects as the Christian condemnation of infanticide and abortion was expansionist. Furthermore, celibacy of the clergy withdrew considerable numbers in France and Spain from the position of family heads; but throughout the sixteenth and seventeenth centuries, the Western world still had such a slender control over the resources of the land on the one hand, and disease on the other, that the mortality rate was still a restrictive force potent enough to offset any expansionist policy. As was emphasized in earlier chapters, birth rates in Europe at this time never reached the potential of *fecundity*, but provided evidence of a degree of control not commonly found in today's 'underdeveloped' areas, or even in many 'developed' areas, mainly through relatively late marriage and the failure of 10 to 15 per cent of females to marry at all.

In the eighteenth century, moreover, the contention that the rights of princes were synonymous with the rights of men was being challenged. The Physiocrats of France began to question the wisdom of uncontrolled population increase, and to point out that Europe was becoming so densely populated that people would soon tend to be pressing against the available food supplies. In 1750 in the United States, Benjamin Franklin also postulated the theory that Europe was almost fully peopled and would increase but slowly thereafter because of the limit of subsistence.

These ideas were the forerunners of important attempts to find a law of population, by which the relationship between man's demographic condition and his material environment could be scientifically explained. The idea that population could continue to increase indefinitely, or that uncontrolled increase would add to the sum total of human happiness, was rejected. The controlling factor, it was considered, was food supply, since the amount of land that could ultimately be brought into production for any community was fixed. This factor must ultimately control the size of the population, for beyond a certain point the law of diminishing returns would begin to operate with regard to agriculture, and people would die from malnutrition and disease, or else check their numbers by other methods, such as restraint from marriage. But whether the check that was applied was of the former kind, i.e. positive, or of the latter kind, i.e. negative, a check must occur because of the pressure of numbers upon available resources.

Thomas Malthus argued along these lines in his *Essay on the Principles of Population*, the first edition of which was published in 1798. Malthus considered that population tended to increase faster than the available food supply. Increased production alone would merely encourage a more than proportionate increase in population. This, to Malthus, was setting the tortoise to catch the hare, and the only way out was to persuade the hare to go to sleep in order that the tortoise should have some chance of overtaking her. In other words, population was to be proportioned to the food supply, and the method he advocated to achieve this end was 'moral restraint'. The scientific and industrial advances of the nineteenth century produced very different results in England, and in the Western world generally, from those postulated by Malthus. The application of scientific techniques to agricultural and industrial production, the development in transport and communication and the opening up of virgin lands in the new world all helped to dispel the Malthusian bogy of pressure of numbers against subsistence and to enable England and other countries to carry populations far in excess of the capacity of the metropolitan country to feed them. Malthus can hardly be blamed for not anticipating these developments. To the demographer and the sociologist, however, Malthus's work constitutes an important advance in technique, despite the author's errors in judgement and his dependence for his basic ideas upon his immediate predecessors, such as Sussmilch, David Hume and Adam Smith, for it denotes an attempt to analyse in detail man's reactions to his environment. In this respect Malthus is a pioneer in the field of human ecology.[2]

Malthus set the style in population theory for half a century, and the most important theories in England during the first half of the nineteenth century followed his lead in the search for a 'natural' law. Later theorists, however, were less pessimistic than Malthus about the pressure of numbers upon resources. Sadler, for example, postulated in 1829 that the fecundity of human beings under similar circumstances varies inversely as their numbers on a given space.[3] This implied a self-regulating mechanism which would prevent overpopulation in the Malthusian sense. Eighteen years later, Thomas Doubleday put forward a similar theory, with emphasis upon material living standards rather than upon density. He considered that there was a constant increase among those who were worst supplied with food, and a decrease among those who lived in a state of affluence, so that in a nation which was poor population would increase, and in one that was 'highly and generally affluent and luxurious' population would decrease and decay. Herbert Spencer carried the search for a natural law a stage further in 1867 when he foresaw the disappearance of population pressure and its accompanying evils as the result of the decreasing fecundity, which would occur as a greater proportion of the individual's energy was used in personal development.

In the twentieth century Corrado Gini[4] rounded off these natural theories by stating that in the process of the rise and fall of nations there is a 'cyclical rise and fall of population'. In its youth a nation displays a high fertility; with increasing numbers, pressure of population begins to be felt, and expansion takes place through war or colonization, or both. Thus, Gini considered, the most energetic section of the population is lost, and of those who remain, the upper classes become relatively sterile as the socio-economic organization becomes increasingly complex, so that the decline in the rate of growth which follows from these factors is the result of a decrease in fecundity, rather than in fertility. Gini was concerned to use both history and demographic data to support Mussolini's Fascist theories of expansion, which required for their success the demise of the world's existing empires, and notably British power in Africa.

The concern of the modern nation-state, as it evolved through the eighteenth and nineteenth centuries, to ensure its own perpetuation was to become a matter of increasing concern in the twentieth century when the decline of the birth rate reached the point where, it was felt, national extinction was the inevitable outcome. As already emphasized, most western European countries had net reproduction rates below unity in the 1930s. In addition, increasing concern was felt about the effect of emigration as an additional drain upon the human resources of the nations of the 'Old World'.

Even in the 1860s and 1870s Bismarck's Germany had discouraged emigration. In 1907 the Imperial Conference of British Countries was also informed that Britain could not afford more than 300,000 emigrants a year because of the falling birth rate. This note was to run through almost every subsequent official inquiry in regard to emigration, at least until the Second World War.

Yet state action had not attained the welfarist outlook that was to come in the 1930s, and where measures to influence the birth rate had been attempted, these were sporadic and had on the whole little support from governments. The nearest approach to a 'pro-natalist' policy was in France, where the birth rate had been low since the beginning of the nineteenth century. In 1860 French naval ratings were granted small child endowments of ten centimes a day. The whole principle of supplementing wages according to the number of dependants was carried a step further when a number of French industrialists applied family allowances to wages in 1891 – a measure which received the support of Pope Leo XIII in his encyclical *De Rerum Novarum*. The system gradually expanded, until by 1914 some thirty leading French industrialists were paying allowances. In addition allowances were then paid by governmental authorities to many lower-income groups.

To some extent the concern in France was matched by thinking in Japan. After the restoration of the Meiji in 1867 measures were taken to stamp out abortion and infanticide, both of which had been common measures of control in the earlier nineteenth and in the eighteenth centuries. Infanticide was classed as murder and imprisonment was decreed for abortion. A number of societies also established funds for paying subsidies to parents on the birth of children.

The advocacy of cash supplements for raising families received a further impetus in France through the works and writings of Dr J. Bertillon and Paul Leroy-Beaulieu between approximately 1890 and 1913. Bertillon founded the '*Alliance Nationale pour l'accroisse-ment de la population française*', a body which was designed both to undertake demographic research and to publicize the dangers of population decline. The society was responsible for establishing an extra-parliamentary commission on population decline in 1902, two years before a Royal Commission reported in the State of New South Wales, Australia, on the decline of the birth rate and the mortality of infants.

Bertillon[5] considered that measures directed towards changing marriage age, changing moral codes or reducing sterility would have little effect on the birth rate. Instead he wanted a steeply graduated system of taxation in favour of parents with children, with complete exemption for those with four children, together with the reservation of the most honorific government posts for members of families of three or more children, an additional vote for married persons, family cash allowances for second and subsequent children, and the suppression of neo-Malthusianism.

Not until after the First World War, however, did the French government institute a family policy along the lines advocated by Bertillon and others, but in the meantime employers were extending the system of additional cash payments to workers with young children. The danger that employers would attempt to cut costs by employing only single persons was minimized by establishing equalization funds out of which all employers belonging to a fund would draw the necessary cash bonuses. These funds were developed in two forms – one covering workers over a wide area in a single occupation, and the other covering a wide range of occupations in a concentrated administrative area.

In 1932 the State gave legal recognition to the system and moved to extend it to cover all industries and occupations. The system was to be extended gradually to ease the burden on industry. But as the birth rate continued to fall concern deepened, and in July 1939 a decree was passed which aimed at improving the well-being of French families to such an extent that it would make the rearing of families an economic possibility. This was the famous *French Code de la Famille*, which gave legislative sanction to many of the ideas of Bertillon and his *Alliance Nationale*.

The provisions of the *Code* were complicated and have been amply explained elsewhere.[6] The main provisions were cash payments for the mother who remained at home to care for her children, and graduated cash allowances which initially were fixed at 10 per cent of the departmental wage for the second child and 20 per cent for each subsequent child. In 1941 this was raised to 50 per cent for the fourth and each subsequent child. Provisions for home assistance for families, subsidized holidays, heavy penalties for practising abortion, and official banning of the sale of contraceptives all added up to a formidable array of legal sanctions and prohibitions in favour of the family. The solid base of the whole scheme remained however the cash family allowances financed by levies on employers and employees, with the state subsidizing for independent workers.

The French worker with four dependent children in 1947 could more than double the basic wage of the Department of the Seine. After the Second World War the amounts of the allowances were at first adjusted as the basic wage was adjusted, but with galloping inflation after 1949 it was felt that this policy was adding to the cost spiral and allowances were pegged to a fixed wage of 10,000 francs a month and the value of the endowments were gradually reduced as a proportion of income. After 1947 contributions for the payment of allowances were also collected by the Social Security Funds, from which the allowances were thereafter paid, thus replacing the administration of the separate family allowance funds.

The French *Family Code* represents the most elaborate attempt by any west European democratic government to arrange its total wage structure according to family needs. The protagonists of the scheme were at pains after the war to attribute the post-war rise in the birth rate to it. Proof of this is difficult, and while the rise in fertility after the war was proportionally greater in France than in any other western European country, one reason was that the rise occurred from a base that was probably the lowest in Europe before the war. In any case the rise was more than equalled in a number of countries outside Europe which had no such elaborate family allowance system (e.g. USA). Nor was France free from the widespread decline in fertility which occurred after about 1960. The French birth rate fell from 23·5 per 1,000 in 1960 to 18·2 in 1963, and again to 16·8 in 1967.

The French system tied endowments to wages and made industry pay. By contrast, pre-war Germany and Italy adopted a thoroughgoing system of state cash bonuses.[7] In Nazi Germany after 1933 birth-control clinics were shut down (although there was no specific measure to prohibit contraception); marriage loans of up to 1,000 RM were payable to those of Aryan stock and of sound health, with the loan repayable over a period of eight years, but with a quarter of the original amount cancelled on the birth of each child. After 1935 special grants of up to 100 RM per child and a maximum of 1,000 RM were payable to couples who satisfied the authorities as to their racial purity and eugenic potential, for the purchase of rural properties; free medical services were also available for expectant mothers and small children. All these cash grants were paid once only, but in addition regular family allowances were also paid. These had been in operation in Germany as far back as 1920 and were financed through equalization funds, much as in France. But for the most part they covered only higher income groups, and in 1936 government allowances were instituted to cover low-income groups with large families. In 1938 these were greatly extended and were made payable for the third instead of the fifth child. In addition, the Germans subsidized holidays, graduated tax in favour of the family, and after 1939 lavished medals on mothers of more than four children.

Again, how far all these measures were responsible for the substantial rise in the German birth rate from 14·7 to 20·3 between 1933 and 1939, is difficult to say; but the German measures did go a considerable way to assist young couples in the business of acquiring a home and rearing children. The undesirable aspect was the association of the whole movement with the campaign for 'Lebensraum' and with the Nazi theories of Aryan superiority.

Germany at least was a low fertility country before the war, which was perhaps the main justification for a pro-natalist policy. On the other hand, the USSR, with an estimated birth rate of over 44 and a rate of natural increase of 23 per 1,000 at the outbreak of the Second World War, had also developed an elaborate system of incentives towards procreation. These may have been encouraged by the knowledge that birth rates were falling quite rapidly in the larger Russian cities. For example, as early as 1926–7 Moscow and the four chief cities of the Ukraine had an average fertility that was barely at replacement level. At this time there were many permissible avenues, including abortion, to family limitation; but in 1936 stern discipline and a thorough-going pro-natalist system were applied. This differed from French and German policies in that a basic aim was not to encourage the mother to return to the home and withdraw from employment, but to help her remain in employment without hardship. Increased social insurance was allocated to employed mothers for the care of infants; maternity leave for a period of sixteen weeks was granted to employed mothers; annual allowances for mothers of six or more children were instituted to the tune of 2,000 roubles a year for five years for each child from the sixth to the tenth, and thereafter for the eleventh and each subsequent child a single grant of 5,000 roubles was made at birth, with 3,000 roubles annually for the next four years. Kindergartens and child-care centres were extended in cities and at places of employment; divorce laws were tightened and abortions were declared illegal except for therapeutic reasons.[8]

The whole trend towards a pro-natalist policy was given a further emphasis in an edict of the Supreme Soviet of 8 July 1944, which instituted greatly extended maternity and child allowances as well as honorific medals and titles to the mothers of large families. The following schedule sets out the position.

Schedule A

Roubles				Birth Order					
	3	4	5	6	7	8	9	10	11 +
Single Grant	400	1,300	1,700	2,000	2,500	2,500	3,500	3,500	5,000
Annual Allowance, paid for 5 years until payment for child of higher order comes into effect		960	1,440	1,680	2,400	2,400	3,300	3,000	3,600
Medals	—	—	2nd class	1st class	Order of Glory 3rd class	Order of Glory 2nd class	Order of Glory 1st class	Order of Mother Heroine Gold Medal & Scroll	

Such measures, together with liberal allowances for unmarried mothers and their children and also widows, and a rapid programme of extending nursery schools and medical services for mothers and infants marked Soviet intention before the Second World War as a determined effort to recognize the family as a basic unit of Soviet social organization. A great deal has been achieved in these aspects of their social policy since then, but if the intention was pro-natalist, the results have scarcely been fruitful, because in 1962 the birth rate of the Soviet Union was estimated at about 22 per 1,000, and in 1967, 17·5 per 1,000, compared with over 40 in 1939. On the other hand, the Soviet suffered grievous casualties during the war, which would greatly reduce the birth rate without any change in marital fertility; but the fall of the crude birth rate over the past two decades or so is too steep to be attributed to war casualties or other changes in the population profile. Doubtless the Soviet pro-natalist campaign after 1944 was in fact an attempt to 'replace' a generation lost in war, but that hope has now gone. The Soviet pattern seems to be one of 'Westernization' in birth rates and family-size patterns.

While the policies outlined have received much publicity as 'pro-natalist' measures, they may well be viewed as part of the development of the welfare state which had other basic motivations than an alteration of family size. Indeed the whole trend from the institution of old-age pensions in the late nineteenth century to the almost universal post-war institution of cash child endowment schemes in the European world has almost certainly had an effect upon the birth rate, but whether *upwards* or *downwards* cannot be proven. One high-income country with perhaps the most comprehensive system of social security in the world, New Zealand,[9] appeared to be leading the race of western countries in procreation, with a birth rate in 1960 around 27 per 1,000. Yet by contrast, another, Sweden, with a system of social security (from which the Labour government which initiated the New Zealand scheme appears to have borrowed a great deal, particularly in regard to its medical scheme) almost as comprehensive and in many ways more consciously directed towards the needs of the family,[10] apparently reaped little of the post-war baby boom and had a birth rate in 1960 under 14 per 1,000. Similarly, England, in which the scheme of security 'from the cradle to the grave' was introduced by Sir William Beveridge[11] experienced only a modest increase in the birth rate (17·2 in 1960) after the war. Furthermore, the return of relative prosperity – and indeed in many countries, the most affluent conditions ever known – have been marked by a widespread decline in birth rates, in the manner indicated in Table 10.1.

It would appear therefore that special 'pro-natalist' measures by the State have not had any marked effect on fertility. On the other hand the comprehensive social welfare systems that have developed throughout most countries of Europe and Europe overseas have had a considerable effect in redistributing incomes in favour of the parents of young children – not merely family allowances, but maternity services, socialized medical and health services for children, State education, school meals, and so on,

Table 10.1 : Crude Birth Rates, Selected Countries 1960 and 1967[12]

Country	Live Births per 1,000 of Population	
	1960	1967
Ireland	21·4	21·1
United Kingdom	17·5	17·4
Switzerland	17·6	17·7
France	17·9	16·8
Sweden	13·7	15·5
USSR	21·2 (1963)	17·5
Canada	26·7	18·0
USA	23·7	17·9
Australia	22·4	19·5
New Zealand	26·5	22·4

These 'free' or 'subsidized' services constitute real benefits to the extent to which they represent a transfer of benefits to the family at the cost of other sectors of the community. Again, however, precise measurement of the demographic effectiveness of these social services is not possible. Until 1961 the American might well have argued that the relatively high birth rate of the USA, around 23 and 24 per 1,000 during the previous fifteen years, was the demographic reaction to prosperous free enterprise, not socialized welfarism; but with the birth rate down below 18 by 1967, that argument also becomes difficult to sustain.

Positive action by States to alter the course of fertility seems therefore to have been of little significance and the change from high to low and controlled fertility must be explained on other grounds. The classical explanation of demographers is 'transition theory' – sometimes referred to by the cynics as demography's only theory – which was formulated in the 1940s. It is not so much a theory, in the sense that it has identified crucial variables in a manner that gives precise understanding of the nature of demographic processes in all places at all times, as an attempt to provide a generalized explanation of the historical experience of Western countries which have moved from the phase of high fertility and high mortality to low fertility and low mortality. The essential element of the theory is the evidence that the process of modernization from an agricultural and rural society towards industrial and urban society lowered mortality which, when accompanied by the impact of such forces as growing individualism and rising

227

levels of personal aspiration, engendered further controls over fertility. As mortality fell, growth rates expanded until fertility control began to reduce the gap between births and deaths. The final phase was the return of low growth rates through controlled fertility in which family size became a highly rational decision, implemented essentially by effective contraceptives and restraint within marriage, without the need to resort to crude Malthusian controls of famine or disease, and was determined by attitudinal changes based on cultural, social psychological and economic factors.

The theory has been increasingly attacked, partly by accumulating historical evidence that indicates many exceptions and variants to the generalized model, and partly because both past and contemporary events have shown that fertility can be changed before the process of industrialization and modernization (accompanied, for example, by a high degree of literacy) takes hold on a society. Historically the theory best describes the processes of demographic change in north-west Europe and Great Britain, but it does not fit the cases of the United States, France or Ireland. The birth rate in the United States showed a declining trend very early in the nineteenth century, but the decline was from a level above 50 per 1,000 before 1830 (which was very much higher than in any north-western European country) to about 35 per 1,000 in 1860 (which was very similar to the western European pattern). As Coale and Zelnik[13] have pointed out, the very high birth rate of the United States of America in the early nineteenth century, compared with European countries, was largely due to the very favourable age composition of the former; an advantage that remained with the USA until about 1870. Other factors were probably the very high proportions of women marrying, early marriage and abundant land and food. However, the decline in the birth rate between 1800 and 1870 was due more to a decline in fertility, associated with higher age at marriage, than to changes in age composition, and Coale and Zelnik again emphasize that by about 1870 total fertility of the United States was lower relative to European experience than was its crude birth rate. In fact in the late nineteenth century, only France had clearly lower fertility than the United States.

In France the decline in fertility appears to have begun even before the French Revolution and by 1830 the birth rate was already below 30 per 1,000. The decline continued steadily and was already below 19 before the First World War. The decline was clearly not associated with 'industrialization' or 'modernization', but may have been, as J. J. Spengler suggests, because of the lack of it, in the sense that social expectations and attitudes changed without commensurate increase in real income.[14] It has also been suggested that a major factor was Napoleon's 'Code Civil' which decreed that a man could dispose freely of only from a quarter to a third of his estate, according to the number of his children – a code that made the large family a severe threat to financial security, especially when the absence of 'modernization' processes did not develop alternative avenues of livelihood. Consequently as rational beings, the French peasantry reduced family size, and in this they found considerable support from the élite of the day. For example, as early as 1851 the Académie Française offered a prize for an essay on the theme that a country was fortunate when *'la sagesse publique et privée'* united to prevent rapid population growth.

In Ireland the factors encouraging restriction of family size may have been similar, that is lack of available land for settlement and absence of alternative employment opportunities, and here the response was essentially celibacy and advanced age at marriage, as well as massive emigration.[15]

While these processes in the USA, France and Ireland virtually contradict demographic transition theory, and while there is other evidence from parish records and other studies to show that birth rates showed declining trends long before the processes of 'modernization' began, the theory does stand in relation to the evolution of societies which *industrialized*, that is in which the majority of the workers earned their livelihood in non-agricultural pursuits and in which the majority of the population lived in towns and cities. Just when the process of 'modernization' (or, to use the more general appellation, of 'industrial revolution') began in each country or area is difficult to determine; but in terms of demographic processes this is less important than the end product of industrial and urban society as defined above. While historians can still find wide variations in birth and death rates in studies of small communities in pre-industrial Europe or America, and while contemporary scholars can still find pockets of extremely high fertility (e.g. the Hutterites of South Dakota, Montana and Canada, with birth rates still probably over 45 per 1,000 and, because they enjoy the extremely favourable health standards of North America, a very low mortality which leaves a growth rate around 4 per cent), the main feature of transition theory remains: no industrialized society has, in the aggregate, sustained pre-industrial levels of fertility.

Now, 'industrialization' is itself a term as generalized as 'transition theory', but it encapsulates a whole range of social, cultural and economic processes that have revolutionized social organization: the shift from subsistence to wage labour, labour mobility, urbanization, the dominance of the nucleated family of parents and children, protection of children from the labour market, compulsory education, literacy, the growth of the nation-state as the boundary within which the lives of people are organized and protected. The list could be extended, and an index of almost any one or any combination of the above factors could be fixed at a point of time which might be taken as the essential dividing line between the 'large family' system and the 'small family' system; but for demographers the change in mortality patterns is still probably the most satisfactory index. While there are some cases, already alluded to, of fertility decline before there was a marked fall in mortality, the more important fact is that among large aggregates of populations forming nation-states there are no cases among European societies of fertility holding up when expectations of life have climbed from the pre-industrial levels of the mid-forties or less to the post-industrial levels of the mid-fifties and more.

An important corollary of this proposition is that, among European societies, once the decline of the birth rate has become associated with the 'modernization' processes referred to above, there are no instances in which the rate was held up above 30, and many cases where it has settled below 20 per 1,000 of population. Completed family size has dropped from something over five to three or fewer children ever born. The forces of change that accompanied the evolution of European societies as nation-states were much more powerful than any measures that the State occasionally attempted to devise to change the demographic drift to controlled fertility. The more advanced the industrial process, the more people turned from the eternal train of reproduction to devote their energies to other aspects of life – European peoples as a whole began to introduce into their private lives what Professor J. A. Schumpeter once aptly called 'a sort of inarticulate system of cost accounting'.[16] The most articulate aspect of the system may well have been the growing realization that the cost of rearing children was rising and that once born, children were expected to live, not to die.

Causal explanation of the emergence of the small-family system of European societies must be in terms of such matters as the transformation of social institutions, economic standards and attitudes and not in techniques of birth control. Today, when the contraceptive pill tends to be accepted as a revolutionary breakthrough – a sort of industrial revolution of contraception – which can begin the process of demographic transition amongst today's high growth, non-European countries, it is well to re-emphasize the fact that the lowest birth rates recorded in history were among European societies at the height of the economic depression of the 1930s, long before the 'pill', or indeed any sudden technological advance in the art of birth control. This was amply illustrated in the Report of the United Kingdom Royal Commission on Population 1949.[17]

The desire to enjoy the pleasures of the sexual act without always accepting its consequences has long been present in human societies.[18] Five different papyri, all dating from between 1900 and 1100 BC, provide recipes for contraceptive preparations to be used in the female vulva. The Book of Genesis provides the story of Onan who practised *coitus interruptus* – or onanism – which indicates that the practice was known to the Hebrews. There is also evidence that Hebrew women knew how to make and use simple pessaries. The writings of Polybius suggest that several forms of birth control were quite widely practised in Rome from the second century BC. Throughout the ages many vile concoctions have been taken orally in the belief that they would impair fecundity. Some of the least disgusting of these refer to hot drinks made from the bark of trees, particularly the willow, yolk of egg, foam from the camel's mouth and saffron. Even within the last two decades there have been reports of a Chinese recipe of swallowing twenty-four live tadpoles within three or four days after menstruation.[19] In the ancient world and in pre-literate societies many crude methods were also used to prevent conception or a live birth, such as expelling semen following intercourse, jumping from heights and massage or placing hot stones on the belly to destroy and expel the foetus.

The Christian religion emphasized ascetism as the moral approach to sexual control: abstinence before marriage, restraint from marriage, and both faithfulness and self-control within marriage.[20] The 'quiver full of arrows' was essentially Old Testament, and moral restraint essentially New Testament doctrine. At the end of the eighteenth century Thomas Malthus was still preaching moral restraint as the only alternative to vice and misery as a check on the tendency of populations to outstrip the means of subsistence. As indicated in earlier chapters, in eastern and northern Europe at least, Malthusian restraint from marriage was one important factor of control; marriage occurred at a relatively late age and frequently 15 per cent of women did not marry at all. The incentive to practise moral restraint was strengthened by the stern teachings of the medieval church; there was probably less contraceptive knowledge among medieval Europeans than among the ancient Hebrews or Egyptians. As emphasized earlier these restraints appear to have been remarkably constant for two or three centuries until the revolutionary change towards younger and universal marriage which became apparent in many 'developed' countries about thirty years ago.

Among European peoples a break with medieval doctrine was becoming apparent by the early nineteenth century.[21] This coincided with the steady and continued growth in the populations of west and northern Europe referred to earlier in this book – not a 'population explosion' as we now envisage the situation in many of the present 'developing' countries, where growth rates are often as high as 3 per cent a year, but a steady growth of 0·5 per cent or so arising from the high fertility of marriages and from the absence of the disastrous waves of killing diseases, such as plague, which had periodically decimated populations in earlier times. But population pressure in the Malthusian sense was probably much less important than the economic, social and cultural revolutions which were sweeping Europe in the late eighteenth and early nineteenth centuries: the beginnings of the industrial revolution; the challenge to traditional beliefs and practices; the overthrow of authoritarian regimes.

In England, in terms of marriage and the family, the main challenge to tradition came from the writings of Francis Place whose *Some Illustrations of the Principles of Population*, published in 1822, openly advocated birth control. His views were supported by influential liberal writers and thinkers of the time. Place also organized the distribution of a series of handbills in which he recommended the sponge as a contraceptive – a method already being used quite extensively in France. Publicity in favour of contraception reached its peak when Mrs Annie Besant and Charles Bradlaugh formed the Freethought Publishing Company and republished Charles Knowlton's *Fruits of Philosophy*, an American book advocating birth control which had first been published in England in 1834 and which had remained in circulation until 1876.[22]

The new edition was countered by the arrest of Charles Bradlaugh and Annie Besant, but between their arrest and trial three months later, 125,000 copies of the *Fruits of Philosophy* were sold, compared with an annual average of about 700 over the previous forty years. The trial, the sentence of guilty and Annie Besant's and Bradlaugh's subsequent successful appeal, followed by the publication in 1877 of the former's new book, *The Law of Population* and the foundation of branches of the Malthusian League throughout the country, gave a tremendous impetus to the birth-control movement. It has been estimated that over a million tracts giving contraceptive advice and information were sold in England between 1876 and 1891.

The influence of these events should not be overrated. In other countries without the stimulus of a Besant-Bradlaugh trial, birth control was spreading and there is fairly clear evidence that a widening range of contraceptive devices were being increasingly resorted to long before the mid-1870s. The insertion of the sponge and other occlusive devices into the vagina was known to be practised in France early in the nineteenth century. The condom or male sheath made its first appearance in the eighteenth century in England. Douches had long been advertised in the name of 'feminine hygiene'. A diaphragm device was invented by a German physician about 1880. The addition to these in the twentieth century of a wide range of spermicidal jellies and creams further increased the efficiency of contraceptive practices. But the age-old method of ornanism or *coitus interruptus* remained a very significant factor until at least the 1930s.[23]

The birth-control movement was not limited to Europe but was equally apparent in the remoter countries peopled by Europeans. An analysis of the vital rates of marriages in Australia and New Zealand indicates that birth control was also spreading in the antipodes in the late nineteenth century. T. A. Coghlan, in *The Decline of the Birth Rate of New South Wales* (Sydney 1903) gave the following figures of legitimate births per 1,000 married women under the age of 45 years:

	1881	1891	1901
New South Wales	336	289	235
Victoria	298	298	229
Queensland	316	328	254
New Zealand	312	276	246

This decline is of particular interest to the history of birth control because it created such great public concern that in 1904 the government of the State of New South Wales appointed a Royal Commission to study the whole matter[24] – the first such Commission ever appointed in the English-speaking world. The Commission (on the Decline of the Birth Rate and on the Mortality of infants in NSW) confirmed Coghlan's findings that the decline was essentially the result of fewer issue to marriages, rather than of changing age composition or changing proportions marrying. It rejected the view that there was any physiological tendency towards lessened fecundity – a theory held by Herbert Spencer who considered that the increasing number of flat-chested girls of higher education were unable to bear a well-developed infant. Attributing the decline of the birth rate essentially to selfishness, associated with a love of luxury and of social pleasures, the Commissioners addressed harsh words to their fellow New South Welshmen:

... The practices involved in the limitation of families are responsible for much physical suffering, for a deadening of moral sensibility, and for a degradation of character among those who resort to them; and these efforts must have an unwholesome influence on the general character of the people who move in an atmosphere so vitiated. Defective health, defective morals, and defective character are already manifesting themselves as a warning of more marked deterioration likely to ensue ...

Precisely what control methods were used in New South Wales and other antipodean colonies at that time, or since, are not known, but many were no doubt acquainted with Annie Besant's methods. In 1879 her Malthusian League had already six subscriptions from ladies in Wanganui, New Zealand, which was then about the southern limit of European settlement! Sydney ladies were unlikely to be less sophisticated. Medical and clerical statements before the

Royal Commission provided fairly ample evidence of the existence of a wide range of birth-control practices. Apart from 'certain rubber goods' which were stopped at the Customs House for a period prior to 1891 because they were classed as 'indecent and obscene', there was no prohibition on the import or manufacture in the country of birth-control appliances, which were stocked by the majority of druggists, both in the city and in country towns. These articles were also hawked from house to house, generally by women attired as nurses. For those who could not secure preventives and abortifacients by these means, numerous midwives, nurses and keepers of lying-in homes and a few medical practitioners were apparently willing to oblige. The evidence before the Commission also indicated that advertisements referring to birth control, 'all objectionable in regard to their patent or latent indecency', appeared freely in newspapers, books and pamphlets of the time. The spread of birth-control literature emanating particularly from the English Neo-Malthusians, was encouraged by a decision of the Full Court of New South Wales in 1888 which sanctioned its publication in the colony. The withdrawal of the sanction again in 1902 did nothing to alter the steady decline in the Australian birth rate, which was already down to about 27 compared with 35 in the early 1880s. Birth control, by whatever method, had clearly arrived to stay in Australia, with considerable effect, sixty years before the contraceptive pill.[25]

The New South Wales Commission also implied that abortions were frequently used to restrict family size. There is ample evidence that abortion has been a very common method of control in many countries going through the demographic transition. Abortions in France were estimated to be as high as 35 or 40 per cent of all conceptions at the end of the nineteenth century, and to be more common than live births in large French towns in 1937. The abortions in Germany after 1918 were placed at between 800,000 and a million a year; a rate comparable with the estimate for French towns in 1937 or of Japan in the 1950s.[26] Studies covering recent years in eastern Europe, where all countries except Albania and East Germany have adopted legislation permitting interruption of pregnancies on very broadly interpreted social indicators, reveal that the numbers of abortions are universally high. In the case of Hungary they have greatly exceeded the number of live births. Consider the figures of Table 10. 2.

Table 10.2 : *Estimated Abortions and Live Births in Selected European Countries*[27] (Figures in thousands)

	Legal abortions	Other abortions	Live births
Hungary (1962)	164	34	131
Bulgaria (1961)	69	20	138
Czechoslovakia (1962)	90	26	217
Poland (1962)	140	70	595
Yugoslavia (1960)	95	62	430

The 'legalizing' of abortions in these countries, in Japan in the 1950s and earlier in the Soviet Union, has generally been undertaken to control a social evil rather than to encourage its spread. It is a recognition of a very widespread practice, and in the case of Japan in particular, its legal recognition is the basis for encouraging other, more socially and medically desirable forms of family planning.

Theoretically, the incidence of abortion could be expected to decline as populations become sophisticated in other methods of control; but the practice of abortion still appears to be very common in all low birth-rate countries. With improvements in medical science and skills it has become relatively safe, even when practised illegally, and is therefore more acceptable than it was in the more 'primitive' times of the nineteenth century, but even when risks of death were high, there seems no doubt that abortion was one of the most widespread methods of preventing live births among many European societies.

The sophistication of western peoples with regard to other methods, whether in Europe or abroad, should not be overrated. In the United Kingdom, for example, an investigation conducted in 1946–7 under the auspices of the Royal College of Obstetricians and Gynaecologists into the contraceptive practices of a national sample of 3,281 women, revealed that among marriages of fewer than seven years duration, 55 per cent of couples had practised contraception and that amongst the contraceptors no less than 43 per cent used *coitus interruptus* only and 57 per cent used appliance methods. An insignificant proportion used the rhythm method.[28]

A United States sample of 2,713 white women taken in 1955 revealed a rather different pattern.[29] Among marriages of less than five years' duration, 65 per cent of couples had practised contraception, and among these 77 per cent used appliance methods, 20 per cent relied on rhythm and only 2 per cent used only *coitus interruptus*. The significance of rhythm in the United States of America compared with the United Kingdom may be substantially accounted for by the higher proportion of Roman Catholics in the United States of America and the interval of ten years between the surveys – years in which much attention was given to research relating to the efficient use of the rhythm method.

The statistics quoted above refer only to the marriages of short duration and therefore still within the years of family formation. When the entire sample is considered, the proportions who had practised contraception are considerably higher. In the United States sample 70 per cent of all couples and 83 per cent of fecund couples had used contraceptives. Jews and Protestants showed the highest usage rate, but among Catholics, 57 per cent of all couples and almost 70 per cent of fecund couples also used contraception, and just over half of the users relied on methods other than rhythm. The majority of the United States couples practising contraception relied on a combination of methods rather than a single method, but some appear to have felt the risk of unwanted pregnancies too great, for a proportion of women – perhaps as high as one in ten – had resorted to sterilization. A recent estimate[30] puts the number of sterilizations among living Americans as high as 1,500,000, and the current number of sterilizations around 100,000 a year, 40 per cent of such operations being on men and 60 per cent on women. Assuming that each of these operations prevents one birth each year, this rate of sterilization would be reducing the annual number of births in the United States by about 14 per cent; but, of course, this is almost certainly not the case because those sterilized would tend to be contraceptors anyway, for whom sterilization had probably become the preferred method.

The findings of some major studies which have been given above emphasize the extent to which contraception has been successfully practised in societies which are now industrialized and highly literate long before the contraceptive pill came on to the market; but they also emphasize that the motivations for fertility control have been so strong among these societies that quite a considerable proportion of women have been prepared to resort to quite drastic measures, such as abortion or sterilization, to prevent unwanted live births. One might reasonably expect that these more drastic, and medically and socially less desirable forms of control might diminish as more 'civilized' methods become widely available.

The illustrations of the nature of controls of the pre-pill era also make it fairly obvious that considerable proportions of the populations of some 'advanced' countries have been practising family planning in defiance of religious doctrine of the time. Before about the 1930s this was the case with all the major branches of the Christian religion. For example, the 1908 Lambeth Conference of the Church of England condemned artificial contraception in all forms. By 1930 this church was weakening, and qualified approval was given. At subsequent meetings the area of approval widened until in 1958 the Lambeth Conference urged responsible parenthood as a duty, meaning by this that the responsible use of birth-control aids within wedlock was approved but that their use outside wedlock for promiscuous purposes was condemned. There seems little doubt now that among those professing Protestant faiths the practice of birth control was quite extensive before the churches officially moved on the matter. An analysis of family size in western European countries suggests strongly that fairly effective birth control was also being practised by at least some Catholics. In Ireland adherence to the Malthusian precept of moral restraint was an important element; Irish men and women married late and high proportions did not marry at all; but changes in marriage patterns were not important elements in the scene in most other countries of falling birth rates.

In Australia, in which about one-fifth of the population was Catholic, the size of completed families, that is the number of children born to women by age 45–9, fell from about five children in 1911 to four children in 1921, and then sharply to an average size of only 2·43 children by 1947. Protestants appear to have led the decline, but the difference appears to have been fairly consistent over the previous twenty-five or so years when the declines in Catholic and non-Catholic families were following parallel curves.[31] All this strongly suggests that Catholics in Australia were behaving much like Catholics in the United States of America and that many couples were practising birth control by onanism or by mechanical methods, for it is now known that the knowledge at that time of rhythm and other methods associated with feminine hygiene were insufficient to have produced such a substantial result.

Doctors had speculated for centuries about the possibility of a sterile period in women and by the late nineteenth century sufficient was known for some use to be made of this period for contraceptive purposes; but it was not until 1930, when Dr Ogino of Japan and Dr Knaus of Austria, working independently, published the results of their researches, that the use of the 'safe' period, or the 'rhythm' method received serious consideration as a means of limiting pregnancies. Both Ogino and Knaus indicated the same method of calculating the length of the sterile or safe period. For example, in a woman whose menstrual periods vary between twenty-five and thirty-one days, the estimated *minimum* period when abstension from intercourse would be necessary in order to avoid the risk of pregnancy would be from the seventh to the twentieth day after the onset of her last menstruation. Irregularities amongst different women and also in each woman over time make a precise determination of each month's safe period difficult. This problem may be partially overcome by studying variations in body temperature. It has been found that immediately after ovulation a woman's body temperature will rise by about 0·3, or 0·4 of a degree and remain at the higher level until a day or two before menstruation and the 'safe' period is estimated to begin the second day after the temperature rise.

While the method as it is now understood can be a significant aid to family planning, and probably fairly effective by itself when used with couples in which the woman has regular menstrual cycles and in which a reasonable degree of moral restraint is practised – that is abstinence for a fortnight each month – its 'safety' is clearly much less than most other pre-pill methods. Studies based on the experience of couples in metropolitan areas of America in 1957[32] suggested that rhythm was not much more effective than douching and had less than half the contraceptive efficiency of condoms or diaphragms.

In terms of permitting effective methods of family planning, the official position of the Roman Catholic Church has not moved substantially since St Thomas Aquinas and St Augustine held contraception in any form to be sinful. Indeed, as has been pointed out, no Christian faith officially moved far from that position until the twentieth century. After about 1850 some leading Catholic theologians argued in favour of permitting the use of the sterile period provided the intrinsic nature of the sexual act (i.e. the

239

begetting of children) was preserved. Some were even prepared to argue that the coital act was an act of love as well as of procreation. Pope Pius XI accepted this philosophy. With this virtual legitimizing of the use of the safe period the Roman Catholic Church appeared to be leading religious reform in the matter of family planning; but the famous 1930 encyclical of Pope Pius XI on Christian Marriage – *Casti Connubii* – seemed to cast the official position back towards the Augustian-Thomist approach, by which any use of marriage to deprive the sexual act of its natural power of procreating life is held to violate the law of God and nature: '. . . since therefore the conjugal act is destined primarily by nature for the begetting of children, those who in exercising it deliberately frustrate its natural power and purpose, sin against nature and commit a deed which is shameful and intrinsically vicious.'[33]

Casti Connubii did not however clearly exclude rhythm, and again there was considerable support for the recognition of the due place of personal as well as procreative aspects of marriage, e.g. its role as an expression of love between the partners.[34] In 1951 Pope Pius XII clarified the Church's position in an address to the Italian Catholic Union of Midwives. Family planning by moral restraint and by 'proper' use of the rhythm method was recognized; the only dispute with non-Catholics remained the means to be employed. Rhythm was now open to Catholics as an aid to family planning, but there had to be serious reason for its employment – such as medical, eugenic, economic, social – and in no case was it to be used to the limit where it avoided the primary duty and very meaning of married life, the conservation of the human race.[35]

Recently the pressure on the Roman Catholic Church has gone further; influential groups of Roman Catholics have declared in favour of further liberalizing of official views, and particularly of recognizing the pill; but officially, the Church will not cross this threshold. The Pope's statement in April 1967 makes one major admission – the clear recognition of the need for population control – but control must be by adherence to the moral law recognized by the Church; and this still excludes the 'pill' as well as all mechanical contraceptive devices. Pope Paul VI's encyclical of July 1968, *Humanae Vitae*, confirmed this view.

There seems little point in searching for a single cause of the demographic transition in that section of the world called 'developed'. There is no single cause: the trend to the small-family system has been but one part of the economic, social and cultural revolution which clearly separates modern developed societies from any societies that have existed before. Parallels may of course be found: the senatorial classes of Augustus's Rome had central heating and practised birth control; but there were few parallels in their social structure and that of Rome today. The masses were still illiterate; death rates were high and expectations of life below those of most of the underdeveloped countries of the present time. The things that mark off present 'developed' society from all other times are universal literacy, metropolitan and urban living, economic affluence within capitalist systems with a vast range of consumer durables available to all but a minority, and above all unique standards of health and life expectancies and virtually universal birth control in all social and economic classes. While the small-family system preceded the development of urbanized industrial society in some cases (e.g. France and Ireland), the remarkable feature of the present world is the similarity of the demographic pattern that now prevails over virtually the whole of Europe, the USSR, and overseas countries peopled by Europeans. Yet this change occurred in the face of opposition from the Christian religion and traditional social and moral sanctions, and seems to have been scarcely affected by the attempts of the State deliberately to encourage larger families, or to redistribute national income as a matter of social justice in favour of the family. The establishment of the small-family system has also cut right across political systems; both the Marxist and Leninist which denied that there was any general law of population and argued that under communism productivity could always outstrip population growth, and mercantilist-capitalist society which believed that continued population growth was a desirable aid to economic development.

Transition theory remains a generalized yet reasonable framework for a *post hoc* explanation of the experience of today's industrial and urbanized societies and does not conflict with more precise explanations in terms of the influence of urbanization or social mobility – or as Dumont[36] conceived it, social capillarity. But those who criticize the theory because it does not appear to be fitting the events of today's 'developing' world are surely assuming that there is a similarity between the world of the twentieth century and that of the nineteenth and eighteenth centuries. In fact, however, the situation is about as different as it could be.

Consider the economic aspect. As Dr Gunnar Myrdal has pointed out, income per head in India in the 1950s was only about a third or a fifth of what it was when today's high-income, developed countries started out on the process of economic growth a hundred years and more ago. As he observed, the latter could 'rise as small islands in an ocean of underdeveloped peoples. . . . Now it is instead the whole "outside world" which is rising and craving for economic development'.[37] Yet none of the great populous Asian countries appeared to have improved its *per capita* income in real terms in the fifteen years following the Second World War. Indeed it is only in the last decade that distinct and apparently steadily rising incomes appear to have taken hold in some of the small Asian countries, such as Taiwan, Hong Kong, Malaysia and Thailand. On the whole, however, investment has been inadequate to raise productive capacity above the rates of population growth which range between 2 and 3 per cent a year.

To the economic problems must be added the problem of mass-illiteracy, the reluctance to change engendered by religious dogma and traditional social customs, and of course the sheer quantity of people to be motivated by a single political system in countries like India, Pakistan or Mainland China.

The situation of the developing countries has generally been painted in these gloomy terms, with the conclusion that until industrialization takes hold, until ignorance gives way to literacy and until religious and customary constraints against social change are weakened, control of the rate of population growth cannot occur in the developing world. In support of such a conclusion the statistic of *per capita* incomes is frequently quoted: if this does not move upwards the conclusion is drawn that no change is occurring throughout society as a whole.

Yet changes of tremendous magnitude and force have clearly been occurring since the Second World War. The first has been the attainment of political independence; another is the application of radio and now television as channels of mass communication which can be used to inculcate new ideas in the minds of the masses without the need for literacy; a third is the improvement that has occurred in agricultural productivity with particular reference to new strains of food grains; a fourth is the increasing mobility of the populations, albeit over short distances and by such simple methods as the bicycle, which also extends the interchange of information and ideas. But more important than all of these is the growing concern of governments themselves, who increasingly want to reverse the phasing of the European demographic transition by first controlling population growth as an aid to economic development instead of treating economic development as the *sine qua non* of controlled fertility. Coupled with this in importance is the growing realization that not only does there appear to be virtually no *serious* opposition to the spread of birth control in any non-Christian religion, but that wherever surveys have been made to test attitudes (and these probably exceed thirty by now) the result has almost always been a large majority of women in favour of limiting family size.[38] This desire was undoubtedly present among a high proportion of European women in the nineteenth century but was seldom made explicit. J. S. Mill, for example, considered that the family was rarely large by the woman's desire; and Queen Victoria herself, writing to her uncle, the King of the Belgians, in 1841, pointed to the very great inconvenience and hardship of a large family: 'Men never think, at least seldom think, what a hard task it is for us women to go through this (childbirth) *very often*.'[39] The Royal Commission in New South Wales in 1904 also noted and disapproved of the desire of women to reduce family size.

In short, despite the outwardly static nature of societies throughout much of the 'developing' world, despite the limited progress of education, and despite the overwhelming preponderance of agriculture in the livelihood of the masses, the climate for the spread of birth control is probably more propitious today in most countries of the ECAFE region than it was in late nineteenth-century Europe; and, perhaps the most significant aspect of all, the situation has been improving so rapidly with regard to mortality – particularly infant and child mortality – that many of these countries are already at the point reached by European countries only thirty to forty years ago. Many of these countries have been adding two or three years to their life span for every five years that elapse, compared with one in five years in Western countries in the nineteenth century. As was emphasized earlier, a number of them have already attained expectations of life at birth of 60 years or more and there is no case yet of a society which, having attained this, has not matched it with a marked fall in fertility. It will be suggested later that many of the small Asian countries may be at, or have already passed this threshold. The prospects in the land masses of Africa and tropical Latin America are more difficult to assess.

The final factor in favour of the rapid spread of birth control among today's developing nations is the public conscience of the developed world. This may have something of the characteristics of a Lady Bountiful – charity for the poor relations – and has been examined with some suspicion on occasions in developing countries on the ground that the developed countries want to exhort birth control in their own interests, i.e. to lower growth rates to prevent, say, Asians or Africans out-breeding the white peoples. Fortunately this suspicion seems to have been buried and, increasingly, developing countries have been accepting, and seeking, technical assistance in the field of population from a wide range of developed countries, particularly from the United States of America.

At the international level the climate of world opinion is seen in the unanimous support of the General Assembly of the United Nations in 1966 for extension of the work of the Economic and Social Council in the field of population – a support in effect for the granting of technical assistance on request of member governments in the field of family planning as well as in other economic, social and health aspects. By 1966 virtually all the Specialized Agencies had agreed to offer assistance in family planning, the World Health Organization being the last to come fully into line. The importance of the population question to the United Nations and its agencies is also seen in the elevation of the Population Branch of the Social Affairs Division to the status of a Division. In the Economic Commission for Asia and the Far East a similar development has occurred. At the meeting of the ECAFE in Canberra, Australia, in 1968, it was agreed that a Population Division should be established, with a planned establishment of fourteen demographers.

On Human Rights Day in December 1966, twelve Heads of State (Colombia, Finland, India, South Korea, Malaysia, Morocco, Nepal, Singapore, Sweden, Tunisia, United Arab Republic, Yugoslavia) representing a wide range of religious and political opinion, issued a statement which declared their belief, *inter alia*:

1 that the population problem must be recognized as a principal element in long range national planning if governments are to achieve their economic goals;

2 that the great majority of parents desire to have the knowledge and the means to plan their families, and that the opportunity to decide the number and spacing of children is a basic human right;

3 that the objective of family planning is the enrichment of human life, not its restriction; that family planning by assuring greater opportunity to each person, frees man to attain his individual dignity;

4 that family planning is in the vital interest of both the nation and the family.

Statements of principle and creed have been matched by deed in the international field to a level not generally recognized, and the extent of international aid which has as its primary objective the control of human fertility might be termed the greatest missionary enterprise of the twentieth century. During the sixteen years 1952–68 the Ford Foundation devoted $100 million to world population problems. Of this 68 per cent was committed in the United States of America, 15 per cent in Asia, 7 per cent in Europe and 5 per cent in Latin America. Over half the funds were spent in reproductive biology (largely in USA and Europe), 27 per cent in training and research in population, and 17 per cent in assistance to family planning programmes.[40]

Another non-governmental international agency which has exerted major influence is the Population Council, founded in the United States of America in 1952 by John D. Rockefeller 3rd, to 'take initiative in the broad fields which in the aggregate constitute the population problem'.[41] Starting with an annual budget of $220,000 in 1953, its activities had grown by 1968 to $11 million. By January, 1968, the Council had spent $41 million. A prominent aspect of the Council's work from the beginning has been the grant of fellowships and awards for training in demography and related fields. By 1968, 529 such awards had been made, of which 404 were to fellows from the less developed countries. In collaboration with the United Nations and national governments, the Council has been a major influence in founding and supporting demographic training and research centres at Bombay, Santiago, and at Cairo. These have been largely concerned with the training of demographers and demographic research, but the Council's

Figure 10.1 : Commitments of major Agencies in Population*

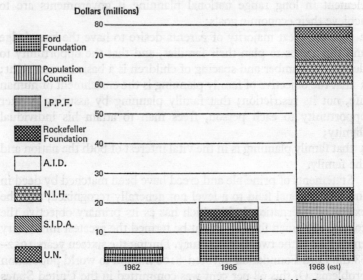

Source: Harkkavy, O., Saunders, L., and Southam, A. (1968) 'An Overview of Demography', *Demography*, v, No. 2, Special Issue, 541–52.

* Absent from this chart are commitments by the Foundation and other agencies on family planning in the United States. In 1968 the Department of Health, Education and Welfare estimates its commitments at $17 million (exclusive of NIH support of research shown in the chart above) for family planning and related activities; the Planned Parenthood Associations and their national federation spend about $5 million on voluntary family planning work. The Ford Foundation will have spent $1 million on domestic family planning in 1968.

influence has gone far beyond this; substantial funds have also been invested in basic research into the physiology of human reproduction, and more recently into the field of family planning. The Council's influence has been exerted, not merely in advisory services to governments (e.g. India and Pakistan), but also in assisting the research that has led to the development of new techniques of controlling fertility. In this respect the greatest influence of the Council has been in the provision of the major part of the funds associated with the development of the modern form of the intrauterine device, the IUCD. The Council obtained the right to grant royalty-free licences for the manufacture of the IUCD in large-scale family planning programmes carried out under government control in the less-developed countries, and under this scheme the coils have been manufactured in Korea, Taiwan, Hong Kong, Pakistan, India, Turkey and Egypt. Whereas the progesterone and oestrogen pills were developed and tested amongst populations in relatively low-income and high-birth-rate regions in Puerto Rico, but have been used so far mainly amongst the women of industrialized and low-birth-rate regions (USA, Australia and New Zealand, Western Europe), the intrauterine coil was developed among industrial and high-income regions but has been the main contraceptive instrument so far in the family planning programmes of the developing countries.

With the exceptions of South Korea and Taiwan, however, the Council has tended to eschew direct involvement with family planning programmes, and to act rather as adviser and to limit direct action to pilot projects, training and evaluation. The Council has been at great pains to appear to come into the picture only at the invitation of governments. There can be little doubt that the influence of the Council has gone far beyond these limits, yet never has it acted other than in the most tactful and diplomatic manner. This remarkable performance owes much to the sagacity of its officers in the field, and most of all to its dynamic President until 1968, Frank W. Notestein.

A third non-governmental agency of growing significance in the field is the International Planned Parenthood Federation, which sprang from a resolution of an international conference on family planning held in Bombay in 1952. The Federation is a union of family planning associations of many countries, bound together by the common theme that all parents have the right of access to the necessary information to enable them to plan the size and spacing of their families. Increasingly the Federation has exerted its influence in developing countries and has recently been able to secure the support of major foundations and governments in sponsoring conferences within regions where the population issue is felt to be particularly acute, as with its conference at Santiago, Chile, in 1967 and in Indonesia in 1969. The Federation sees its most important role, in the words of its Secretary-General until 1968, Sir Colville Deverell, as acting before governments become committed 'by persuading the intelligensia of the need for governmental concern, and by creating a climate of public opinion which will convince the politicians that governmental action meets a popular demand'.[42] In addition to this clearly 'pressure group' function, the Federation seeks to set up voluntary associations in each country, and particularly in urban areas, which can give advice, disseminate information, set up model clinics to dispense and evaluate new methods of contraception, and generally to act as a co-ordinator among those concerned with family planning. Until recently the work of the IPPF in developing countries was mainly in Asia, but its regional conference at Puerto Rico in 1964 and its international conference at Santiago in 1967 indicate its growing influence in other high-growth regions. The IPPF was also assisting family planning activities in eighteen African countries by 1968. With an estimated annual expenditure of $4·5 million in 1968, IPPF has clearly become one of the major non-governmental institutions now concerned with reducing the world's birth rate.

Substantial as the efforts of these non-governmental agencies may be, they are now far outstripped by the efforts of others with governmental affiliations. It has been estimated that the commitment of major agencies (governmental and non-governmental) in the field of population in 1968 alone would be approximately $80 million, compared with less than $20 million in 1965 and only $5 million in 1962. By 1968 by far the largest contributor was the United States Agency for International Development (AID), with a commitment for that year of $35 million and a professional staff of fifty-five devoting all or most of their time to population and family planning activities (see Figure 10. 1).

The origin of this major official interest in the United States to the population question goes back to the Draper Commission of the Eisenhower administration, which recommended in 1959 that the United States government should provide assistance, on request, to help nations with their population problems. The report was not supported by the President, but three years later the policy of assistance was affirmed by President Kennedy, himself a Roman Catholic, in terms that went far beyond the official position of the Church of Rome, both then and now. Official activity by the United States was modest until about 1966, after which the pace quickened. In 1967 President Johnson established the Office of War on Hunger with AID to focus increased attention on the problems of food and population, and the Population Branch of the Health Service became the Population Service. Through this service population officers were designated to overseas countries. In the same year contraceptives were included in the items for which financial assistance could be provided. The assistance is given only on request and it is emphasized that such assistance must not infringe the right of individuals to decide for themselves both the size and timing of children; but nevertheless, the clear aim of AID activity in the population field is to reduce national birth rates. As the Foreign Assistance Act of 1967 states:

. . . voluntary family planning programs to provide individual couples with the knowledge and medical facilities to plan their family size in accordance with their own moral convictions and the latest medical information can make a substantial contribution to improve health, family stability, greater individual opportunity, economic development, a sufficiency of food, and a higher standard of living.[43]

When this Act became law in January 1968, President Johnson's AID administration urged missions to take all practicable steps, short of any suggestion of coercion, to see that 'Congressional intent is carried out to the fullest', and the earnestness of Congress's intent is seen in the surge of available funds from $4·7 million in 1967 to $35 million in 1968. Latin America, East Asia and South East Asia have so far received the main attention. Aid covers many aspects of population, but assistance to research, operation and evaluation of family planning constitutes the major part of assistance given through AID. As a recent commentator has said:[44]

The ultimate goal of the AID population and family planning program is to improve health, well being, and economic status of peoples of the developing countries by improving the conditions of human reproduction in these societies.

It is proposed to move towards the achievement of this goal by support of broad gauge population and family planning programs, designed to make family planning information and services fully available to and used by all elements of these societies.

It is believed that the world population crisis can be largely solved by the expansion of human knowledge, freedom, and availability of information and means so that women everywhere need reproduce only if and when they choose.

These may be optimistic words, with some major implications not yet tested by research. They may also imply that the course of the world's birth rate can be changed basically by investment in technical know-how without the counterpart of social change. Yet they are perhaps no more than a reasonable expectation resulting

249

from such extensive involvement in the population issue. Moreover the cases cited above by no means encompass all international effort. To them should be added the involvement of the UN Population Division, the ECAFE Population Division, the work of the specialized agencies, and the technical assistance and research sponsored by other governments, such as those of the Netherlands, the United Kingdom, and particularly Sweden. The expected expenditure of the Swedish International Development Agency (SIDA) in the field of population in 1968 was $8 million.

Writing in 1968 of the work of the Population Council, Professor Notestein[45] modestly states that the Council has been effective partly because it came on the scene when the time was ripe, 'a fact that has more to do with the luck and wisdom of our founders than with the sagacity of our staff', and adds that one of the very special attractions of the field in which the Council works has been 'the opportunity it affords to use scientific skills in the social, biological and medical fields in ways that visibly contribute to the solution of one of the world's most pressing sets of problems'. There are still the cynics who consider that all this effort of social engineering by the developed nations on behalf of the developing nations cannot succeed until the latter pull themselves up by their own bootstraps to higher levels of living, literacy and governmental efficiency. In other words until economic and social change towards modernization has become clearly established, the issue of population control cannot be solved. This is essentially a *Western* view, still widely held but increasingly challenged, not only by those managing the organization discussed in this chapter, but also by the leaders of the countries in which the problem of control is most acute. They are aiming at reversing the traditional transition process by tackling the problem of population control first, as an aid to the initiation of policies to bring about economic and social change, rather than the reverse. The initiation of such policies is so recent that it would be quite unrealistic to have expected substantial results by now, for they are scarcely fifteen years old yet in any country; but a summary of their present extent, when added to the supplementary efforts of the governments and institutions discussed in this chapter, add up to an attack on the population issue which is unique both in its theoretical assumptions and in the extent of its operation.

The first government to institute a policy with the deliberate objective of reducing the rate of population growth was that of India, in 1950. By 1968 over twenty countries of the developing world had accepted the principle of family planning programmes aimed at reducing fertility and, including communist China, about 65 per cent of the population of the developing world was living in countries in which governmental funds were being used for this purpose. The movement has spread most rapidly in Asia, where about 80 per cent of the people live under governments favouring family planning, compared with only 20 per cent in Africa and 15 per cent in Latin America. Of the thirteen largest developing countries with populations exceeding twenty-five millions, only three were not committed by 1969: Brazil, a Catholic country, Nigeria and Burma. There was also a high correlation between levels of literacy and *per capita* income. Of the countries with 75 per cent or more of the children enrolled in the first and second grades, eleven governments favoured official activity in the field of family planning, as against only three which had no official policy. By contrast, in countries with educational enrolments below 75 per cent the majority of the governments had no official policy on family planning. In countries with *per capita* incomes above $250 a year, eleven governments favoured and six had no policy with regard to family planning; and below that level the majority again had no policy. Countries without policies included most of those with very high birth rates, above 45 per 1,000 of population, whereas the majority of those with rates around 40 or lower favoured family planning; but as those with the lower birth rates also tended to have much lower death rates than the very high-fertility areas, they often had the highest growth rates, sometimes exceeding the 3 per cent level.[46] The very significant fact is that all the 'giants' of Asia are now committed, although one of them, China, is outside the sphere of technical assistance now being so extensively operated through the instrumentalities discussed earlier in this chapter.

The details of the development of family planning programmes in the developing world have been described elsewhere[47] and will therefore not be repeated at length here; but some of the salient features need emphasizing to indicate the magnitude of the effort when related to *per capita* income and to the virtual absence of those religious, social or cultural barriers that stood for so long – and theoretically and rather pathetically still formally (although no longer effectively) stand with the Church of Rome – in the way of birth control among the European and Christian world.

The Indian government started cautiously and rightly began by emphasizing research to assess attitudes to birth control, to educate parents and to try and win support for action programmes. It was generally found that resistance was low, and indeed that the majority of women wished to limit family size – a finding common to almost all the fifty or more surveys that have been conducted in many countries since then. Government allocations for family planning were at first modest, at $330,000 in the first five-year plan. This increased to $4·5 million in the second plan, and then leapt to $54 million in the third plan.

An extended family planning programme introduced in 1963 aimed at initiating a decline in the Indian birth rate from the prevailing rate of around 41 to 25 per 1,000 in 1973. This period also saw the break away from traditional methods of birth control to the introduction of such new methods as the intrauterine coil, sterilization, the consideration of liberalization of abortion, and the raising of the legal age of marriage. Some saw in the downward trend of the birth rate in these five years in some cities, such as Bombay, Poona and Madras, the first signs of success, but the third five-year programme was still on too small a scale and too fraught with administrative problems to have any major influence on the nation's growth rate.

The most significant event of these years was the appointment of a United Nations Technical Assistance Mission at the request of the Indian government to examine ways and means of improving the efficiency of India's attack on the birth rate.[48] The extended programme of 1963 had optimistically aimed eventually to provide 90 per cent of the married adult population with knowledge of family planning methods, primarily through a vast network of health centres reaching from the cities down through the villages and into the rural population. The UN Mission saw at once that the plan could not be quickly implemented, and certainly not within a decade as initially planned, for it involved securing the cooperation of all States, the training of a veritable army of doctors, educators, nurses, midwives and other workers. Yet the basic administrative approach was right: a major problem was the difficulty of educating people in the use of traditional contraceptives. The Mission saw in the intrauterine device, the loop, a potential breakthrough in the problem, for here was a contraceptive method which was cheap, reversible, highly effective and comparatively safe. The Mission felt that the loop would be as acceptable to Indian women as it had been elsewhere, for example in Taiwan and South Korea; but it was recognized that success in the programme would require more than one method and that much would depend upon the rapid development of other new, cheap and efficient contraceptives. Moreover there were methods acceptable to Indians which were not highly favoured elsewhere, and these should be persisted in. Hence the mission strongly recommended that the sterilization programme, already supported in most States and already vigorously put into effect in Maharashtra, should be intensified. In addition, the more acceptable traditional contraceptives, such as the condom, should be made much more freely available. Techniques were however seen as only part of the programme; efficient administration at both central and State levels would be required, to institute effective educational programmes, to get doctors and nurses co-operating at the village levels and to 'sell' contraception to the masses. In this last respect particular emphasis was laid on the importance of instructing women in contraceptive methods immediately after childbirth.

The Mission expressed the view that, if vigorously put into effect, the programme they proposed could render possible a reduction of the Indian birth rate by about a third in ten years. 'If this target is reached the rate of population growth would decline from 2·4 per cent at present to 1·6 per cent by 1975 and under 1 per cent before 1985.' But having stated this, the Report of the Mission emphasized that their programme meant changing deeply rooted habits of thought in a nation containing a seventh of the population of the entire world, and then translating the changed outlook into innumerable actions, and doing all this 'before economic and social factors can play their classical role in bringing about a major reduction of the birth rate'.[49]

The Indian government has certainly reacted vigorously to the Report of the UN Mission. In the fourth five-year plan for 1966–71 the budget for family planning has been lifted to $306 million, compared with only $54 million in 1961–5. A Cabinet Committee on Family Planning has been established (actually before the UN Mission reported) a member of which is the Minister for Health and Family Planning, with a chain of responsibility flowing from this through all States. Figure 10·2 illustrates the organizational plan. The object of this structure is to provide a fully equipped family welfare centre for every 800,000 people, a sub-centre for every 10,000 people, and to have ultimate 40 per cent of the married couples of child-bearing age practising contraception by the use of the loop, sterilization or conventional contraceptives. The targets to 1971 are:

1 Loop insertions: 17 million (i.e. 20 per cent of women of reproductive age).

2 Conventional contraceptives (mainly condoms): 400 million pieces a year

3 Sterilizations: 6 million

By March 1967 1,700,000 IUCD insertions had been achieved, mostly in Punjab, Maharashtra, West Bengal, Kerala and Mysore. In addition it was estimated that 2·3 million sterilization operations had been carried out on parents with two or more children, and there were then over 3,000 hospitals and some 260 mobile units staffed to carry out such operations free of cost. To increase the supply of trained workers five central training institutes, twenty-seven State training centres and seventeen central field units had been established. State training centre personnel were being trained at the Central Family Planning Institute in New Delhi by the close of 1966 at the rate of ninety a year. Incentive payments encourage health service doctors to operate family planning schemes. Doctors are paid sums varying from Rs.5 to Rs.10 for vasectomies and tubal ligations if they perform this work over and above their normal duties. In Uttar Pradesh lady doctors are paid Rs. 300 for the first fifty clinic insertions of IUCDs and Rs. 2 for each additional insertion, and persons presenting themselves for IUCD insertions are authorized to receive Rs. 5. Payments are also made in some areas to 'motivators' who encourage others to adopt family planning. The Department of Family Planning had also authorized a 'task force' of two hundred general practitioners and fifteen specialists to operate in areas where personnel are short. It was estimated that by the end of 1966 each 'task force' doctor could account for 5,000 insertions a year. A new development in December 1966 was the approval by the Indian Council for Medical Research of the import and private sale of oral contraceptive pills. All these steps are backed by a vigorous mass education programme, using all the media from television to puppet shows, to keep family planning prominently and continuously before the masses.[50]

Figure 10.2 : The Administration of Indian Family Planning

Cabinet Committee on Family Planning

(Prime Minister and Minister for
Planning Finance, Health, Food
and Agriculture)

Minister for Health and Family Planning

Central Family Planning Council

(State Ministers of Health and
Family Planning, Health experts,
representatives of voluntary
organizations)

Secretary, Department
of Family Planning

Commissioner for
Family Planning

Six Regional Family
Planning Offices

The early efforts of India in the field of population control were treated with great scepticism by many Western observers. There can scarcely be any doubt about the magnitude of the present effort. To have expected results by now, in 1969, would be unrealistic; but if good government and administrative efficiency is maintained, the human and financial investments now being made in family planning may bring results in the near future. Scepticism is giving way to respect for the herculean task the governments of India have set themselves. Reviewing the scene early in 1967, Dr Sheldon J. Segal, the Director of the Bio-Medical Division of the Population Council, wrote:[51]

In a period of less than two years India has doubled the number of couples initiating effective contraception. By the end of 1966 approximately 4 per cent of couples in the reproductive age group had adopted the practice of family planning. By April 1967 it may be possible to detect a trend in the rate of acceptors. Meanwhile, there is a basis for optimism. The administrative structure has been carefully designed to reach remote villages and crowded urban centres; the funds that have been provided are ample, the priority given to the program is clearly evident, and the leadership imparted by the newly-organized Department of Family Planning is outstanding. The shortage of trained personnel is a problem India must confront in many facets of her economic and social development effort. With the most efficient utilization of available manpower for family planning, India's objective of reducing the birth rate to 25 per 1,000 can be achieved. Until the present program has had a longer period of operation, it is not possible to determine the time span that will be required.

The cautious optimism in these words may be fully justified. By mid-1968, and compared with the estimates given above for some fifteen months earlier, it was estimated that IUCD insertions had risen to 2·5 million, an increase of 800,000, and that sterilizations had risen to 4·5 million, an increase of 2·2 million. It appears therefore that the sterilization programme is well on its way to the target of 6 million, but that the loop programme is lagging far behind the 17 million target. However this must be considered against an extended programme in traditional contraceptives as well as the possibility of the mass introduction of the contraceptive pill if, as seems likely, costs of manufacture and distribution can be greatly reduced.

If India is to achieve the target of reducing the national birth rate from 41 to 25 per 1,000 of population between 1966 and 1975, some 85 million births will have to be prevented, compared with the numbers that would occur if birth rates remained at the 1966 level. Dr Agarwala, Director of the Demographic Training and Research Centre at Chembur, has estimated that to achieve this target the number of births to be prevented in 1966–7 should have been 791,000 rising to 1,642,000 in 1967–8 and so on, as family planning spreads, to a saving in the last year (1975–6) of 10,797,000. His lower estimate is that the actual performance of birth prevention in 1966–7 may have been between about 652,000 and 751,000, and in 1967–8 between about 985,000 and 1,123,000.[52] Such estimates must be treated with some reserve, but if they can be accepted they suggest that India has already gone a considerable distance in preventing births; but they also suggest an increasing lag in 1967–8 below the target figure, compared with the previous year, which implies that even greater efforts will have to be made in the future if the saving of 85 million births in the decade is to be achieved.

In Pakistan government policy with regard to population control has been broadly similar to that in India. Sporadic attempts to spread family planning were made by voluntary agencies in the 1950s, and some support was given by government; but a fully structured government policy was not introduced until the 1960s. In the second Five Year Plan (1960–5) a National Research Institute of Family Planning was set up, together with five family planning, training and research institutes and a number of clinics, all with considerable technical assistance from abroad. This was essentially an experimental period. In the third plan for 1965–70 the government instituted a major scheme with a budget of 12 cents a head a year, to total 300 million rupees. In *per capita* terms this is about equivalent to the Indian budget for 1966–71. The goal in the Pakistan plan was to reduce the national growth rate from 3 per cent to 2·5 per cent a year by 1970, and to reduce this further by 1985 to 1·5 per cent. Again this is broadly similar to the Indian goal, but Pakistan has to start from a higher fertility level, probably nearer 50 births per 1,000 of population, compared with 40 in India.

By 1968 the Pakistan government had over 50,000 persons employed in the programme and about an equal number of agents registered for distribution of conventional contraceptives. The government programme, again as in India, has been based so far primarily on IUCD insertions, sterilizations and the use of conventional contraceptives. Sterilizations seemed to have settled by 1968 to about 21,000 a month; but the number of IUCD insertions was still rising sharply (with an estimated 69,000 a month between January and June 1968), as were the sales of conventional contraceptives (estimated at 14,500,000, January–June 1968). The number of couples practising contraception at the end of each year was estimated to have increased as follows over the first three years of the programme:[53]

	1965–6	1966–7	1967–8
IUCDs	206,100	578,200	959,900
Sterilizations	5,400	53,800	317,000
Conventional	363,300	971,500	1,641,200
Total	574,800	1,603,500	2,918,100

While the whole programme was estimated to have reached only 12 per cent of eligible women by August, 1968, the progress over three years has been striking, particularly in such a large population in which literacy levels are so low and the problems of effective communication so great. Moreover, if the estimates of contraceptive users are correct, and assuming that a high proportion of these are *new* users, the savings in births must have been considerable already, as it appears to have been also in India. In both countries the dimensions of the performance of government policy are sufficient to raise some hopes that deliberate public policy can bend down growth rates in a massive way without first achieving the traditional features of economic and social change that have traditionally been accepted in transition theory as the essential forerunners of controlled fertility.

The situation in the other great Asian giant, Communist China, is much more difficult to assess, but the evidence is fairly clear that following an official attitude before 1957 which accepted the traditional Marxist–Leninist approach that under the communist system production would always be sufficient to meet the requirements of the population, there has been a marked change in favour of a reduction of the rate of population growth. This change appears to have coincided with the economic failure of the 'Great Leap Forward' planned in 1957. However even before 1957 some prominent Chinese scholars were stressing the advantages of reducing the rate of population growth.

In 1955 the non-communist world began to applaud the news that the Communist government of China was apparently encouraging a birth-control campaign.[54] In 1954 Deputy Shao Li-tzu, addressing the National Congress, stated that while Lenin had pointed out that the working class had no place for Neo-Malthusianism, he had also emphasized that this did not mean that Communist society should not discard all laws seeking to punish abortion and to prevent the propagation of medical theories on contraception. Many statements made by Chinese leaders in the following years, while attacking Malthus, yet emphasized the desirability of birth control to space births and to protect the health of mothers and children. These were followed by the establishment in 1957 of a national committee to guide birth-control research. The movement was vigorously supported by Ma Yen-Ch'u, President of Peiping University.

Such statements, together with the fact that there had been an easing of restrictions on abortions since 1954, all seemed to point to the beginnings of a vigorous birth-control movement. The fact that measures seriously advocated included swallowing, whole and alive, fresh tadpoles for several days after menstruation (fourteen the first day and ten more the following day to achieve sterility for five years – by shock presumably), should not be taken as evidence that a vigorous campaign by an authoritarian government in China would not have had considerable success. Other measures advocated had the ring of modern thinking and hard realism.

But in October 1957 the advocates of birth control, and particularly Ma Yen-Ch'u, were vigorously denounced. Ma stood his ground, but was dismissed from Peiping University in 1960, at the age of 76 years. Whether the dismissal was due to his advocacy of birth control or because he opposed the new policy of a labour-intensive approach instead of a capital-intensive approach to economic growth, is not clear. Quite likely his dismissal had more to do with his economic theories than with his advocacy of birth control, for some who visited China after 1957 and others who studied quasi-official press and journal articles claimed that while *officially* the Chinese communists had 'buried Malthus', they were not in fact preventing the dissemination of birth-control knowledge.[55] The concern of the government in 1957 seems to have been rather not to encourage the view that birth control was essential to the improvement of living standards. One suggestion was that the government abandoned its official advocacy of birth control in 1957 when it knew that bumper harvests were being reaped, but these were to give way in subsequent years to lean agricultural returns. After 1957 writings in support of family planning seemed to be permitted again, provided they were at the same time anti-Malthusian. A writer in 1959 stated in the *Peiping Review*, for example, that 'in denouncing the reactionary Malthusian theory, Marxists did not in any way exclude the necessity of the planned limitation of population growth in the future development of society'. The irony of the current Chinese situation is that the measures being advocated to limit population growth seem to be thoroughly Malthusian and capitalist: moral restraint through postponement of marriage and reduction of the family to two or three children. Precisely what measures are being used to achieve these ends are not known, but it is reported that large quantities of traditional contraceptives are imported through Hong Kong.

Turning to the smaller countries of the ECAFE region it is now easier to list countries which have *not* accepted the principle of birth control and family planning, whereas twelve years or so ago it was difficult to list many who had either accepted the principle or appeared to be much concerned about it. A few illustrations indicate how far some have gone.[56]

The government of South Korea sponsored a family planning programme in May 1964. Two years later over 2,200 workers had been put in the field. The objective was to reduce a growth rate of about 3 per cent to 2 per cent a year by 1971 as an aid to economic plans to raise living standards. Major but not exclusive reliance was placed on insertions of intrauterine coil devices (IUCD). It is estimated that the attainment of the target objective will require one million IUCD insertions, 200,000 vasectomies, and 300,000 regular users of traditional contraceptives. That there was a strong desire or motivation for smaller families from the outset is implied in the facts that the target figures for the 1965 official programme (including 200,000 loop insertions) were attained and that in addition there was evidence of extensive control practised outside the official programme, with abortion playing a very significant role. In 1965 abortions in Seoul were estimated at one for every two live births.

By the end of 1967 the accumulated IUCD total was put at 1,020,000, and by that time the coil programme had been supplemented by 102,000 vasectomies and the introduction of oral contraceptives. It was then estimated that about one in five eligible women were practising contraception and these, with the sterilized and infertile, would mean that over a third of women of childbearing age were virtually without serious risk of pregnancy.

In Taiwan a similar programme developed, although not directly under government control. Here one IUCD had been inserted by 1966 for every twelve women in the child-bearing years. The monthly rate of insertions had then reached approximately five per 1,000 women in the child-bearing ages and funds to continue this level of activity had been assured up to 1970, the *per capita* cost of the IUCD programme being about 2·5 cents a year. In late 1964 the Economic Planning Board also approved a ten-year health plan in which family planning was an integral part.

In 1968 the government of Taiwan introduced its own pro-gramme, with the target of reducing the birth rate to 24·1 by 1973. By June 1968, 440,000 IUCDs had been inserted, supplemented by 1,200 sterilizations, and the oral contraceptive had been intro-duced with an estimated 45,000 users. About a third of the eligible couples of Taiwan were then estimated to be practising effective contraception and the birth rate seemed well on the way to its target, being about 28 compared with about 36 per 1,000 in 1963.

While the cases cited are the most advanced examples of vigor-ous action by governments to reduce fertility, similar objectives now hold in many countries. In Ceylon, the government instituted a programme in 1965, and in co-operation with a number of international agencies, particularly the Swedish International Development Agency, has established 400 clinics as part of the maternal and child health service. In Hong Kong government and voluntary agencies are operating some 60 clinics, using IUCDs and now mainly oral contraceptives, in a plan to reduce the birth rate to 20 per 1,000 by 1970. It is estimated that 41 per cent of eligible women are practising family planning. In Malaysia the government instituted a programme in 1966 and by 1968 some forty clinics were operating. Nepal had instituted its programme in 1966. In Singapore the government has a plan to reduce the birth rate to 20 per 1,000 and it is estimated that over 40 per cent of eligible women were practising contraception by the end of 1968. Thailand began a three-year family health programme in 1968. In Turkey old anti-contraceptive laws were repealed in 1965 and a Family Planning Law has been laid down to implement a national programme through the Ministry of Health and Social Assistance. A major objective is a reduction of illegal abortion which is estimated to have been running at the rate of one abortion for every two live births. In the United Arab Republic a Supreme Council for Family Planning was set up in 1965, and by 1968 family plan-ning facilities were available in 1,700 maternal and child health centres and the voluntary Family Planning Association was responsible for a further 360 centres. The movement has thus broken through any religious and cultural barriers that may have been thought to exist in the predominantly non-Christian coun-tries. It is also having considerable success in countries where Roman Catholicism is a powerful influence. In the Philippines the central government remains uncommitted but voluntary clinics are developing without government opposition. There were over 300 such clinics by the end of 1968. Both United States AID and the Population Council are active in the Philippines. In Latin America there are now voluntary family planning movements in almost every country, and interest has been stimulated by the holding of the Eighth International Conference of the International Planned Parent Federation in Chile in 1967 – a major and carefully planned piece of international co-operation by almost all the major voluntary agencies set up to spread family planning. In Chile the government has agreed in principle to an official programme; in Columbia the government set up a programme in 1967; Costa Rica did the same in 1968, as did the Dominican Republic. Of the major continents of the developing world, only Africa remained substantially outside the influence of family planning but there are signs that the movement is beginning to take hold there too.

A schedule of the objectives of official policies and an account of the efforts of voluntary agencies can easily overestimate the effectiveness of such efforts. Nevertheless the acceptance of the principle of reducing population growth by deliberate government action and the encouragement given by so many governments to voluntary agencies to propagate non-governmental family planning programmes within their countries constitute an entirely new approach to the population issue. It is unique in the world's history and is the response to a unique demographic situation with regard to the width of the gap that now exists in many areas between the levels of fertility and mortality. Other aspects of the modern programmes which are in marked contrast to the experience of the Western, Christian world are the apparently few resistances to almost any method. Male and female sterilizations are an integral part of many of the programmes. There has been virtually no opposition to any of the traditional or modern methods of preventing conception. By far the most important to date have been the traditional methods, but the IUCD has been of major significance in eastern Asia. In the newer programmes oral contraceptives appear to be gaining popularity rapidly, and with the very great improvements in the efficiency of the progesterone pill and a marked reduction in its unit cost, particularly where governments are prepared to organize bulk purchase, the oral contraceptive is coming within the means of increasing numbers of women in developing countries. However, up to 1968 the pill was of much greater importance to the developed than to the developing countries, but even in the former it had by no means supplanted more traditional methods. Total world consumption in 1966 and 1967 was estimated at about 9·5 and 12·8 millions respectively, broadly distributed as follows:[57]

	July 1966	July 1967
United States of America	5,000,000	6,500,000
Latin America	1,600,000	1,934,000
Australia and New Zealand	590,000	670,000
United Kingdom	415,000	700,000
Europe, including USSR	690,000	1,200,000
Canada	450,000	750,000
Far East	307,000	507,000
Near East and Arab Republic	273,000	320,000
Africa	100,000	122,000
	9,425,000	12,703,000

While these figures no doubt need to be accepted only as rough approximations, they are small enough to indicate that the pill had not taken over the job of birth control by 1967, particularly in the developing world. On the other hand, its impact on the developing world was considerable and was clearly growing rapidly. By far the greatest users, measured as a proportion of the female population at risk, were in Australia and New Zealand, and later figures here suggest that the popularity of the pill has grown enormously since 1967. An estimate published in a journal of the Commonwealth Department of Health puts the users by June 1969 in Australia alone as high as 750,000, or more than one in four of the women between ages 15 and 49.

A. S. Parkes wrote in 1961 that 'established methods of birth control are so crude as to be a disgrace to science in this age of technical achievement'. He added that 'they are such as to be virtually useless to those most needing assistance – illiterate and overcrowded peoples . . .'[58] Certainly the plastic coil, IUCD, and the pill are not the final answer and when analysed do in fact seem crude instruments.

The IUCD is suitable only for women who have already borne a child: this is no real handicap as all national programmes aim to

263

reduce higher-order births, not to prevent women having two or three children. It has to be inserted into the cervix by a doctor or by a para-medical officer trained for the job, and before attempting to insert the IUCD a thorough medical examination should be made because it is generally not advisable to use the method if there are any physiological abnormalities. At least 10 per cent of women eject the device: close examination of the Taiwan programme has also revealed that a further 30 or 40 per cent deliberately have had the device removed because of discomfort or other reasons. A few cases of perforation of the uterus occur: it is considered advisable for users to have periodical pelvic examinations at least once a year and preferably every six months. Yet the fact remains that the IUCD – the loop – with over 90 per cent guarantee to its wearer against pregnancy, is the instrument which has brought family-planning knowledge and practice to millions of couples in the 'developing' world, particularly in Asia, and those who for one reason or another reject this method are not necessarily lost contraceptors, for all programmes are backed by other more traditional methods to which many will tend to turn.

While the IUCD might retain some advantages for the 'developing' countries – e.g. its cheapness, its effectiveness from first insertion until its removal – the oral contraceptive is clearly gaining ground rapidly, particularly in developed societies. The pills are also much more efficient today than when they were first swallowed by the women of Puerto Rico and Haiti, about fifteen years ago.

The pill is the product of hormonal science and its origin goes back to the end of last century when it was suggested that it might be the endocrine gland in the ovary which produces the hormone, progesterone, which is responsible for inhibiting ovulation during pregnancy. Later researches confirmed the hypothesis and proved further that a second hormone, oestrogen, also inhibited ovulation. In a normal menstrual cycle, the rejection by the menstrual flow of the unfertilized egg cell or ovum is followed by the production of gonadotropic hormones which begin again the process of preparing an ovum for release and preparing the lining of the uterus for the reception of the egg, should it be fertilized. If the egg is fertilized and implanted, nature prevents further ovulation through the action of the two hormones progesterone and oestrogen, which act upon the pituitary gland to cease production of the gonadotropic hormones. The oral contraceptive, by introducing progesterone and oestrogen artificially cheats the pituitary, as it were, into thinking that implantation has occurred and so it acts to prevent ovulation. Experience has shown that while oestrogen is the principal inhibitor, a combination of oestrogen and progesterone, taken on a twenty-day cycle, produces almost one hundred per cent security against ovulation, and therefore protection against pregnancy.

Considerable side effects have been recorded: nausea, increase in weight, blotching of the skin. There have been reports of death from thrombophlebitis and of fears of carcinogenic consequences arising from constant use. So far the worst fears appear to have little substance and continual research is improving the pill, particularly by discovering that the dosage of the hormones can be greatly reduced without impairing their efficiency. Today, women using oral contraceptives need use in twenty days only the equivalent of what was formerly taken in two days. The pill is clearly here to stay and looks like being by far the most efficient contraceptive yet produced; but too much should not be claimed for it, and it is certainly only one phase in the evolution of birth-control methods.

Science is turning increasing attention to the male, for whom the only effective contraceptive so far has been the condom and sterilization. Ways have already been found to inhibit the production of spermatozoa in experimental animals without impairing sexual activity. So far, however, the greater part of research enterprise seems to be concentrated on the female, to find more efficient preventives than the daily pill. One promising approach is a subdermal implant that may emit a low dosage of progesterone sufficient to protect a woman from pregnancy for up to a year. Other researchers are working on the idea of inactivating the female egg after fertilization, by preventing it from becoming implanted in the uterus, a process which takes place about a week after fertilization. Theoretically this method limits any artificial action to the third week only of the menstrual cycle. Another line which has been followed is the possibility of immunizing females against spermatozoa: it has already been established that antibodies do occur among some couples, thus producing anti-immunization, and further studies of such conditions may lead to the possibility of simulating the antibodies.

The reports of such experiments, together with a rapidly increasing expenditure of funds, and the backing of the major birth-control organizations, provide considerable grounds for believing that the 'scientific revolution' with regard to the understanding and control of human fertility has still to come. The 1970s may yet see a scientific breakthrough in fertility control as revolutionary for the twenty-first century as Jenner's vaccine against smallpox was for the nineteenth century. And lest it be felt that science is working against the trend of world public opinion in these matters, it should be emphasized that survey after survey in the developing countries has revealed the yearning desire of women to free themselves of the burden of unwanted pregnancy. As Notestein has written:[59]

More than thirty surveys have been undertaken (with the support of the Population Council) in more than a score of countries . . . in an effort to substitute hard information for popular lore, both lay and professional, to the effect that in the newly developing countries there is little knowledge of the means of controlling fertility and less interest in the subject. Indeed the typical upper-class attitude that the peasants are too traditionally minded, if not too stupid, to be interested in family planning has done much to weaken the efforts of local leadership in support of family planning.

Virtually without exception, these surveys . . . have shown that substantial majorities (60–70 per cent) of the women say that they want to limit their fertility. Obviously this does not mean that they want only two children. But they do not want unending childbearing. Some motivation for restriction is present. . . . The discovery through such surveys that the public is indeed interested in family planning has done much to turn the subject from a political liability to a political asset.

This chapter has attempted to point out the vast contrast between the situations that existed when European birth rates declined and the present situation in today's high-birth-rate areas and to suggest that the application of transition theory that fitted the nineteenth century may have only very limited relevance to the twentieth and twenty-first centuries. The religious and moral prejudices, social customs and economic theories which worked against fertility control in the nineteenth century now have little relevance in the predominantly non-Christian world now seeking to reduce its growth rates. This revolutionary difference of attitudes and the positive activities of governments, backed by substantial and growing international assistance and increasing scientific endeavours in the field of fertility control, bring entirely new dimensions to the subject. Instead of waiting for social and economic change to induce the conditions for fertility control, which is the classic concept of transition theory, the developing world is trying to implant fertility control as an essential first step in inducing those social and economic changes which will help to raise living standards. The classical process is going into reverse. Can it succeed?

Chapter 11

Retrospect and Prospect

Will the population control policies succeed? And what is to be the measure of success: a growth rate of 1 per cent, or population stability? Is it a matter of techniques or of social change? Do the historical processes so commonly fitting into the framework of transition theory provide an immutable law?

The population situation in the world today is unique: unique indeed from almost any angle. For the developed, industrialized countries it is unique in its distribution, with the majority of the people herded into cities; it is unique in its conquest of mortality to the point at which, reproductively speaking, the complete elimination of death would make little difference to reproductive potential. With regard to the pattern of nuptiality, the situation is perhaps not unique but has nevertheless developed a pattern which suggests the most revolutionary change for two or three hundred years in many countries, with very much higher proportions of adults marrying during the last twenty years or so than appears to have been the case in the measurable past. And associated with this change in nuptiality, the pattern of the developed world is unique in the degree of rational control now exercised over fertility, without which growth rates could exceed 4 per cent a year if mortality could be held down to present levels. There is, however, no sign that such an explosion will occur amongst the developed countries: indeed with the narrowing of social, economic and religious differentials, it is quite apparent that effective birth control is almost a universal phenomenon amongst developed societies. There are pockets of high fertility which go almost to the limits of human fecundity, such as among the Hutterite communities of North America; but such cases are quite exceptional. Over aggregates of populations within national boundaries the patterns of fertility – and mortality – have come to look remarkably similar whether one goes from capitalist United States to communist Soviet Union, from protestant United Kingdom to catholic Italy, or from the heart of Europe to the European settlements of the antipodes.[1]

268

These people have been learning to live with life expectations of about seventy years, or with reproductive immortality, with their average completed family size of not more than three children. With generation replacement now possible with an average of less than 2·2 children per marriage, the process of child-bearing has become an episode of married life, not its continuing and major function. This is probably the greatest social revolution of our time. As the methods of preventing unwanted pregnancy have become increasingly efficient, and as the social and religious taboos have weakened and society has become increasingly permissive in sexual matters, the response has been on the whole, not more promiscuity, but a more rational and in many ways more stable approach to marriage. More young couples enter into marriage; and for countries where the relevant statistics exist, more of these couples want to have children, for compared with the 1930s and 1920s the proportion remaining without issue seems to have decreased; but the majority cease bearing children after two or three births - a process which may be over within the first six years of married life, and frequently before a wife has attained the age of 30 years.

This is the unique family pattern of the twentieth century: its evolution has been so rapid that social customs, attitudes and institutions have not yet been fully adjusted. The majority of young women are in paid employment before marriage and in many cases the establishment of a home after marriage is financially a joint venture. Most women leave employment during the child-bearing process, but increasing proportions again seek employment after their two or three children have been born. Marriage remains from this point a sexual, social and frequently economic partnership, but has no further procreative function for the greater part of its duration. Increasingly children have also become the responsibility of society: free enterprise in reproduction is almost unique to the United States, for in most other developed countries the State subsidizes birth through maternity allowances, subsidizes medical and hospital care after birth and assists parents with the cost of rearing children by child endowments. The nature of these 'pro-natalist' measures has been outlined in the previous chapter. Yet none of these measures to transfer income in favour of those with young children seems to have made any substantial difference to the evolution of the small-family system. For years until recently family size has been higher in free enterprise America than in socialized Britain, France or Sweden; yet all have moved in the same direction towards a remarkably uniform family system, which is the most efficient reproductive unit that mankind has ever experienced. The loss by death, either of mother or child in the process of childbirth is negligible; death after birth until the process of begetting the next generation has been completed is of minor importance, demographically speaking; and so far each generation seems to show enough propensity to reproduce to sustain population growth at levels between about 0·5 and 1·0 per cent a year – levels which, if sustained, will add significantly to the world's future population.

Historically speaking, such rates of increase are greater than those which have applied throughout much of human history, but they appear extremely modest compared with the rates ranging between 2 and 3 per cent a year which apply throughout many parts of Asia, Africa and Latin America. Nor does there seem to be any reason to worry unduly about the capacity of the economies of the developed countries to produce ample nutriment and shelter. Their problem is not lack of resources but the distribution and management of these in a manner that will make possible the continuation of civilized life: control of air and water pollution, city reorganization, decongestion of traffic flows. Until the solution to these problems is in sight, an even greater reduction in growth rates might be assumed to be desirable, but there is little evidence that growth rates could be so lowered (or raised) at the behest of governments. It has been shown in Chapter 10 that the establishment of the small-family system was apparently little affected by the policies of some governments to provide substantial economic and social incentives to increase natality. There was ample evidence in the economically depressed years of the 1930s that parents tended to reduce fertility by postponing births and to 'make up' many of these postponed births when economic conditions improved again. There was also ample evidence, in the United States of America, western Europe, Australia and New Zealand, that the generation marrying after the Second World War responded to the relative prosperity by marrying younger and showing higher fertility than the pre-war generation; but this was a shifting forward to younger ages of family formation rather than any reversion to substantially larger completed families. The widespread decrease in fertility since 1960 in many developed countries in Europe and overseas indicates how strongly entrenched the small-family system is.[2]

The 'small-family system' as applied to developed, or low birth-rate areas (i.e. with birth rates of approximately 20 or less per 1,000 of population) means a completed average family size for each woman of around three children. At today's marriage patterns, this means a completed family size of about 3·2 children per *married* woman, which seems to be the 'ideal' family size as expressed by European women of the United States in response to recent surveys.[3] This may be compared with the average completed family of more than five children per marriage found among European women in the eighteenth and nineteenth centuries (See Chapter 4). If this is the extent of the reduction in family size of today's developed countries, in the face of religious and moral opposition and despite the efforts of many governments to increase fertility, is it not possible that the application of modern contraceptive techniques – along the lines observed in Chapter 10 – will achieve similar reductions in today's developing countries, particularly when there appears to be so little opposition to their introduction?

Certainly none of the governments of today's developing countries who have instituted family planning programmes are as

Figure 11.1 : Models of the Demographic Transition

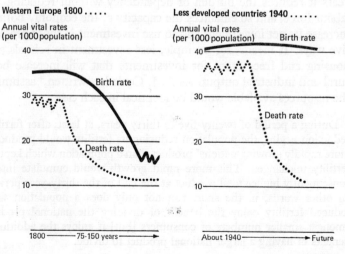

Western Europe 1800 . . . . .   Less developed countries 1940 . . . . . .

Annual vital rates (per 1000 population)   Annual vital rates (per 1000 population)   Birth rate

sanguine as this. India's policy is perhaps the most ambitious, aiming to reduce the birth rate from 40 to 25 in approximately ten years. Pakistan, with a considerably higher fertility aims to reduce the birth rate from 50 around 1960 to 40 by 1970. Some of the smaller countries are more ambitious. Taiwan aims to bring annual growth rates down between 1965 and 1973 from 3·02 to 1·86 per cent, with a reduction of birth rates from about 36 to 24 per 1,000 of population. Ceylon has a broadly similar objective. Turkey is more modest, aiming to reduce growth rates from about 3 per cent to 2 per cent. Malaysia aims to bring its growth rate down from 3·0 to 2·2 per cent in twenty years. Thus in none of these countries does the population policy now being implemented imply an early cessation of growth: on the contrary the attainment of present objectives will still leave them growing at considerably faster rates than the current rates among most non-Asian countries outside Latin America. The objectives of the present programmes are thus moderate: their emphasis is upon techniques of birth control as a first step, as an aid to social and economic change, and not as an event which is entirely dependent upon such change. The objectives are also economically sensible, given the size of populations and the limited natural and capital resources. The prevention of births, even on a modest scale, can change the structure of a population quite markedly in favour of a higher level of net investment, for initially and for a period of at least twenty-five years it reduces the burden of dependency without reducing the labour force, and so enhances the capacity of the economy both to increase its net investment and to use investment in more productive ways. It means, for example, less investment in schools and housing and frees more for investments that will increase both rural and industrial output. As A. J. Coale has written,[4] assuming the resources available would be identical in each case:

During a period of twenty-five to thirty years, at least, after fertility reduction begins, the population reducing its fertility would produce a more rapidly growing national product than a population which kept its fertility unchanged. This more rapid growth would cumulate into a consequently higher total product at the end of the thirty-year period. In other words, in the short run not only does a population with reduced fertility enjoy the benefit of dividing the national product amongst smaller numbers of consumers [but] it enjoys the additional benefits of having a larger national product to divide.

As Coale goes on to show, the initial advantages of a lower dependency ratio which would flow from a reduction in fertility would be followed in the longer run by a reduced rate of growth of the work-force and a consequent opportunity of increasing the stock of capital per worker. Both processes would give an impetus to economic growth, and the process would be particularly important in most of the already densely populated developing countries in which the growth of the population of working age is already outrunning the capacity of new rural frontier areas to absorb it. Therefore, on the assumption that there are immediate net economic advantages in an induced decline in fertility, the policies of the countries which concentrate on techniques seem soundly based, and if their limited demographic objectives succeed they may prove an important stimulus to long-term economic and social change. The implied interrelation of techniques on the one hand and economic and social change on the other has been overlooked by some of the critics of current policies who appear to pin their faith on either one approach or the other, rather than on their combination.

The most extreme statement of faith in the capacity of techniques to reduce growth rates comes from Donald J. Bogue in an article 'The End of the Population Explosion' published in 1967[5]. He sees the population crisis as a passing phenomenon of the twentieth century, and concludes:

The trend of the worldwide movement toward fertility control has already reached a state where declines in death rates are being surpassed by declines in birth rates. Because progress in death control is slackening and progress in birth control is accelerating, the world has already entered a situation where the pace of population growth has begun to slacken. . . . From 1965 onward, therefore, the rate of world population growth may be expected to decline with each passing year. The rate of growth will slacken at such a pace that it will be zero or near zero at about the year 2000, so that population will not be regarded as a major social problem except in isolated and small 'retarded' areas.

Bogue sees the onset of this revolutionary downward trend in growth rates, not as a result of economic and social change (i.e. the classical transition theory), but in improved contraceptive technology and the increasing support of governments for crash birth-control programmes, leading to the massive adoption of effective control measures by uneducated people.

273

The naïvety of the conclusions is so astonishing in the light of all known facts, that it is difficult to treat Bogue seriously. He completely overlooks the revelations of surveys to the effect that, while women in developing countries apparently want to free themselves from unwanted pregnancies, desired family size is generally around four children, which is sufficient to sustain substantial growth in most existing or expected mortality conditions. He also overlooks the fact that the developing countries in which birth rates are falling tend to be those in which social and economic change are occurring at a very rapid rate (e.g. Taiwan). He grossly overstates the case for contraceptive technology and crash programmes and ignores the difficulty of preventing growth in populations with life expectations of sixty or more years.

By contrast, another well-known American demographer, Kingsley Davis,[6] has tended to overstate the case against current birth-control programmes. Davis attacks the current family planning programmes for their lack of clear objectives – do they mean population 'control' or merely population 'planning'? They do not aim to stop population growth, but to cut growth rates by about one half, as a necessary first step in the process of social and economic change. This point seems to have been largely ignored by Davis who complains that the programmes should not be referred to as control or planning programmes 'because they do not attempt to influence the factors responsible for the attributes of human population'. Nor, he adds, should they be called 'fertility control' programmes 'because they do not try to affect most of the determinants of reproductive performance'. Davis emphasizes that family planning programmes which only aim – as most do – at allowing individuals to have as many children as they wish, can only reduce reproduction to the extent that unwanted births exceed wanted births, and such a limited objective would still leave an extremely high rate of multiplication – a point completely ignored by Bogue. Therefore, argues Davis, the social structure must be changed, by deliberate policy, 'so as to regulate births in accord with the demands of the collective welfare' a process that would require political power far beyond that which is likely to be in the hands of public health officials, nurses and midwives. 'Changes basic enough to affect motivation for having children would be changes in the structure of the family, in the position of women, and in the sexual mores.' Davis argues that the family planners, by operating from the basic assumption of the preservation of the family of desired size, ignore this fundamental need to change motivations. He then goes on to favour measures by the State which would have the opposite objectives to those pro-natalist policies of the 'developed' countries of the recent past which were discussed in Chapter 10, measures such as discouraging marriage, raising the marriage age and rewarding non-familial rather than familial roles. Here he joins with Professor S. Enke[7] in suggesting that governments should pay people to be sterilized, should meet all costs of abortion and abort all illegitimate pregnancies, should charge substantial fees for marriage licences, and should construct a tax system providing *disincentives* rather than *incentives* for child-bearing. Noting that twenty-seven European countries give cash payments to parents having children, Davis suggests that family allowances be reduced, that income-tax exemptions for children might be abolished; that paid maternity leaves should be reduced, that women should be encouraged to work, that public housing priorities should not be based on family size, that educational aids to married students should cease . . . and so on.

By this point the reader begins to wonder what Davis means in political terms by inducing basic changes in motivations *against* children, and, remembering how little effect the totalitarian regimes of Germany and Italy had in their *pro-natalist* objectives, how effective his *anti-natalist* proposals might be, so long as couples desire children, which apparently they do. That he tends to overstate the economic bases of motivations is suggested in his concluding remarks that the fact that the net reproduction rate of Sweden had been below replacement level for thirty-four years before 1963 was 'because of the economic depression'. He might also have observed that Sweden had one of the most comprehensive policies of social security in the world in favour of the family,[8] which seems to suggest that motivations might not be changed as readily as he seems to imply by his proposed disincentives, which also carry substantial totalitarian overtones at the political level. Nevertheless Davis has performed a major service in emphasizing how difficult it is in modern societies, in which mortality no longer exercises the degree of control that it did in the past, to induce anything like stability in human populations.

But if Bogue is too optimistic, Davis does seem to be a little too pessimistic about the role of family planning in reducing the rate of population growth. The very fact that the movement is spreading so rapidly is itself a sign of changing attitudes, and attitudes do not readily change without accompanying social change. Furthermore, the growing number of governments prepared to implement policies and to invest very substantial public funds to *restrict* growth rates is an entirely new phenomenon. Davis ignores the extent to which an induced reduction in birth rates (even though it operates only through those sectors of the population who want to control family size – e.g. the third or quarter of women at risk who are prepared to come to the clinics) can in turn affect the process of economic development and social change. Yet too much should not be expected. The history of the relative ineffectiveness of pro-natalist policies does not encourage the opinion that anti-natalist policies will be very much more effective, unless they are associated with other changes in the economic and social systems of the countries in which they operate. The one advantage which the anti-natalist policies have is that they are generally being applied in societies where there is increasing evidence that women want fewer children. In other words, the initial motivation to slower growth rates is already there. However, knowledge is much too imprecise yet to permit prediction of the effectiveness of the population policies now being implemented in developing countries, and as some of the countries with vigorous family planning programmes in which the birth rate has fallen are also those which have also clearly undergone major social and economic changes, the isolation of the precise influence of each of the many variables involved is an extremely difficult task. The cases of Japan and Taiwan illustrate this point.

Japan is the clearest example of a non-European country that has completed a major demographic transition in the present century, or more precisely in the forty years following 1920. The story of this transition has been completely documented and recounted in the scholarly work of Dr Irene Taeuber,[9] and therefore need not be described in detail here. The relationship of birth and death rates in Japan between approximately 1920 and 1960 provides an almost perfect illustration of the classical transition theory. The Japanese population had been fairly stable for over a century before 1850. Even in the nineteenth century there appears to have been a considerable degree of control over fertility through recourse to abortion, infanticide and primitive methods of contraception. These traditional methods of control to maintain a stationary population in a peasant society began to break down as Japan's contacts with the Western World widened. Early population figures and vital rates were almost certainly deficient, but the fact of a substantial and increasing rate of growth in the latter half of the nineteenth century is certain. The estimated population of 27,200,000 in 1852 had increased to 34,600,000 in 1876, and to 46,732,000 in 1902.[10] Up to this point the increase cannot be clearly attributed to falling death rates. Before 1850 and running well back into its history, Japan had suffered heavy mortality from dysentery, typhoid, smallpox and malaria. Contact with European peoples after 1850 eventually helped to check some of these, but initially brought both new diseases and more virulent strains of old ones. Taeuber writes that over 250,000 deaths were recorded from a cholera outbreak in 1860 in Tokyo alone, that dysentery reached a peak in 1893, and that vaccination against smallpox did not become effective until towards the end of the century.

All these factors kept death rates high until well into the twentieth century, but at the same time constraints on fertility seem to have weakened and birth rates rose from a recorded 25·2 per 1,000 in 1875–9 to 33·6 in 1910–14. The general trend is illustrated in Table 11. 1.

Table 11.1 Vital Rates of Japan 1875–1919[11]

Period	Population in thousands	Birth Rate Per 1,000	Death Rate Per 1,000	Natural Increase per 1,000
1875–9	35,111	25·2	18·0	7·2
1895–9	43,248	30·6	20·7	9·9
1915–19	55,527	32·4	22·5	9·9

The suggestion of increasing fertility is supported by an increase in children aged 0–4 per 1,000 women aged 15–49 from 490 in 1888 to 559 in 1913. Precisely how changes in marriage patterns might have affected this trend is not clear, but at the end of the period the proportions of young men and women who were married were very high, corresponding approximately to the recent peak rates in the United States, Australia, New Zealand and a number of western European countries. In 1920, for example, the proportions of young Japanese men and women who were married were as follows:

Age	Men	Women
20–24	27·4	64·9
25–29	70·6	85·7
30–34	87·6	89·4

In summing up the situation of Japan between about 1870 and 1915, Taeuber concludes:[12]

. . . the initial impact of economic modernization tended towards an increase in fertility. . . . In Japan, the amelioration of economic conditions, wider opportunities for employment, and the increase of social mobility presumably resulted in, or were accompanied by, a reduced incidence of family limitation. Children who were not needed to replace their parents in the villages could migrate to the developing cities, to employment outside agriculture, or to the Empire. The same matrix of values that sanctioned abortion or infanticide now sanctioned the rates of childbearing so often presumed to be an inherent characteristic of the peasant society.

From about 1920 until the end of the Second World War, the two most significant demographic trends in Japan were a shift towards higher marriage age and a steady decline in death rate. The proportions married moved quite markedly at younger ages towards the patterns then prevailing amongst European-type populations which were discussed in earlier chapters, that is with about a third of young women married between ages 20 to 24 years. The trend is summarized in Table 11.2. On the other hand the fertility of young married women remained fairly constant, but the shift in marriage patterns and a decline in fertility of older women brought some decline in crude birth rates. But the death rate moved downward steadily, to expand growth rates markedly between 1920 and 1925, and to sustain these rates around 1·3 to 1·4 per cent over most years until the Second World War.

These vital indices could be measured against the major changes that had occurred in Japanese society over these decades, marked by rapid urbanization, industrialization, increased rural productivity, and the attainment of almost universal literacy, to present an almost perfect pattern for the proponents of transition theory. By 1950 marriage patterns, fertility and life expectation (with

278

Table 11.2: Vital Indices of Japan, 1925–50[13]

| Year | Proportion of Women who were Married | | | Legitimate Female Births per 1,000 Married Women | | | | Crude Birth Rate per 1,000 | Crude Death Rate per 1,000 | Natural Increase per 1,000 |
	Age 20–24	Age 25–29	Age 20–24	Age 25–29	Age 30–34	Age 15–49			
1925	67·1	87·6	164·8	145·5	124·2	105·6	34·8	20·3	14·5
1930	60·1	87·6	161·4	137·9	116·1	101·2	32·4	18·2	14·2
1940	45·2	82·8	161·9	145·5	117·4	98·6	29·4	16·4	13·0
1950	42·7	79·1	158·8	135·8	93·7	81·5	28·1	10·9	17·2

infant mortality as low as 60 and e_0^0 at almost 61 years in 1950) were all well on the way to the traditional end product of the demographic transition. Thus the final decline of fertility in Japan, after a temporary post-war boom which took birth rates over 33 per 1,000 in 1947, 1948 and 1949, was a continuation of a longer-term trend going back to at least 1920, and was not a sudden post-war phenomenon. What appeared to have been new was the sudden revival of abortion as the method of control, but here again this method had a long tradition in Japan until at least the middle of the nineteenth century. It should also be remembered that in the terminal stages of the demographic transition of many European countries abortion was, and still appears to be, a major method of restricting fertility.

Immediately before the war the Japanese government opposed the birth control movement, but the influx of over five million Japanese from abroad immediately after the war and the baby boom which raised the birth rate to 34 per 1,000 in 1947 raised new fears of 'overpopulation'. A Population Problem Council was set up under Cabinet control in 1948 and in the same year the Eugenic Protection Law was passed, initially to permit the manufacture and dissemination of contraceptives; but before the new policy became really effective there was evidence that induced abortion was increasing rapidly and the Law was amended in 1949 to greatly liberalize the grounds on which induced abortion could be legally obtained. An important objective was, not to use abortion as the primary method of population control, but to minimize the harmful effects of clandestine operations and to provide a basis for the spread of more socially desirable forms of birth control.[14] However, there is now little doubt that the legalizing of abortion greatly assisted its spread, and estimates that the number of abortions was spreading rapidly encouraged the government to disseminate information about contraception 'to eliminate the bad influence of abortions upon the mother's health'.[15] It took some time for these government measures to show results, and abortions continued to rise to a peak of 1·17 million in 1955 (when they were estimated to be 68 per cent of all live births) after which they dropped to 955,000 in 1963, and to about 650,000 in 1965. However induced abortion still seems to be a prominent method of preventing unwanted births and the number of cases appears to have risen since then to over 700,000 in 1968.

In reviewing the factors that were most conducive to the creation of such a high motivation to family planning among the Japanese, Muramatsu lists a number of factors – the high degree of literacy, universal education and the desire of parents to give advanced training to their children, the influence of mass media, the impact of the post-war constitution giving equal rights of inheritance to children, the emancipation of women, the high degree of urbanization, and the historical heritage of population limitation going back for a century. Many of these are traditional in the classic transition cycle, but Muramatsu[16] gives considerable weight to the deliberate policy of the government as a factor accelerating the later phases of the process.

In the field of voluntary fertility regulation, the basic motivation is important on one hand, but at the same time to make available certain practical means of known effectiveness is no less significant, on the other hand, especially when the decline in fertility must be brought about within a short period of time . . . one would probably conclude that the real merit of the government's efforts [in bringing down Japan's birth rate in the fifteen years to 1965] lies in the planning all over the country, rapidly and extensively, since the official sanction and endorsement of family planning by the government meant a great deal to the general public. . . . But at the same time, one may be equally justified in speculating that the low level of fertility in Japan would have been reached anyway, sooner or later even if there had been no such government-sponsored efforts at all. . . .

Japan is the one clear case of a major Asian population completing the process of demographic transition, but its course has been very different from that which other Asian governments are now trying to induce. To begin with its initial level of fertility was comparatively low; it also had a tradition of population control; and the country had been thoroughly 'Westernized' (in terms of literacy, urbanization, etc). before the final transition occurred. It should also be emphasized that the decline in fertility never caught up with the decline in mortality, for, as Table 11.3 shows, even the low birth rate of 18·6 in 1965 was still giving a rate of natural increase of over 1 per cent, for by this time the Japanese enjoyed a life expectation which compared favourably with the most affluent Western societies.

Kingsley Davis[17] has used the Japanese case in support of his argument that social and economic change must be present before

281

THE GROWTH AND CONTROL OF WORLD POPULATION

Table 11.3: Vital Indices of Japan 1950–65

	Rates per, 1000 of Population			Infant Deaths per 1,000 live Births	Expectation of life at birth, persons
	Live Births	Deaths	Natural Increase		
1950	28·1	10·9	17·2	60·1	57·9
1955	19·3	7·8	11·5	40·0	66·0
1960	17·2	7·6	9·6	30·8	67·8
1965	18·6	7·1	11·5	18·5	70·3

any substantial fall in fertility can be experienced and observes that in the few additional countries of Asia in which there has been a decline in fertility, this decline may again have been as much the response to economic and social change as it was to family planning policies. He observes, for example, that there had been a fall in the registered births per 1,000 Taiwanese women between ages 15–49 from as early as 1952 (e.g. from 198 in 1952 to 170 in 1963). The decline accelerated after that (to 149 in 1966), but while the decline after 1963 coincided with the implementation of the family planning programme, it also coincided with rapid economic development, an increased rate of urbanization, housing shortages and other indices typically associated with the onset of fertility decline.

Taiwan and the other countries of Asia in which there has clearly been a decline in fertility – e.g., South Korea, Singapore, Hong Kong – are not only marginal in quantitative terms to the vast population of Asia, but are also areas in which economic and social change has been most in evidence. Compared with the situation in which the mass of the peasantry of India or Pakistan live, they are affluent and economically developed societies. They have also already reached a fairly advanced degree of literacy. Nevertheless the efforts to influence fertility patterns now being made in the 'giant' countries of Asia are on such a different scale from anything that has been attempted before, and are of such recent origin, that a final pronouncement cannot yet be made upon them. One cause for optimism is the support found for the family planning programmes in the many surveys that have been carried out, and the absence of any strong moral or religious opposition. The Japanese experience also suggests that when a government is prepared to adopt extreme measures, such as legalizing abortion, the process of decline can be accelerated. Other Asian countries have not followed

282

the Japanese in this regard, and as Davis implies, they still begin with the proposition that parents must be allowed to have their desired number of children – say three or four – and at current mortality levels this still implies a relatively high growth rate. To this extent the current policies of the governments of India, Pakistan and elsewhere are still 'pro-natalist', but to attempt to put more than a brake on growth rates, and to legislate against the family as Enke and some other economists have suggested could run the risk of losing mass support. The limited objectives of the present policies of India, Pakistan, and the many other countries cited in Chapter 10, appear politically more realistic than a thorough-going 'anti-family' policy.

If this is accepted, then the situation envisaged by Bogue, of world population stability by the twenty-first century, will certainly not occur. Indeed from the evidence of both the developing and developed countries of the world today there seems little to support such a view. With death now so unimportant, and with marriages so much more frequent in the young childbearing age groups than they appear to have been for centuries past, the 'developed' countries are likely to go on increasing at rates between 0·5 and 1·0 per cent so long as the average family size by the end of a woman's child-bearing life continues to be between 2·5 and 3·0 children. Probably there is no *urgent* need to alter this pattern: the countries in which these patterns exist are affluent; they have enough rural surpluses to feed at least twice their existing populations, and there seem enough industrial and fuel resources at their disposal to keep their societies in affluent living for the next hundred years or so. Still, even if their growth rates average about 0·75 a year, they will have to plan for populations twice their present size within a century and, as will be suggested later, this prospect is beginning to cause some concern.

The major *problem* of population remains, however, the reduction of the uniquely high growth rates of the 'developing' world; and within these regions the problems are undoubtedly most acute among the Asian giants. Despite the extremely high growth rates of many parts of Latin America, particularly tropical America, this zone has the potential to carry populations several times as large as at present. The problem there is political rather than one of resources: how to redirect investment to increase efficiency in the use of ample human and material resources, how to increase the mobility of labour and how to extend international co-operation amongst governments.

Much the same may be said of Africa. Growth rates are high, but there are still ample land and other resources. A feature of Africa has been the very considerable labour mobility. But with growing nationalism this is tending to be restricted rather than encouraged – a restriction that can only bring new problems rather than solve existing ones. Again a crucial element is the need for stable and co-operating governments rather than incipient over-population.

In India, Pakistan, Indonesia and probably Mainland China, the problem of the ratio of population to resources is much more acute, although some of the most gloomy prognostications of a few years ago appear to have been unfounded. Writing in 1963 and emphasizing that *per capita* incomes of three-quarters of the population of the ECAFE region were still below $100, Simon Kuznets concluded[18] that the levels in 1961 were still barely above those of 1938 for most countries, and that in many populations growth was tending to outstrip the growth in *per capita* product. The only clear exception to this was Japan. Writing in 1967, Kuznets still found a negative correlation between population growth and *per capita* product in many areas, particularly in Asia and Africa,[19] but he appears to have been a little more optimistic than in 1963, emphasizing that the underdeveloped countries control substantial resources, that they have the opportunity to apply modern technology – without the cost of having to develop it – to utilize those resources, and that they should be able to divert sufficient funds from current into capital product to raise the rate of economic growth. He sees the core of the problem in inadequate internal social and political institutions rather than in basic resources and capital.

While opinions about the world's resources tend to range from extreme pessimism to absurd optimism, the current opinion seems to be settling towards cautious optimism. The extreme of pessimism is the prognostication of Professor Erlich[20] who sees the world disintegrating by the 1980s through vast famines, if these are not preceded by plague and thermonuclear war; and the extreme optimism is perhaps Mr Colin Clark[21] who sees little difficulty in the world carrying five or six times the present population. The recent spectacular improvements in strains of food grains (such as maize, sorghum and millets) and the growing evidence of the willingness of the peasants of India and Pakistan to improve rural productivity by the use of fertilizers does at least lean towards Mr Clark rather than to Professor Erlich, particularly as far as food production is concerned. An Australian economist, raising the question whether the growth rate of agricultural production in India can be lifted sufficiently to take care of both the population increase and rising standards of food consumption, before population control makes a major contribution, answers that this can be done and adds that the most encouraging thing of all from the economists' point of view is the discovery that 'the inertia of a traditional society and a traditional agriculture will succumb to the attraction of incentive prices, a new high-yielding technology and assured supplies of inputs and credit in support of that technology'.[22] What he sees happening in India is already well advanced in many of the smaller Asian countries. The production of food (as the 1968 world wheat situation indicates) is not the problem, but rather its distribution through sound economic policies that can assist the developing countries.

The situation regarding fuel and mineral resources seems no less promising, at least for the next fifty years or so, given reasonable international trading arrangements. The greatest users of these resources will continue to be the slower growing but most affluent societies, but their exhaustion does not seem to be an immediate prospect.[23]

Yet optimism should not run too far, and certainly not to the extreme of Bogue who suggests the complete cessation of population growth by the twenty-first century. In this case resources would be ample; but the evidence is all against such stability. The most optimistic view warranted by the scene of 1968 would seem to be about a halving of the world's growth rate by the end of the century and this will have to occur through increasingly efficient control of human fertility, for it is quite evident that no government of the 'developing' or the 'developed' world will voluntarily permit death to resume its historical role as the controller of human growth rates. All this assumes the absence of the ultimate human folly, nuclear war, an event which would make nonsense of all the discussion presented so far. Assuming man does avoid this ultimate folly, what then appears to be the minimum growth pattern for which the world must prepare for the remainder of the century?

285

First consider the summary position of the world between about 1960 and 1965 and the variation between major continental areas, as illustrated in Table 11.4. The world's growth rate in 1960–5 has been estimated at 1·8 per cent a year and if it is stabilized at this level the world's population will double in approximately thirty-three years, that is just before the twentieth century is out. The fastest growing continent is Latin America (with a rate that would double population in twenty-three years) followed by Africa (doubling in about thirty years), and then Asia (doubling in about thirty-five years). Only Europe falls below a 1 per cent growth rate, but even its rate of 0·8 per cent would double its population within 86 years. Nowhere does there seem to be the prospect of population stability or growth rates even beginning to approach the levels that have prevailed over most of human history before the nineteenth century.

Table 11.4: Rank Order of Growth Rates of Major Continental Regions of the World, 1960–65

	Rate of Increase per cent a year	Estimated Rates per 1,000 Births	Deaths
The World	1·8	34	16
Latin America	2·8	40	11
Africa	2·3	46	23
Asia	2·0	38	18
USSR	1·5	22	7
North America	1·3	22	9
Europe	0·8	18	10

Recent projections prepared by the Population Branch of the Department of Economic and Social Affairs of the United Nations[24] indicate that if recent levels remain constant, the world's population could grow from 2,998 million in 1960 to 7,522 million by the end of the century. This assumes only a continuation of mortality declines, at a rate that will add six months to the life expectation at birth among the less developed regions with the passing of each year of time, but with diminishing rates of gain as levels of life expectancy rise towards an ultimate maximum e_0^0 of 73·9 years. The most significant determinant of future growth will be fertility rather than mortality, and in the light of trends already observed indicating some decline and of the major campaigns now in hand to reduce birth rates, an assumption of 'no change' in fertility is probably too pessimistic.

Consequently the United Nations' projections include assumptions of fertility decline, based on the generalized proposition that once such a decline sets in, the birth rate (adjusted for age and sex) will be 90 per cent of its initial value after ten years, 70 per cent after twenty years, and will eventually settle at 50 per cent. The projections then give 'high', 'medium' and 'low' variants according to the time at which fertility decline is assumed to commence, and the projections of world population within these limits are, in millions:

	1960	1980	2000
'High' variant	2,998	4,551	6,994
'Medium' variant	2,998	4,330	6,130
'Low' variant	2,998	4,147	5,448

It is assumed here that the 'medium' variant is the most plausible proposition for the future. It will in fact assume a 'saving' of 1,392 millions of people by the year 2000 compared with the assumption that fertility would remain constant, and this is taken here as the maximum that might be expected from birth control between now and the end of the century.

Therefore, given the schedule of change implied in Table 11.5, the population of major regions would be as shown in Table 11.6.

The implications of these growth patterns are clear. Even among the 'developed' countries the total increase this century would continue to make major demands upon both agricultural and industrial resources – a fact too often overlooked in considering projections of populations – but the increase of European peoples seems very modest compared with the staggering growth of Latin America and Africa, in which populations may increase by almost 200 per cent between 1960 and 2000.

It will be seen from Table 11.5 that these projections are based upon very considerable reductions in birth rates in today's most fertile areas, with the birth rate of South Asia coming down from 43 to 27 per 1,000 between 1960–5 and 1995–2000. The assumed decreases are less in Latin America or Africa, but this assumption seems reasonable, for as yet birth control has taken very little hold

287

Table 11.5: Schedule Showing Assumed Trend of Crude Birth, Death and Natural Increase Rates per 1,000 of Population Applied in the Projections of Table 11. 6*

| | 1960–65 | | | 1975–80 | | | 1995–2000 | | |
	BR	DR	NI	BR	DR	NI	BR	DR	NI
WORLD†	33·9	15·9	18·0	31·6	12·8	18·8	25·7	9·3	16·4
North America	22·6	9·2	13·4	23·6	9·2	14·4	22·2	7·9	14·3
Latin America	39.6	11·2	28·4	37·2	8·4	28·8	30·3	6·2	24·1
Europe	17·8	10·0	7·8	16·4	10·4	6·0	15·9	11·2	4·7
USSR	22·1	7·2	14·9	19·9	7·3	12·6	19·3	8·7	10.6
South Asia‡	43·0	18·9	24·1	38·6	14·1	24·5	26·9	7·9	19·0
East Asia§	32·6	18·9	13·7	27·3	14·3	13·0	19·9	10·5	9·4
Africa	45·5	22·5	23·0	44·6	18·1	26·5	40.0	13·1	26·9
Oceania‖	25·0	10·8	14·2	25·5	9·5	16·0	25·3	9·6	15·7

* Based on UN Department of Economic and Social Affairs, *World Population Prospects as Assessed in 1963*, New York 1966, 34-6.
† Includes all areas except Israel, Cyprus, Hong Kong, Mongolia, Macao and the Ryukyu Islands, Polynesia and Micronesia.
‡ South Asia includes: India, Pakistan, Iran, Afghanistan, Ceylon, Nepal, Bhutan, Sikkim and the Maldive Islands (Middle South Asia).
Indonesia, Viet-Nam, The Philippines, Thailand, Burma, Malaysia and Singapore, Cambodia, Laos, Portuguese Timor, Brunei (South East Asia).
Turkey, Iraq, Saudi Arabia, Syria, Yemen, Jordan, Lebanon, The Protectorate of Southern Arabia, Muscat and Oman, Palestine (Gaza Strip), Kuwait, Aden, Bahrain, Trucial Oman and Qatar (South West Asia).
§ East Asia includes: Mainland China, Japan, Korea, China and Taiwan.
‖ Not including Polynesia and Micronesia.

Table 11.6 : Estimates of World Population, in Millions (Based on rates and trends illustrated in Table 11. 5)

	Numbers			Increase per cent		
	1960	1980	2000	1960–80	1980–2000	1960–2000
WORLD	2,998	4,330	6,130	44	42	104
North America	199	262	354	32	35	78
Latin America	212	378	628	78	66	196
Europe & USSR						
Europe	425	479	527	13	10	24
USSR	214	278	353	30	27	65
Total	639	757	880	18	16	38
Asia						
South Asia†	865	1,420	2,171	64	53	151
East Asia‡	794	1,041	1,287	31	24	62
Total	1,659	2,461	3,458	48	41	108
Africa	273	449	768	64	71	181
Oceania	16	23	32	44	39	100

† South Asia includes: India, Pakistan, Iran, Afghanistan, Ceylon, Nepal, Bhutan, Sikkim and the Maldive Islands (Middle South Asia).
Indonesia, Viet-Nam, The Philippines, Thailand, Burma, Malaysia, Cambodia, Laos, Portuguese Timor, Brunei (South East Asia).
Turkey, Iraq, Saudi Arabia, Syria, Yemen, Israel, Jordan, Lebanon, the Protectorate of Southern Arabia, Cyprus, Muscat and Oman, Palestine (Gaza Strip), Kuwait, Aden, Bahrain, Trucial Oman and Qatar (South West Asia).
‡ East Asia includes: Mainland China, Hongkong, Mongolia, Macao, Japan, Korea, China, Taiwan and the Ryukyu Islands.

Figure 11.2: Retrospect and Prospect: The Distribution of the World's Population in the Year 2000

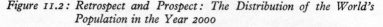

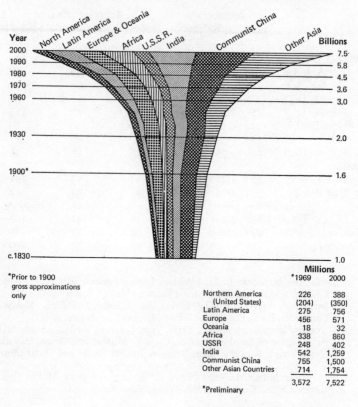

*Prior to 1900
gross approximations
only

*Preliminary

	Millions	
	*1969	2000
Northern America	226	388
(United States)	(204)	(350)
Latin America	275	756
Europe	456	571
Oceania	18	32
Africa	338	860
USSR	248	402
India	542	1,259
Communist China	755	1,500
Other Asian Countries	714	1,754
	3,572	7,522

Based on assumption of constant fertility levels

Source: United
Nations (basic data)

on these continents. While it is assumed in Table 11.5 that growth rates will also decline in all major areas except Africa, the rates shown for 1995–2000 are still considerable. This follows from the assumption that for the less developed regions mortality decline will continue throughout the rest of the century. The decline could well exceed the assumed levels in the case of Africa and Latin America, where current mortality is still very high, but the main determinant of growth in all regions for the rest of this century will be changes in fertility.

The projections given in Table 11.6 will considerably alter the

Figure 11.3: *Relative Rates of Population Growth by Major Regions 1920–2000*

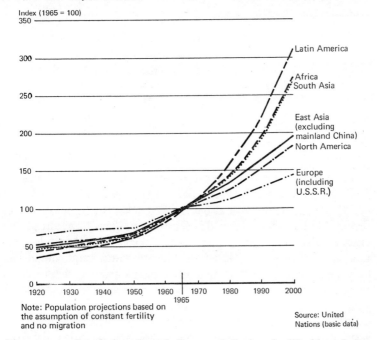

Note: Population projections based on the assumption of constant fertility and no migration

Source: United Nations (basic data)

Figure 11.4: *Population Growth Past and Projected: World and Less Developed Countries (LDCs)*

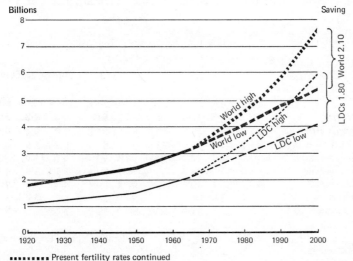

━━━━━ Present fertility rates continued
━ ━ ━ ━ 30% Reduction in growth rates by 2000

291

distribution of the world's population. Taking Europe and USSR combined as a base of 100, the pattern would be:

	1960	2000
Europe and USSR	100	100
Africa	43	87
North America	31	40
Latin America	33	71
Asia	260	393
Oceania	3	4

The implications of these projected population growth rates for food production and land use have already been mentioned; but additional problems must also arise. Whatever the future course of fertility and mortality, the 'developing' countries have already an enormous stock of young persons as a result of past trends (particularly falling mortality) whose education and employment can only be achieved by diverting investments from agriculture. In most countries these young people, classified as persons aged 0–14 years, represent over 40 per cent of the populations of 'developing' countries. In a few cases they approach 50 per cent. Under the assumptions in the above projections, there will be little relief from this burden of young dependency until after 1980. The age distributions based on the projections of Table 11.6 are given in Table 11.7.

Table 11.7: Age Composition of Populations Implied in Table 11.6
(Proportions per cent in each age group)

	Age 0–14			Age 15–64			Age 65 and Over		
	1960	1980	2000	1960	1980	2000	1960	1980	2000
World*	36·4	35·8	32·4	58·7	58·4	61·2	4·9	5·8	6·4
North America	31·3	29·9	29·8	59·7	60·7	61·3	9·0	9·4	8·9
Latin America	41·7	42·1	38·0	55·0	53·9	57·7	3·3	3·9	4·3
Europe and USSR	27·4	24·1	24·6	64·0	64·1	63·1	8·6	11·8	12·3
South Asia	41·0	41·7	34·6	55·9	54·7	60·9	3·1	3·6	4·6
East Asia	36·1	32·2	26·5	59·7	62·4	66·1	4·2	5·4	7·4
Africa	43·1	43·6	42·3	54·2	53·6	54·5	2·7	2·8	3·2
Oceania	31·7	30·8	31·6	60·5	60·9	59·9	7·8	8·3	8·5

* Excluding population of the Ryukyu Islands, Israel, Cyprus, Polynesia and Micronesia.

Whatever the course of future fertility,[25] the numbers of young people reaching working age must double in many 'developing' countries over the next fifteen years. Agricultural development, which still provides the livelihoods of 70 or 80 per cent of the workers in many countries, will of course remain crucial for many years ahead, but increasing proportions must move into non-agricultural occupations. The economic boom associated with rising *per capita* incomes has never been achieved and sustained without the rapid transfer of populations to urban areas, even in the past when growth rates did not exceed 1·5, or even 1 per cent a year. This urbanization process is already markedly in evidence in many areas of rapid growth. For example, major cities of India (such as Bombay, Delhi, Madras) have been growing at 5 and 6 per cent a year compared with an all-India growth rate of 2·1 or 2·2 per cent. In Pakistan, Karachi has been growing at about 4·5 per cent compared with some 2 per cent for the whole country. Bangkok has achieved almost 7 per cent growth in recent years in a national average of 3·2 per cent. Kuala Lumpur and Singapore stand similarly in relationship to Malaysia; and Taipei with 4·5 to 5 per cent is outstripping Taiwan's 3·5 per cent growth.

The shift from agriculture raises in turn the question of investment resources for education and occupational training – a crucial aspect of any policy which aims at bringing about the economic and social changes associated with birth control. Many of the smaller Asian countries in particular (e.g. Taiwan, Thailand, Malaysia) have made considerable progress in the field of education, but the objective of universal literacy will continue to require rates of investment far in excess of the rates of population growth. The following figures taken from a paper presented to the Asian Population Conference of 1963[26] illustrate the dimensions of this problem. In the Philippines, 73 per cent of children aged 7–13 were estimated to be at school by 1957. To reach a target of 100 per cent enrolment in a six-year school programme by 1980 would involve a threefold increase in numbers. In Indonesia, also with an estimated 73 per cent enrolment ratio in 1960, the increase to reach 100 per cent enrolment by 1980 was calculated at 2·23 times the school population of 1960. In India the task is even more formidable, for here it was estimated that only 40 per cent of the children of 6–13 years were at school in 1961, and this in a five-year school programme. The aim of increasing the duration of schooling to eight

293

years and reaching 100 per cent enrolment would increase the school population in the twenty years 1961–81 from 32 million to 113 million, or by a factor of 3·5. India's problem is, however, small compared with that of Pakistan, where enrolment ratios of children aged 5–9 in 1961 were as low as 35 per cent. Lifting that to 100 per cent and raising the duration of schooling from five to eight years by 1981 would require an increase in school children from 4·5 millions to 32·4 millions, or more than a seven-fold increase!

Educational training and the relocation of labour have direct political implications, for success in these fields as in family planning, requires stable and efficient government; and both require the development of a market economy for agricultural and industrial products.

Figure 11.5 ; Age Distribution – Child Dependency, 1966

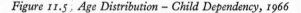

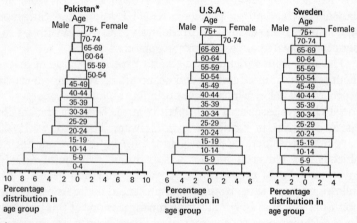

*Projected by U.S. Bureau of the Census [1965]

The demographic issues now facing 'developing' countries, unique in terms of the speed of growth as well as in the vast numbers involved, cannot be solved by a unilateral approach. With regard to the basic requirement of food, the race between Malthus's hare of population growth and tortoise of food production still goes on, with the latter showing some signs at least of catching up a little. The next step, which is now being recognized in the forward planning of high growth regions is to sustain the balance between food production, social investment and industrial investment. Thwarted by their failure to reach this desideratum in face of ever expanding population growth rates, many of the 'developing' countries have now, as we have seen, turned to a new line – in Malthusian terms how to persuade the hare to go to sleep for a while. The limited success so far should not be interpreted as inability to bring about curbs to growth. The experiments now being tried are at most a decade old. The demographic transition of today's 'developed' countries of western and northern Europe and Europe overseas took from fifty to seventy years to accomplish. The trends this century in eastern Europe and Japan are reminders that events can move faster in the twentieth century. The new element in the present situation of the 'developing' areas is the widespread determination of governments to act and to lead their people towards the goal of population control; but they need at least another decade to see if they can produce results. Whatever the success of the major efforts now being made, however, there seems little chance that the 6,000 million figure will not be reached by the end of the century, or indeed that this will not be doubled again in the twenty-first century to 12,000 million.

Any estimate about the twenty-first century is necessarily highly conjectural, whereas, given the absence of nuclear war, the doubling of the world's population this century seems a positive certainty. In other words, in little more time than the average age span between parents and their children, as many people may be added to the world's population in one generation as in the whole of man's history to the present. For thousands of years man's existence on earth was a struggle between the forces of life and death. Now man appears to be perfecting the power to defer death at least to the expectation of seventy years. The great gap that still exists in life expectation between the rich and poor nations of the world tends to obscure the facts both that there are few areas today where these expectations are not far in excess of earlier centuries, and that the lower expectations of around fifty years are leaping ahead towards the levels that now prevail in the high income, industrialized countries. As man approaches the biblical ideal of three score and ten years as his birthright, he becomes a unique creature reproductively. As emphasized at the beginning of this chapter, he will come to replace an incredibly wasteful reproductive system, with its high wastage through death, by an extremely efficient system which, for the purposes of reproduction, practically eliminates death as a controlling factor. With expectations of life at seventy years, to which he seems to be inexorably moving, mankind must rely on efficient birth control to keep populations within the capacities of his social and economic systems to provide for his welfare. The desperate attempts of many governments of the less developed societies to reverse the course of history by making population control an aid to, rather than a consequence of, improvement of their economic and social systems, have been discussed in Chapter 10; but few who live in modern industrial societies seem yet to realize either the uniqueness of their own position or what any relaxation of the very effective fertility controls now practised by them could mean to their own economic and social systems. Nor do they seem to be conscious of the implications of their own growth rates of around 1 per cent.

In this regard a message from President Nixon to Congress on 18 July 1969 is of particular interest. He drew attention to the fact that the 1967 population of 200 million Americans would increase at current growth rates to 300 million by the year 2000, and added:

This growth will produce serious challenges for our society . . . many of our present social problems may be related to the fact that we have had only fifty years in which to accommodate the second hundred million Americans . . . We have thus had to accomplish in a very few decades an adjustment to population growth which was once spread over centuries. . . .

The President went on to question whether existing cities can cope with this influx, as the vast majority of the next hundred million Americans will have to be accommodated in urban areas. As an alternative the National Commission on Urban Growth has recommended the creation of a hundred new communities of 100,000 people in each, but this would accommodate only 20 million or a fifth of the total increase. To accommodate the full 100 million persons would mean the creation of a new city of 250,000 persons each month until the end of the century! Such colossal tasks, when combined with other major problems of preserving natural resources and controlling water and air pollution, seem almost insuperable,[27] Yet they have to be solved if industrial society as we know it is to persist. The President concluded his statement by proposing a 'Commission on Population Growth and the American Future' which should examine: the probable course of population growth and distribution to the year 2000; the resources in the public sector of the economy that will be required to deal with the anticipated growth; and ways in which population growth may affect the activities of Federal, State and Local government. The President ended his message with a call to extend family planning services with Federal support in order that 'no American woman should be deprived access to family planning assistance because of her economic condition'. Thus the assumption appears to be, even in the world's most affluent and free-enterprise society, that restraints on population growth by social policy are still necessary.[28]

Clearly therefore the demographic patterns of the modern world have revolutionary implications for both the 'developed' and the 'developing' societies. The greatest problem is how to force the pace of reducing the uniquely high growth rates of the 'developing' world, and the next decade is likely to give fairly clear indications as to whether the policies reviewed in the previous chapter are going to succeed; but those living in the affluence of the developed world cannot close their eyes to the uniqueness of their own position and to the social, economic and cultural implications of their abolition of death as a significant phenomenon – reproductively speaking.

As emphasized at the beginning of this book, some who observe the present 'population explosion' decry it as if a great shadow of impending doom had spread upon the world; yet the astonishing growth rates of the world today must be accepted as a triumph of man over his environment. The point to emphasize is not that half of mankind is still illiterate and undernourished, but that in half the world man has escaped sufficiently from the controls of the past to become literate and to look forward to his heritage of three-score years and ten. This is a tremendous achievement, but the victory will not be won until the stirrings of the developing world, and particularly of Asia, are brought to their fulfilment of controlled population and expanding productivity. Mankind has in fact to go against the historical trend of evolution, as the authors of the preface to the United Nations' population projections have so succinctly put it:[29]

Deliberate thinking . . . has so increased this rate [of population growth] that the very nature of the evolutionary process has thereby been changed. . . . Faced with the problem of checking this growth, we are swimming against the tide and, in extremity, having discovered how to increase the flood waters we now also possess the means of arresting them. It now depends upon us whether this awakening consciousness within the stream of life ends in failure or success. If tomorrow mankind loses the desire to live or, more correctly, to survive, the history of life on earth will have lost all meaning.

Thus the problems associated with the control of population growth are not peripheral to man's existence, but fundamental to it. With so much achieved already, there is not yet cause for despair. And the time? Fifty years, or at most, a century. In any case, it is so short that a demographer facing up to *his* facts of life, and hearing man's cry for 'peace in our time on earth', is morally bound to add 'and population control'.

References

CHAPTER I

1 United Nations Department of Economic and Social Affairs, 1967, *Demographic Yearbook*.

2 For outlines of the problems of assessing the growth and size of world, national and regional populations see UN: Department of Social Affairs, 1953, *The Determinants and Consequences of Population Trends*, Population Studies No. 17; Department of Economic and Social Affairs, 1963, *Population Bulletin No. 6 with special reference to the situation and recent trends of mortality in the world*; and 1965, *Population Bulletin No. 7 with special reference to conditions and trends of fertility in the world*, New York

3 There are many standard texts dealing with methods of demographic analysis, but four basic works are the UN, Department of Economic and Social Affairs: 1952, Manual I: *Methods of Estimating Total Population for Current Dates*, Population Studies No. 10; 1955, Manual III: *Methods of Appraisal of Quality of Basic Data for Population Estimates*, Population Studies No. 23; 1956, Manual II: *Methods for Population Projection by Sex and Age*, Population Studies No. 25; 1967, Manual IV: *Methods of Estimating Basic Demographic Measures from Incomplete Data*, Population Studies No. 42.

4 Figures in this table are derived from: W. S. Thompson, 1959, *Population and Progress in the Far East*, Chicago, p. 12; A. M. Carr Saunders, 1936, *World Population*, Oxford, p. 42; UN, Department of Economic and Social Affairs, 1966, *World Population Prospects as Assessed in 1963*, Population Studies No. 41.

5 Sources of these figures are *UN Demographic Yearbooks*.

6 Adapted from UN, 1966, op. cit., p. 37.

7 UN, Department of Economic and Social Affairs, 1958, *The Future Growth of World Population*, New York, p. v.

CHAPTER 2

1 For histories of censuses see: Australia, Commonwealth Bureau of Census and Statistics, 1917, *Census of the Commonwealth of Australia, 1911*, Vol. I (Statistician's Report), Melbourne; F. E. Linder, 1959, 'World Demographic Data' in P. M. Hauser and O. D. Duncan, eds., *The Study of Population*, Chicago, pp. 321–60; and United Nations, Department of Social Affairs, 1953, *The Determinants and Consequences of Population Trends*, Population Studies No. 17.

2 For an appraisal of King's estimates see D. V. Glass, 1950, 'Gregory King's estimate of the population of England and Wales, 1695', *Population Studies* III, No. 4, pp. 338–74.

3 For the history of the development of vital registration systems see F. Lorimer, 1959, 'The development of Demography', in P. M. Hauser and O. D. Duncan, op. cit., pp. 124–79; and more generally Part II (Development and Current Status of Demography) of this book.

4 The early history of population theories is summarized and documented in UN, 1953, op. cit., Chapter III. See particularly also C. E. Stangeland, 1904, *Pre-Malthusian Doctrines of Population* (Studies in History, Economics and Law, edited by Faculty of Political Science, Columbia University, XXI, No. 3), New York. Also, the extremely valuable article and bibliography by F. Lorimer, 1959, op. cit.

5 T. R. Malthus, 1803, *An Essay on the Principle of Population*; or *A View on its Past and Present Effects on Human Happiness, with an Inquiry into our Prospects Respecting the Removal or Mitigation of Evils which it Occasions*, London.

6 M. T. Sadler, 1830, *The Law of Population: a treatise, in six books, in disproof of the super-fecundity of human beings, and developing the real principle of their increase*, Vols I, II, London.

7 F. le Play, 1866, *La réforme sociale en France déduite de l'observation comparée des peuples européens*, Vols I–IV, Paris.

8 A. Dumont, 1890, *Dépopulation et civilisation. Etude démographique*, Paris.

9 New South Wales, Australia, Legislative Assembly, 1904, *Report* of the Royal Commission on the Decline of the Birth Rate and on the Mortality of Infants in New South Wales, together with copies of Commissions, Diagrams, Statistical Evidence and Statistical Exhibits, etc., Vol. I.

10 T. H. C. Stevenson, 1920, 'The fertility of various social classes in England and Wales from the middle of the nineteenth century to 1911', *Journal of the Royal Statistical Society*, LXXXIII, Part III, pp. 401–44.

11 For an outline of their contribution and a bibliography of their major works see F. Lorimer, 1959, op. cit.

12 Derived from F. Lorimer, et al., 1954, *Culture and Human Fertility*, Paris, UNESCO; T. E. Smith, 1960, 'The Cocos-Keeling Islands: a demographic laboratory', *Population Studies*, XIV, No. 2, pp. 94–130; and R. Titmuss and B. Abel-Smith, 1960, *Social Policies and Population Growth in Mauritius*, London, p. 273.

13 L. I. Dublin and A. J. Lotka, 'On the true rate of natural increase', *Journal of the American Statistical Association*, New Series, XX, No. 150, pp. 305–39.

14 F. Lorimer, 1959, op. cit., p. 156.

CHAPTER 3

1 J. C. Russell, 1958, 'Late ancient and medieval population', *Transactions of the American Philosophical Society*, XLVIII, Part 3.

2 A. P. Usher, 1930, 'The history of population and settlement in Eurasia', *The Geographical Review* (USA), XX, No. 1, pp. 110–32.

3 E. S. Deevy, 1960, 'The human population', *Scientific American*, CCIII, No. 3, pp. 195–217.

4 A. P. Usher, 1930, op. cit.

5 J. D. Durand, 1960, 'The population statistics of China, AD 2–1953', *Population Studies*, XIII, No. 3, pp. 209–56.

6 K. Davis, 1951, *The Population of India and Pakistan*, Princeton, pp. 24 ff.

7 For a summary and appraisal of these estimates of the ancient world see United Nations, Department of Social Affairs, 1953, *Determinants and Consequences of Population Trends*, Population Studies No. 17, Chapter II.

8 Ibid.

9 J. C. Russell, 1948, *British Medieval Population*, Albuquerque.

10 M. M. Postan, 1950, 'Some economic evidence of declining population in the later Middle Ages', *Economic History Review*, 2nd series, No. 3, pp. 221–46.

11 D. V. Glass, 1950, 'Gregory King's estimate of the population of England and Wales, 1695', *Population Studies*, III, No. 4, pp. 338–74.

12 A. Landry, 1945, *Traité de démographie*, Paris.

13 G.B.Riccioli, 1661, 'De versimili hominum numero', *Geographiae et hydorographiae reformatae*, Bologna, pp. 630–34.

14 W. F. Willcox, 1931, 'Increase in the population of the earth and of the continents since 1650' in W. F. Willcox (ed.) *International Migrations*, Vol. II, New York, pp. 32–82.

15 A. P. Usher, 1930, op. cit., pp. 130–32.

16 K. Davis, 1951, op. cit.

17 J. D. Durand, 1960, op. cit.

18 O. van der Sprenkel, 1953, 'Population statistics of Ming China', *Bulletin of the School of Oriental and African Studies*, XV, Part 2, pp. 286–326.

19 Ping Ti Ho, 1959, *Studies on the Population of China, 1368–1953*, Cambridge, Mass.

20 A. M. Carr Saunders, 1936, *World Population*, Oxford.

21 W. F. Willcox, 1940, *Studies in American Demography*, Ithaca, pp. 511–40.

22 UN, 1953, op. cit., p. 11.

23 J. C. Russell, 1958, op. cit.

24 J. D. Durand, 1960, op. cit.

25 F. Lorimer, et al., 1954, *Culture and Human Fertility*, Paris, UNESCO, p. 176.

26 J. C. Russell, 1958, op. cit.

CHAPTER 4

1 For presentation and discussion of these estimates see A. M. Carr Saunders, 1936, *World Population*, Oxford; W. S. Thompson, 1942 and later editions, *Population Problems*, New York; and United Nations, Department of Social Affairs, 1953, *Determinants and Consequences of Population Trends*, Population Studies No. 17, New York.

2 J. C. Russell, 1948, *British Medieval Population*, Albuquerque.

3 G. Chalmers, 1802 ed.: first published 1786, *An Estimate of the Comparative Strength of Great Britain*, London. King's estimates were published as an appendix to Chalmers's 1802 edition, together with a short life of King. See D. V. Glass, 1952 'The population controversy in eighteenth century England', *Population Studies*, VI, No. 1, pp. 69–91.

4 D. V. Glass, 1952. op cit.

5 G. T. Griffith, 1925, *Population Problems of the Age of Malthus*, Cambridge.

6 See J. T. Krause, 1958, 'Changes in English fertility and mortality, 1781–1850', *Economic History Review*, 2nd Series, XI, No. 1, pp. 52–70.

7 G. T. Griffith, op. cit., p. 18.

8 Based on H. Gille, 1949, 'The demographic history of the northern European countries in the eighteenth century', *Population Studies*, III, No. 1, pp. 3–65.

9 H. Gille, 1949, op. cit.

10. Ibid. p. 43.

11 See H. Gille, 1949, op. cit.; J. T. Krause, 1958–9, 'Some implications of recent work in historical demography', *Comparative Studies in Society and History*, I, pp. 164–88; and J. W. Eaton and A. J. Mayer, 1954, *Man's Capacity to Reproduce: The Demography of a Unique Population*, Glencoe.

12 For a discussion of the late eighteenth and early nineteenth centuries see J. T. Krause, 1958, op. cit.

13 T. McKeown and R. G. Brown, 1955, 'Medical evidence related to English population change in the eighteenth century', *Population Studies*, IX, No. 2, pp. 119–41; and T. McKeown and R. G. Brown, 1962, 'Reasons for the decline of mortality in England and Wales during the nineteenth century', *Population Studies*, XVI, No. 2, pp. 94–122.

14 G. M. Trevelyan, 1946, *English Social History*, London, p. 290.

15 K. F. Helleiner, 1957, 'The vital revolution reconsidered', *The Canadian Journal of Economics and Political Science*, XXIII, No. 1, pp. 1–9.

16 H. J. Habakkuk, 1953, 'English population in the eighteenth century', *Economic History Review*, 2nd series, VI, No. 2, pp. 117–33.

17 For a study of the converse of this argument, that is economic and social factors inhibiting marriage and fertility, see K. H. Connell, 1950, *The Population of Ireland, 1750–1843*, Oxford.

18 T. McKeown and R. G. Brown, 1955, op. cit.

19 M. Greenwood, 1948, *Medical Statistics from Graunt to Farr*, Cambridge, p. 44.

20 J. T. Krause, 1958, op. cit.; 1958–9, op. cit.; and 1959, 'Some neglected factors in the English Industrial Revolution', *Journal of Economic History*, XIX, No. 4, pp. 528–40.

21 K. F. Helleiner, 1957, op. cit., p. 8.

22 J. L. and B. Hammond, 1947, 2nd edition, *The Bleak Age*, West Drayton.

23 The most complete study of the many patterns and variations in the population growth of the European world through the seventeenth to the end of the nineteenth century is to be found in D. V. Glass and D. E. C. Eversley, eds., 1965, *Population in History*, London. This reprints most of the classical articles on the history of population – e.g. by Marshall, Chalmers, Habakkuk and others – and also contains a great deal of new material based on both the United Kingdom and the continental countries of Europe, as well as of USA.

24 K. H. Connell, 1950, op. cit.

25 See J. J. Spengler, 1938, *France Faces Depopulation*, Durham.

26 See F. Lorimer, 1946, *The Population of the Soviet Union: History and Prospects*, Geneva (League of Nations).

27 Figures derived from W. S. Thompson, 1942, op. cit., *passim*.

28 A. Landry, 1945, *Traité de démographie*, Paris, p. 515.

29 J. J. Spengler, 1956, 'Notes on France's response to her declining rate of demographic growth' in J. J. Spengler and A. D. Duncan, eds., *Demographic Analysis*, Glencoe, pp. 588 ff.

30 J. J. Spengler, 1938, op. cit.

31 A. Landry, 1945, op. cit., p. 161.

32 Ireland Republic, 1954, *Commission on Emigration and other Population Problems, 1948-1954*, Dublin, p. 118.

33 F. Lorimer, et al., 1954, *Culture and Human Fertility*, Paris, UNESCO, p. 174, quoting unpublished MS. of D. V. Glass.

34 Quoted in F. Lorimer, et al., 1954, op. cit., p. 174.

35 W. S. Petersen, 1960, 'The demographic transition in the Netherlands', *American Sociological Review*, xxv, No. 3, pp. 334-47.

36 T. McKeown and R. G. Brown, 1955, op. cit.

37 Adapted from J. Hajnal, 1965, 'European marriage patterns in perspective' in D. V. Glass and D. E. C. Eversley (eds.), *Population in History*, London, p. 102.

38 From R. R. Kuczynski, 1936, *The Measurement of Population Growth*, London, pp. 216-20.

CHAPTER 5

1 M. L. Hansen, 1940, *The Atlantic Migration, 1607-1860*, Cambridge, Mass.

2 See United Nations, Department of Social Affairs, 1953, *Determinants and Consequences of Population Change*, Population Studies No. 17, New York, p. 12; A. M. Carr Saunders, 1936, *World Population*, Oxford, p. 48; and A. Landry, 1945, *Traité de démographie*, Paris, p. 410.

3 For a summary history of this emigration see UN, op. cit., 1953, pp. 100 ff.

4 W. D. Borrie, 1958, 'Immigration' in *The Australian Encyclopaedia*, v, pp. 65–75.

5 W. D. Borrie, 1938, *Immigration to New Zealand*, unpublished MS., Library of University of Otago, Dunedin.

6 For a history of migration from Europe during the nineteenth century and until the great depression of the 1930s, see M. R. Davie, 1936, *World Immigration with Special Reference to the United States*, New York; and W. F. Willcox, 1931, *International Migrations*, Vol. II, New York.

7 UN, 1953, op. cit., p. 100.

8 Adapted from C. and Irene B. Taeuber, 1958, *The Changing Population of the United States*, New York, p. 56.

9 For a detailed analysis of the economic factors in the great Atlantic migration see B. Thomas, 1954, *Migration and Economic Growth*, Cambridge.

10 For a discussion of these attempts to foster the 'redistribution of the white population of the Empire', as Winston Churchill described the purpose of the Empire Settlement Act of 1922 and its antecedent, the Dominions Royal Commission, see W. D. Borrie, 1949, *Immigration, Australia's Problems and Prospects*, Sydney; and G. F. Plant, 1951, *Oversea Settlement, Migration from the United Kingdom to the Dominions*, London.

11 See, for example, F. W. Notestein, et al., 1944, *The Future Population of Europe and the Soviet Union*, Geneva, The League of Nations; and Enid Charles, 1935, 'The effect of present trends in fertility and mortality upon the future population of England and Wales and upon its age composition', *London and Cambridge Economic Series*, Special Memorandum No. 40, pp. 1–19.

12 For a detailed treatment of these see D. V. Glass, 1940, *Population Policies and Movements in Europe*, Oxford.

13 See particularly the *Final Report* of the UK Oversea Settlement Board for 1938 (Cmd 5766).

14 Council of Europe, Consultative Assembly, Committee on Population and Refugees, 1954, *Survey of the Situation and and Development of the European Populations*, p. 15.

15 G. Frumkin, 1951, *Population Changes in Europe Since 1939*, London, pp. 162–64.

16 UN, Department of Economic Affairs, Research and Planning Division, Economic Commission for Europe, 1948, *A Survey of the Economic Situation and Prospects for Europe*, p. 197.

17 W. S. Petersen, 1955, *Planned Migration, the Social Determinants of the Dutch-Canadian Movement*, Berkeley.

18 Hilde Wander, 1951, *The Importance of Emigration for the Solution of Population Problems in Western Europe*, The Hague.

19 See International Labour Office, 1959, *International Migration 1945–1957*, Geneva; and J. B. Schechtman, 1962, *Post-War Population Transfers in Europe*, Philadelphia.

20 For a detailed history of the International Refugee Organization see Louise W. Holborn, 1956, *The International Refugee Organization*, Oxford.

21 The figures on which the estimates of migration to and from Europe are based are derived from ILO, 1959, op. cit. and official published statistics of the countries concerned. For a discussion of the problems of definition and interpretation of these statistics see B. Thomas, 1961, *International Migration and Economic Development, A Trend Report and Bibliography*, UNESCO Population and Culture Series, Paris. Also, UN, Department of Economic and Social Affairs, 1955, *Analytical Bibliography of Migration Statistics 1925–1950*, Population Studies No. 24; and 1949, *Problems of Migration Statistics*, Population Studies No. 5, New York.

22 The 8 countries were: Belgium, Denmark, Italy, Netherlands, Portugal, Spain, Sweden, West Germany, the United Kingdom.

23 UK Oversea Settlement Board, *Reports* for 1960 and 1961 (Cmd 1243 and 1586), and *Statistics* for 1961–3 (Cmd 1905, 2217, 2555), London.

24 United Kingdom, Parliament 1965, *Immigration from the Commonwealth*. Presented to Parliament by the Prime Minister (Cmd 2739), London.

25 United Kingdom, Parliament, 1965, op. cit.

26 After 1963 the United Kingdom experienced a net loss, due largely to booming immigration to Canada and Australia until the end of 1967. Thereafter the movement to Canada slackened, although the Australian flow continued strongly, and a net loss

of 63,000 for the year 1966–7 (July–June) was again reduced to only 19,000 in 1968–9. For the whole period 1953–68, the United Kingdom almost certainly gained slightly more people that it lost.

27 B. P. Hofstede, 1964, *Thwarted Exodus: Post-War Overseas Migration from the Netherlands*, The Hague, Appendix 3 and estimates for 1963 based on official Netherlands statistics.

28 Figures compiled from ILO, 1959, op. cit. and from Federal Republic of Germany, *Statistical Yearbooks*.

29 ILO, 1959, op. cit. and Italy, Official Statistics, *Movimento con L'Estero*, Persona espatriate e rimpatriate . . .

30 It must be emphasized, however, that the figures for these countries can only be taken as approximations of broad movements. The figures on which the following discussion of Spain and Portugal is based, with particular reference to Latin America, are derived from ILO, 1959, op. cit., and from estimates kindly prepared by ILO for the preparation of a paper by the author for the World Population Conference, Belgrade, 1965 ('Trends and patterns in international migration since 1945', background paper for Session B.9). The author accepts full responsibility for the interpretations now based on those figures.

31 S. Agapitidis, 1961, 'Emigration from Greece', *Migration*, I, No. 1, pp. 53–61; also statistics in *International Migration*, 1963, I, No. 3, p. 214.

32 A. C. Zammit, 1963, 'Malta and Migration', *International Migration*, I, No. 3, pp. 178–82. It should be noted that the figures presented by Zammit are higher than those given in ILO, 1959, op. cit., p. 78, which appears to exclude emigration to the United Kingdom.

33 See S. H. Eisenstadt, 1954, *The Absorption of Immigrants*, London; 1956, 'Cultural assimilation and tensions in a country of large-scale immigration: Israel', *International Social Science Bulletin*, VIII, No. 1, p. 53; and ILO, 1959, op. cit.

34 ILO, 1959, op. cit., and USA *Statistical Abstracts*.

35 ILO, 1959, op. cit., and *Canada Yearbook*.

36 A recent estimate states that from 1952–66, 2,074,000 persons emigrated to Canada, an average of 138,000 a year. The losses

appear to have been relatively slight. Census analysis shows
that the *net* gain from immigration 1951–61 contributed about
27 per cent of total intercensal population growth. See L. W.
Jones, 1969, 'The amount and structure of immigration into
Canada and the United States'. Paper prepared for *London
Conference* of the International Union for the Scientific Study
of Population.

37 Canadian Minister for Citizenship and Immigration, 1962,
speech delivered at an Immigration Conference, Toronto, on
March 9, and printed in *Migration*, II, No. 2, pp. 61–72.

38 Derived from official statistics of the Commonwealth Bureau of
Census and Statistics, particularly *Demography* (annual) and
quarterly bulletins of oversea arrival and departures.

39 C. A. Price, 1962, 'Overseas migration to and from Australia,
1947–61', *Migration*, II, No. 2, pp. 21–34; 1969, 'International
migration – Australia and New Zealand, 1947–68'. Paper prepared for the *London Conference* of the International Union for
the Scientific Study of Population.

40 C. A. Price, 1969, op. cit. puts the number of persons arriving
June 1947 to June 1968 'intending permanent settlement' at
2,335,000 of whom 1,900,000 were still alive and residing in
Australia by the latter date, when about one in five persons in
Australia was a post-war immigrant or the offspring of one. He
estimates that over the whole period 1947–68, immigrants and
their children were responsible for 58 per cent of the national
population growth.

41 L. Katzen, 1963, 'South African immigration and emigration
in the post-war period', *International Migration*, I, No. 3,
pp. 183–91; and Republic of South Africa, Bureau of Statistics,
Monthly Bulletin of Statistics.

42 See note 30 above.

43 D. Kirk, 1946, *Europe's Population in the Interwar Years*,
Geneva, p. 99.

44 UN, 1953, op. cit., p. 101.

45 ILO, 1959, op. cit., pp. 137–59.

46 Ibid., pp. 141–6.

47 Ibid.

48 These figures are derived from population estimates and birth and death records from official sources and UN *Demographic Yearbooks* 1960 and 1962. The pattern revealed here may be compared with figures by Edith Adams, 1969, 'International migration trends affecting Europe in the 1960s'. Paper prepared for *London Conference* of the International Union for the Scientific Study of Population. There are small differences in Miss Adams' figures for 1950–60 and mine for 1957–61, but the pattern is the same. She also carries the calculations over a greater range of countries and includes a table for 1960–6 in which the figures for the countries listed in Table 5.4 show a continuation of the 1950–60 trend, with, however, a significant reversal of trend in Ireland. Her figures for 1960–6 are (in thousands; gain = +; loss = −):

Federal Republic of Germany	1,980	Netherlands	60
France	1,591	Switzerland	323
United Kingdom	229	Greece	−226
Ireland	−122	Portugal	−195
Belgium	149	Spain	−801
		Italy	−471

49 The material which follows is based upon an unpublished MS, kindly supplied in 1965 by the International Labour Office, prepared for a conference in Latin America; and also upon T. Lynn Smith, 1959, 'Migration from one Latin American country to another', in *Proceedings*, Vienna Conference of the International Union for the Scientific Study of Population, pp. 695–702.

50 UN, 1953, op. cit., pp. 105–6, and UN, 1951, '*International Migrations in the Far East During Recent Times*, Population Bulletin No. 1, New York.

51 ILO, 1959, op. cit., pp. 60–70.

52 Government of India, *Census of 1951*, Vol. I.

53 ILO, 1959, op. cit., pp. 121–6.

54 Hong Kong Census, *Report on 1961 Census*, by K. M. A. Barnett, Vol. II, Tables CVI–CVIII.

55 G. McT. Kahin (ed.), 1963, *Major Governments of Asia*, Cornell, 2nd ed., p. 686.

56 International Labour Organisation unpublished MS., 'Les Migrations Internationales en Afrique', prepared in 1962.

57 *International Labour Review*, 1957, 'Interterritorial migrations of Africans south of the Sahara', LXXVI, No. 3, pp. 292–310.

58 Ibid.; also ILO, 1959, op. cit., pp. 157–9.

59 T. E. Smith and J. P. C. Blacker, 1963, *Population Characteristics of the Commonwealth Countries of Tropical Africa*, Institute of Commonwealth Studies Papers, No. 9, London.

60 Unpublished information from surveys, supplied by Dr J. C. Caldwell. See also M. Prothero, 1968, 'Migration in tropical Africa', in J. C. Caldwell and C. Okonjo (eds.), *The Population of Tropical Africa*, London, pp. 250–63.

61 United Nations, High Commissioner for Refugees, 1963, *Report*, General Assembly: Eighteenth Session Supplement No. 11, p. 14.

62 For a recent assessment of the extent and nature of this migration see Margaret G. Marchant, 1969, 'Aspects of external migration in countries of eastern and southern Africa, 1960–6', Paper prepared for the *London Conference* of the International Union for the Scientific Study of Population.

63 For discussions of these aspects see B. Thomas (ed.), 1958, *The Economics of International Migration*, London, especially Chapter 2, 'Effects produced in receiving countries by pre-1939 immigration' by J. J. Spengler.

64 For a discussion of the economic significance of immigrants' remittances to their homelands see W. D. Borrie, 1966, 'International migration as related to economic and demographic problems of developing countries' in *World Population Conference, Belgrade 1965, Volume I: Summary Report* Moderator's statement, Meeting B9, New York, pp. 138–45.

65 See T. H. Silcock, 1958, 'Migration problems of the Far East', Chapter 18 in B. Thomas (ed.), *Economics of International Migration*, London.

CHAPTER 6

1 For a review of trends in fertility, mortality and growth rates of industrialized countries with special reference to the twentieth

century see: United Nations, 1953, *Determinants and Consequences of Population Trends*, Population Studies No. 17, New York; A. M. Carr Saunders, 1936, *World Population*, Oxford; D. V. Glass, 1940, *Population Policies and Movements in Europe*, Oxford (2nd ed. published in 1967); A. Sauvy, 1958, *De Malthus à Mao Tse-Tung : le problème de la population dans le monde*, Paris; M. Reinhard, A. Armengaud and J. Dupaquier, 1968, *Histoire générale de la population mondiale*, 3rd ed., Paris; UN Department of Economic and Social Affairs, 1958, *Recent Trends in the Fertility of Industrialized Countries*, Population Bulletin No. 27; 1963, *Population Bulletin No. 6, with special reference to the situation and recent trends of mortality in the world;* 1965, *Population Bulletin No. 7, with special reference to conditions and trends of fertility in the world,* New York.

2 For an admirable review of the trends and factors associated with the onset of controlled fertility see National Bureau of Economic Research, 1960, *Demographic and Economic Change in Developed Countries*, Princeton.

3 R. R. Kuczynski, 1936, *The Measurement of Population Growth*, London.

4 New South Wales, Australia, Legislative Assembly, 1904, Vol. I, *Report* of the Royal Commission on the Decline of the Birth Rate and on the Mortality of Infants in New South Wales, together with copies of Commissioner's Diagrams, Statistical evidence, and Statistical exhibits, etc.

5 National Birth Rate Commission (UK), 1917, Vol. I, *The Declining Birth Rate : its causes and effects*, London: 1920, Vol. II, *Problems of Population and Parenthood*, London.

6 Reproduced from W. D. Borrie, 1948, *Population Trends and Policies*, Sydney, p. 9.

7 See D. V. Glass, 1940, op. cit., W. D. Borrie, 1948, op. cit., A. Sauvy, 1958, op. cit., J. A. Banks, 1954, *Prosperity and Parenthood*, London; J. A. and Olive Banks, 1964, *Feminism and Family Planning in Victorian England*, Liverpool; and P. Fryer, 1965, *The Birth Controllers*, London.

8 See D. E. C. Eversley, 1959, *Social Theories of Fertility and the Malthusian Debate*, Oxford.

9 A. Dumont, 1890, *Dépopulation et civilization. Etude démographique*, Paris.

10 E. Lewis-Faning, 1949, 'Report on an enquiry into family limitation and its influence on human fertility during the past fifty years', United Kingdom, *Royal Commission on Population*, Papers, Vol. I, London.

11 N. E. Himes, 1936, *Medical History of Contraception*, Baltimore, p. 251.

12 United Kingdom, Royal Commission on Population, 1949, *Report* (Cmd 7695 for 1949), London, p. 38.

13 W. D. Borrie, 1948, op. cit., p. 114.

14 United Kingdom, Royal Commission on Population, 1949, op. cit., p. 29.

15 For an early US study see F. Lorimer and F. Osborne, 1934, *Dynamics of Population*, New York. The analysis of differentials also formed a major component of the extensive Indianapolis studies conducted by P. K. Whelpton, C. V. Kiser and others. For a review see Milbank Memorial Fund, 1958, *Thirty Years' Research in Human Fertility*, New York.

16 See Enid Charles, 1943, 'Differential fertility in Canada, 1931', *Canadian Journal of Economics and Political Science*, IX, No. 2., pp. 175–218.

17 C. Burt, 1946, *Intelligence and Fertility*, Occasional Papers No. 2, Eugenics Society, London.

18 F. W. Notestein, et al., 1944, *The Future Population of Europe and the Soviet Union*, Geneva, The League of Nations pp. 83 ff.

19 G. Frumkin, 1951, *Population Changes in Europe since 1939*, London.

20 Based on J. A. Rowntree, 1966, 'Falling age at marriage and decrease in celibacy', Council of Europe, European Population Conference, 1966, *Official Documents of the Conference*, Vol. I, No. 8, Strasbourg.

21 It was apparent, however, at the London (1969) Conference of the International Union for the Scientific Study of Population that the study of nuptiality in developed countries is beginning to attract the attention of an increasing number of demographers.

22 Judith Hubback, 1955, 'The fertility of graduate women', *Eugenics Review*, XLVII, No. 2, pp. 107–13.

23 Gwendolyn Z. Johnson, 1960, 'Differential fertility in European countries', National Bureau of Economic Research, op. cit., pp. 26–72.

24 C. V. Kiser, 1960, 'Differential fertility in the United States', National Bureau of Economic Research, ibid., pp. 77–116.

25 R. Freedman, P. K. Whelpton, A. A. Campbell, 1959, *Family Planning, Sterility and Population Growth*, McGraw Hill.

26 From official statistics and UN *Demographic Yearbooks*.

27 A. J. Coale, 1967, 'Factors associated with the development of low fertility: an historical summary', in United Nations, Department of Economic and Social Affairs, *World Population Conference, Belgrade, 1965, Volume II*, Meeting B.2, New York, pp. 205–9.

CHAPTER 7

1 J. D. Durand, 1960, 'The population statistics of China AD 2–1953', *Population Studies*, XIII, No. 3, pp. 209–56. See also Ta Chen, 1958, 'New China's population census of 1953 and its relations to national reconstruction and demographic research', *Bulletin de L'Institut International de Statistique*, XXXVI, No. 2, Stockholm, pp. 255–71.

2 Ping-ti Ho, 1959, *Studies on the Population of China, 1368–1953*, Cambridge, Mass.

3 Ibid., Ch. 1.

4 Ibid., p. 23.

5 I. Taeuber and Wang Nai-Chi, 1959, 'The population reports of the Ch'ing dynasty and the growth of China's population', *American Association for the Advancement of Science*, Section K, Chicago.

6 L. Silberman, 1960, 'Hung Liang-Chi: a Chinese Malthus', *Population Studies*, XIII, No. 3, pp. 257–65.

7 L. Silberman, 1960, op. cit.

8 S. Chandrasekhar, 1959, *China's Population: Census and Vital Statistics*, Hong Kong.

9 J. S. Aird, 1960, 'The present and prospective population of mainland China', in Milbank Memorial Fund, *Population Trends in Eastern Europe, the USSR and Mainland China*, New York, pp. 93–133.

10 See J. S. Aird, 1961, 'The size, composition and growth of the population of mainland China', *International Population Statistics Reports*, US Bureau of the Census, Series P–90, No. 15; and, 1968, 'Estimates and projections of the population of mainland China, 1953–86', ibid., Series P–91, No. 17.

11 K. Davis, 1951, *The Population of India and Pakistan*, Princeton, p. 27.

12 Ibid., pp. 33, 34, 68, 85.

13 S. N. Agarwala, 1965, 'Effect of a rise in female marriage on the birth rate in India', *Papers Contributed by Indian Authors to World Population Conference, Belgrade, Yugoslavia, 1965*, Office of Registrar General, India, pp. 267–70.

14 K. G. Basavarajappa and M. I. Belvalgidad, 1967, 'Changes in age at marriage of females and their effect on the birth rate in India', *Eugenics Quarterly*, XIV, No. 1, pp. 14–26; and J. W. Eaton and A. J. Mayer, 1954, *Man's Capacity to Reproduce. The Demography of a Unique Population*, Glencoe, p. 16.

15 See S. N. Agarwala, 1965, loc. cit, and K. G. Basavarajappa and M. I. Belvalgidad, 1967, loc. cit.

16 W. S. Thompson, 1959, *Population and Progress in the Far East*, Chicago, p. 120, and United Nations *Demographic Yearbooks*.

17 W. S. Thompson, 1959, op. cit., p. 276.

18 D. Kirk, 1967, 'Prospects for reducing natality in the underdeveloped world', *Annals*, American Academy of Political and Social Science, 369, pp. 48–60.

19 F. Yusuf, 1967, 'Some recent estimates of fertility of Pakistini women, based on PGE data', *Paper to Seminar on Population Problems in the Economic Development of Pakistan*, Pakistan Institute of Development Economics, Karachi.

20 M. A. Khan and L. L. Bean, 1967, 'Interrelationships of some Fertility Measures in Pakistan', *Journal of Pakistan Institute of Development Economics*, VII, No. 4, pp. 504–18.

315

21 For a historical summary of the growth of the population of Indonesia see W. S. Thompson, 1959, op. cit., pp. 345 ff.

22 N. Keyfitz, 1965, 'Indonesian population and the European industrial revolution', *Asian Survey*, v, No. 10, pp. 503–15.

23 J. N. Bhatta, 1961, 'Source and reliability of demographic data in Indonesia', *Dinas Geografi*, Publication No. 11, Djakarta; Tangoantiang, n.d., 'An Estimate of Basic Demographic Parameters for Indonesia as of Around 1960', unpublished manuscript; and UN *Demographic Yearbook*, 1967.

24 N. Keyfitz, 1965, op. cit., p. 508.

25 Kartono Gunawan, 1967, 'The growth of population in Djakarta during the intercensal period 1930–1961', unpublished paper for session X, *International Union for the Scientific Study of Population*, Sydney Conference.

26 Loc. cit.

27 Ibid.

CHAPTER 8

1 Carmen M. Miro, 1966, 'The population of twentieth century Latin America', in J. M. Stycos and J. Arias (eds.), *Population Dilemma in Latin America*, Washington, pp. 1–32.

2 Figures from United Nations, *Demographic Yearbooks*.

3 UN *Demographic Yearbooks*, and *Population Reference Bureau*, 1969, 'World Population data sheet', Washington.

4 For a summary of the estimated trend of mortality in Latin America, see Population Reference Bureau, 1967, 'Punta del este, 1961–1967: early dawn of a demographic awakening', *Population Bulletin*, XXIII, No. 3, pp. 45–83.

5 Population Reference Bureau, 1967, op. cit.

6 Sources as for Tables 8.1 and 8.2.

7 T. Lynn Smith n.d. (c. 1963), 'The growth of population in Latin America' in *The Population of the World*, Forum Lectures of the Voice of America, p. 107.

8 Adapted from Milbank Memorial Fund Quarterly, 1965, *Components of Population Change in Latin America*, XLIII, No. 4, Part 2, p. 199. Much of the material which follows in this chapter is based upon this volume.

9 Population Reference Bureau, 1967, op. cit., p. 66.

10 Carmen M. Miro, 1964, 'The population of Latin America, *Demography*, I, No. I, p. 36.

11 Figures adapted from Carmen M. Miro and F. Rath, 1965, 'Preliminary findings of comparative fertility surveys in three Latin American cities', in Milbank Memorial Fund Quarterly, op. cit., pp. 41 and 45.

12 Population Reference Bureau, 1967, op. cit.

13 J. M. Stycos and J. Arias (eds.), 1966, op. cit., p. x.

CHAPTER 9

1 See A. M. Carr Saunders, 1936, *World Population*, Oxford.

2 F. Lorimer, 1968, in W. Brass, A. J. Coale, et al., *The Demography of Tropical Africa*, Princeton, p. 4.

3 A. M. Carr Saunders, 1936, op. cit., p. 300.

4 R. R. Kuczynski, 1948–49, *Demographic Survey of the British Colonial Empire*, Vol. I, 1948, West Africa; Vol. II, 1949, South and East Africa, Oxford.

5 United Nations, Department of Social Affairs, 1953, *Determinants and Consequences of Population Trends*, Population Studies No. 17, New York, p. 18.

6 Ibid., p. 19.

7 J. C. Caldwell and C. Okonja (eds.), 1968, *The Population of Tropical Africa*, London, p. 4.

8 Ibid., p. 30.

9 W. Brass, A. J. Coale, et al., 1968, op. cit.

10 Adapted from J. C. Caldwell and C. Okonja (eds.), op. cit., pp. 182–4.

11 A. J. Coale, 1968, 'Estimates of fertility and mortality in tropical Africa', in J. C. Caldwell and C. Okonja (eds.), op. cit., p. 186.

12 A. M. Carr Saunders, 1936, op. cit., pp. 302–3.

13 J. C. Caldwell, 1968, *Population Growth and Family Change in Africa: The New Elite in Ghana*, Canberra, Chapter 5.

14 E. Van de Walle, 1968, in W. Brass, A. J. Coale, et al., op. cit., Chapter 5.

15 Ibid., pp. 205–18.

16 A. J. Coale, 1968, op. cit., p. 186.

17 United Nations, Department of Economic and Social Affairs, 1966, *World Population Prospects as Assessed in 1963*, Population Studies No. 41, New York, p. 201.

18 Ibid., p. 219.

19 UN, *Demographic Yearbook*, 1967.

20 Ibid.

21 UN, Department of Economic and Social Affairs, 1963, *Population Bulletin No. 6 with special reference to the situation and recent trends in mortality in the world;* See also 1965, *Population Bulletin No. 7 with special reference to the condition and trends of fertility in the world*, New York.

22 L. T. Badenhorst, 1950, 'The future growth of the population of South Africa and its probable age distribution', *Population Studies*, IV, No. 1, pp. 3–46.

23 Adapted from L. T. Badenhorst, 1950, op. cit.; and from UN *Demographic Yearbook*, 1967.

24 L. T. Badenhorst, 1950, op. cit., p. 23.

25 UN *Demographic Yearbook*, 1967.

CHAPTER 10

1 For a summary of pre-Malthusian ideas see C. E. Stangeland, 1904, *Pre-Malthusian Doctrines of Population*, New York; see also A. M. Carr Saunders, 1936, *World Population*, Oxford; D. V. Glass, 1940, *Population Policies and Movements*, Oxford; W. D. Borrie, 1948, *Population Trends and Policies*, Sydney.

2 The term *ecology* seems to have been coined by Ernest Haecel in 1869 as an aspect of animal and plant biology. It was first used in the study of human societies by Robert E. Park in 1915. 'Human ecology' is concerned with the relation of human organisms to their environment. For a discussion of human ecology see L. Wirth, 1945, 'Human Ecology', *The American Journal of Sociology*, L, No. 6, pp. 483–8.

3 For an outline of post-Malthusian theories of population see W. S. Thompson, 1942, *Population Problems*, New York. See also Chapter 2 above.

4 C. Gini, 1930, 'The cyclical rise and fall of population', *Population*, Harris Foundation Lectures 1929, Chicago, pp. 4–25.

5 J. Bertillon, 1911, *La dépopulation de la France*, Paris.

6 For example, D. V. Glass, 1940, op. cit.; and W. D. Borrie, 1948, op. cit.; also see Hope T. Eldridge, 1954, *Population Policies: A Survey of Recent Developments*, Population Investigation Committee and the International Union for the Scientific Study of Population.

7 See C. W. Guillebaud, 1941, *The Social Policy of Nazi Germany*, Current Problems Series, Cambridge; and W. D. Borrie, 1948, op. cit., Chapter XII.

8 W. D. Borrie, 1948, op. cit., p. 190.

9 See W. B. Sutch, 1966, *The Quest for Security in New Zealand, 1840 to 1966*, Oxford.

10 See Alva Myrdal, 1945, *Nation and Family. The Swedish Experiment in Democratic Family Planning and Population Policy* (2nd ed.), London.

11 Sir Wm Beveridge, 1944, *Full Employment in a Free Society*, London.

12 From United Nations, *Demographic Yearbooks*.

13 A. J. Coale and M. Zelnick, 1963, *New Estimates of Fertility and Population in the United States*, Princeton.

14 J. J. Spengler, 1938, *France Faces Depopulation*, Durham. See also A. Landry, 1945, *Traité de démographie*, Paris.

15 K. H. Connell, 1962, 'Peasant marriage in Ireland: its structure and development since the famine', *Economic History Review*, 2nd Series, XIV, No. 3, pp. 502–23.

16 J. A. Schumpeter, 1947, *Capitalism, Socialism and Democracy*, London, p. 157.

17 E. Lewis-Faning, 1949, *Report on an Inquiry into Family Limitation and its Influence on Human Fertility During the Last Fifty Years*, United Kingdom Royal Commission on Population, Papers Vol. I, London.

18 For a history of contraception, see N. E. Himes, 1936, *Medical History of Contraception*, Baltimore.

19 H. Y. Tien, 1963, 'Birth control in mainland China: ideology and politics', *Milbank Memorial Fund Quarterly*, XLI, No. 3, pp. 269–90.

20 See R. M. Fagley, 1960, *The Population Explosion and Christtian Responsibility*, Oxford.

21 See J. T. Noonan, 1965, *Contraception, A History of its Treatment by Catholic Theologians and Canonists*, Harvard.

22 P. Fryer, 1965, *The Birth Controllers*, London. See also above, p. 135.

23 See, for example, E. Lewis-Faning, 1949, op. cit.

24 See note 4, Chapter 6, *supra*.

25 W. D. Borrie, 1948, op. cit., Chapter IV.

26 D. V. Glass, 1940, op. cit., Chapter IV and VI.

27 C. Tietze, 1964, 'The demographic significance of legal abortions in eastern Europe', *Demography*, I, No. 1, p. 120.

28 E. Lewis-Faning, 1949, op. cit.

29 N. B. Ryder and C. F. Westoff, 1966, 'Use of oral contraception in the United States, 1965', *Science*, 153, No. 3741, pp. 1199–1205.

30 C. F. Westoff and N. B. Ryder, 1967, 'The United States: the pill and the birth rate 1960–65' in Population Council, *Studies in Family Planning*, No. 20, pp. 1–3.

31 L. H. Day, 1964, 'Fertility differentials among Catholics in Australia', *Milbank Memorial Fund Quarterly*, XLII, No. 2, pp. 57–83. See also W. D. Borrie, 1969, 'Recent trends and patterns in fertility in Australia', *Journal of Bio-Social Science*, I, pp. 57–70.

32 C. F. Westoff, R. G. Potter, P. C. Sagi and E. G. Mishler, 1961, *Family Growth in Metropolitan America*, Princeton; and C. F. Westoff, R. G. Potter and P. C. Sagi, 1963, *The Third Child*, Princeton.

33 For a scholarly study of the history of doctrine of the Roman Catholic Church on the subject of birth control, see J. T. Noonan, 1965, op. cit.

34 H. Doms, 1939, *The Meaning of Marriage*, London.

35 J. T. Noonan, 1965, op. cit, pp. 446 ff.

36 A. Dumont, 1890, *Dépopulation et civilization, Etude Démographique*, Paris.

37 G. Myrdal, 1959, 'Indian Economic Planning', *Population Review*, January, pp. 16–32.

38 See, for example, United Nations, Department of Economic and Social Affairs, 1961, *The Mysore Population Study*, Population Studies No. 34, New York, and the KAP (Knowledge, attitudes, practice) studies carried through in Taiwan, South Korea, Singapore, Malaysia and elsewhere.

39 Quoted in A. M. Carr Saunders, 1936, op. cit., p. 110.

40 O. Harkkavy, L. Saunders and A. L. Southam, 1968, 'An overview of the Ford Foundation's strategy for population work' *Demography*, v, No. 2 (Special Issue), pp. 541–52.

41 For an outline of the work of the Population Council see F. W. Notestein, 1968, 'The Population Council and the demographic crisis of the less developed world', in *Demography* (Special Issue), op. cit., pp. 553–60.

42 Sir Colville Deverell, 1968, 'The IPPF – its role in developing countries', *Demography* (Special Issue), op. cit., pp. 574–7.

43 Quoted in R. T. Ravenholt, 1968, 'The AID Population and Family Planning Program – Goals, Scope and Progress', *Demography* (Special Issue), op. cit., p. 563.

44 R. T. Ravenholt, 1968, op. cit., p. 571.

45 F. W. Notestein, 1968, op. cit., p. 533.

46 B. Berelson, 1969, 'National family planning programs: where we stand', *Studies in Family Planning*, No. 39 (Supplement), Population Council, New York.

47 See particularly, Population Council, 1963–, *Studies in Family Planning*, No. 1–, New York.

48 United Nations, Department of Economic and Social Affairs, 1966, *Report on the Family Planning Programme of India*, Programme of Technical Assistance, New York.

49 Ibid., p. 10.

50 The Embassy of India, Washington, 1968, *The Quiet Revolution, Family Planning in India*. This pamphlet is almost certainly too optimistic about the success of the plan, but on the other hand many statements by western sceptics have undoubtedly

been too pessimistic. See also Government of India, 1969, *India: Family Planning since 1965* (Ministry of Health, Family Planning and Urban Development, Department of Family Planning).

51 S. J. Segal, 1967, 'Indian economic policy and the Fourth Five Year Plan', International Bank for Reconstruction and Development, IV, March, *Family Planning*.

52 S. N. Agarwala, 1968, 'How are we doing in family planning in India?', *Demography* (Special Issue), op. cit., pp. 710–13.

53 E. Adil, 1968, 'Measurement of family planning progress in Pakistan', *Demography* (Special Issue), op. cit., pp. 659–65.

54 H. Y. Tien, 1962, 'Population control: recent developments in mainland China', *Asian Survey*, July, pp. 12–16; and 1963, 'Induced abortion and the population control in mainland China', *Marriage and Family Living*, February, pp. 35–43.

55 S. Chandrasekar, 1959, *China's Population, Census and Vital Statistics*, Hong Kong.

56 See B. Berelson, 1969, op. cit.

57 H. Levin, 1968, 'Commercial distribution of contraceptives in developing countries: past, present and future', *Demography* (Special Issue), op. cit., pp. 941–6.

58 A. S. Parkes, 1961, 'The menace of overpopulation', *New Scientist*, No. 238, pp. 566–70.

59 F. W. Notestein, 1968, op. cit., p. 558.

CHAPTER 11

1 For a perceptive note on the sociological aspects of fertility see R. Freedman, 1962, 'The sociology of human fertility', *Current Sociology*, X/XI, No. 2, pp. 35–68.

2 For studies of family formation and size in post-war 'developed' countries, see, for example: R. Freedman, P. K. Whelpton, and A. A. Campbell, 1959, *Family Planning, Sterility and Population Growth*, McGraw Hill; C. F. Westoff, R. G. Potter, et al., 1961, *Family Growth in Metropolitan America*, Princeton, and 1963, *The Third Child*, Princeton; National Bureau of Economic Research, 1960, *Demographic and Social Change in*

Developed Countries, Princeton; L. H. and Alice T. Day, 1964, *Too Many Americans*, Boston; M. Biraben, 'Fertility trends in western Europe', Council of Europe, European Population Conference, 1966, *Official Documents of the Conference*, I, No. I. Also the following papers presented to the *London Conference* of the International Union for the Scientific Study of Population, 1969: K. G. Basavarajappa, 'Trends in age-duration specific fertility rates of non-Maoris in New Zealand, 1936–66'; W. D. Borrie, 'Fertility in Australia a review of recent trends'; and J. Henripin, 'Evolution de la fécondité au Canada depucis la dernière Guèrre mondiale'.

3 See, for example, Judith Blake, 1968, 'Are babies consumer durables', *Population Studies*, XXII, No. I, p. 12.

4 A. J. Coale, 1963, 'Population and economic development', in P. M. Hauser, (ed.), *The Population Dilemma*, The American Academy, Prentice Hall, pp. 46–49.

5 D. J. Bogue, 1967, 'The end of the population explosion', *The Public Interest*, VII, pp. 11–20.

6 K. Davis, 1967, 'Population policy: will current programs succeed', *Science*, 158, pp. 730–9.

7 S. Enke, 1960, 'The economics of government payments to limit population', *Economic Development and Cultural Change*, VIII, No. 4, Part I, pp. 339–48. See also R. A. Easterlin, 1966, 'On the relation of economic factors to recent and projected fertility changes', *Demography*, III, No. I, pp. 131–53.

8 See Alva Myrdal, 1945, *Nation and Family. The Swedish Experiment in Democratic Family Planning and Population Policy* (2nd ed.), London.

9 Irene B. Taeuber, 1958, *The Population of Japan*, Princeton.

10 Ibid., pp. 23 and 41.

11 Ibid., p. 50.

12 Ibid., p. 55.

13 Adapted from Taeuber, op. cit., pp. 213, 265, 311.

14 M. Muramatsu, 1967, 'Policy measures and social changes for fertility decline in Japan', in United Nations, Department of Economic and Social Affairs, *World Population Conference Belgrade, 1965, Volume II*, Meeting A1, New York, pp. 96–9.

323

15 Ibid.

16 Ibid.

17 K. Davis, 1967, op. cit.

18 S. Kuznets, 1964, 'Growth and structure of national product. Countries in the ECAFE region, 1950–61', in ECAFE, *Asian Population Conference and Selected Papers, New Delhi 1963*, New York, pp. 128–42.

19 S. Kuznets, 1967, 'Population and economic growth', *Proceedings of the American Philosophical Society*, III, No. 3, pp. 170–93.

20 P. Erlich, 1967, 'Paying the piper', *New Scientist*, XXXVI, No. 575, pp. 652–62.

21 C. Clark, 1967, *Population Growth and Land Use*, London.

22 Sir John Crawford, 1967, 'The Malthusian spectre in India', *Australian Journal of Science*, XI, No. 10, pp. 383–90.

23 H. Brown, J. Bonner, J. Weir, 1957, *The Next Hundred Years*, New York. Also S. Mudd (ed.), 1964, *The Population Crisis and the Use of World Resources*, Vol. 2, World Academy of Art and Science, The Hague.

24 UN, Department of Economic and Social Affairs, 1966, *World Population Prospects as Assessed in 1963*, New York.

25 For a review of fertility trends see United Nations, Department of Economic and Social Affairs, 1965, *Population Bulletin No. 7 with special reference to conditions and trends of fertility in the world*, New York.

26 UNESCO, 1964, 'Implications of population trends for planning educational programmes' in ECAFE, 1964, op. cit., pp. 90–96.

27 The fear of relative 'overpopulation' in developed countries may be spreading. The information presented by Miss Jean Thompson of the UK Registrar-General's Office, to a Conference held in London by the Institute of Biology, in September 1969, seems to have raised this fear in the minds of at least of those attending. Official projections indicate a population by the year 2000 of 66 million, or 12 million more than in 1969. The greater part of this increase is expected to occur in south east England. Some, reacting to this information, see the need

for more drastic family planning if population growth is not 'to swamp available land and food resources by the year 2000'. (*The Times*, 26 September 1969).

28 See United States, President's Committee on Population and Family Planning, 1968, *Report on Population and Family Planning, the transition from concern to action*, Washington.

29 UN, Department of Economic and Social Affairs, 1958, *The Future Growth of World Population*, Population Studies No. 28, New York, p.v.

Index

Abel-Smith, B., 30 n
Abortion, 54, 252, 259–61. *See also* regions and countries
Abortifacients, 235
Adams, Edith, 116 n
Adil, A., 257 n
Africa: age composition, 16, 292; birth control, 205–6; birth rates, 202–3, 207; censuses, 199, 201–2; death rates, 202–3, 207–8; density, 43, 213; estimates of population, 6, 43, 52, 154, 199–201, 207, 213; expectations of life, 208; fertility rates, 202–6; growth rates, 11, 200–1, 208, 284, 286; infant mortality, 31, 202–3; inter-continental movement, 117, 121–4; marriage, 206; migration, 121–7, 284; mortality, 202–3; natural increase, 204, 209; projections, 286, 289–92; refugees, 121–4; resources, 284; rural/urban movements, 124; vital rates, 11, 207–8, 213
Agarwala, S. N., 166 n, 168 n, 256 n
Age composition: 16–17, 292; dependent groups, 292; working groups, 292. *See also* regions and countries
Age profiles, 17, 139, 294.
Age specific birth (fertility) rates. *See* Birth (fertility) rates, age specific

Agency for International Development (AID), 248–9, 262
Agipitidis, S., 106 n
Agriculture, 67, 154, 159, 173
Aird, J. S., 163 n, 163
Ancient populations, 42, 216
Algeria, growth rate, 200
Andes, ancient population, 42
Angola, enumerations, 201
Arabs, 107, 118
Arias, J., 180 n, 196 n
Armengaud, A., 128 n
Arensberg, C. M., 79
Argentina: birth rate, 182–3; growth rate, 182–3
Asia: age composition, 16, 292; birth rate, 286; death rate, 286; density, 15, 43; estimates of population, 6, 43, 52, 57; fertility decline, 282; growth rates, 10–11, 286; international migration, 118–19; marriage, 9; migration flows, 117–18; migration policies, 118, 121; natural increase, 286; per capita income, 242; post-war migration, 118; projections, 288–92; refugees and forced migration, 118; social change, 242–3; sources of immigrants, 117–18; vital rates, 11, 133
Asian Population Conference (1963), 293 n
Australia: births by duration of